– JESUS –

When Is He Coming?

Robert Y. Jackson

– JESUS –

When Is He Coming?

A detailed study of when Scripture indicates Jesus is coming, both in the Rapture for the church and in His Second Coming.

Robert Y. Jackson

AuthorHouse™
1663 Liberty Drive
Bloomington, IN 47403
www.authorhouse.com
Phone: 1-800-839-8640

First published by AuthorHouse 09/17/2011

ISBN: 978-1-4634-1580-8 (sc)
ISBN: 978-1-4634-1582-2 (hc)
ISBN: 978-1-4634-1581-5 (ebk)

Library of Congress Control Number: 2011909516

Printed in the United States of America

This book is printed on acid-free paper.

Table of Contents

Introduction

Is the time of Jesus' coming still known ONLY to God? How we answer that question determines our approach to the end-time prophecies in Scripture. The answer that's most commonly taught and accepted is that God is indeed the only one who knows *when Jesus will come again,* and also ***that no one else CAN know when He will come until the moment He actually descends from heaven with a shout to receive His church.*** *Those who accept that answer* normally don't even bother to ask the question — ***when will He come again?*** *Therefore, the first question we have to address in this book is* ***whether or not it is God's will and plan for believers to know ahead of time when Jesus is going to come again.*** Accordingly, we'll begin by carefully considering what Jesus said about *when He will come again.*

A few days before Jesus was crucified, He told His disciples the temple would be destroyed with not one stone left upon another. His disciples assumed He was talking about the end of the age, and asked Him the following questions. ***"Tell us, when shall these things be? And what will be the sign of Your coming, and of the end of the age?*** *(Matthew 24: 3).* In His answer to that question, one of the things Jesus said was, ***"...of the day and hour no one knows, not even the angels of heaven, but My Father only."*** *(Matthew 24: 36).* Mark's account of this incident even included the Son — Jesus Himself — among those who didn't know the day and hour of His return *(Ref: Mark 13: 32).* Therefore, ***at that point in time,*** *it indeed was true that God the Father was the only one who knew the day and hour when Jesus will come again.* However, after Jesus was crucified and resurrected, He said something that revealed *the knowledge of when He will come again was* ***THEN*** *no longer limited* ***ONLY to the Father.*** He said, ***"All authority has been given to Me in heaven and on earth."*** *(Matthew 28: 18).* ***After*** Jesus was given ***"ALL authority," it's inconceivable that He still didn't know when He will come back to the earth.*** Also, He gave us a promise that the Holy Spirit was going to take everything He received from the Father

and declare it to us, for He said, ***"I still have many things to say to you, but you cannot bear them now. However, when He, the Spirit of truth, has come, He will guide you into <u>ALL TRUTH</u>; for He will not speak on His own authority, but whatever He hears He will speak; and HE WILL TELL YOU THINGS TO COME. He will glorify Me, for HE WILL TAKE OF WHAT IS MINE AND DECLARE IT TO YOU. ALL THINGS THAT THE FATHER HAS ARE MINE. Therefore I said that He will take of Mine and declare it to you."*** *(John 16: 12 - 14).*
Not only has Jesus been given ***<u>ALL THINGS</u>*** *that the Father has,* but He also promised that the Holy Spirit, *who came at Pentecost,* will take *those things* ***that now belong to Jesus*** *and declare them to us.* This strongly indicates that *the knowledge of when Jesus will come again* is now available to believers by the revelation of the Holy Spirit. We have assurance this interpretation is correct, because God confirmed this same truth through the Apostle Paul.

In the last few verses of the fourth Chapter of I Thessalonians, Paul described what is going to happen when Jesus comes for His church. Then he began the fifth Chapter by revealing *that although those who are lost won't know when Jesus is coming, that doesn't apply to believers for he said,* ***"But concerning the times and the seasons, brethren, you have no need that I should write to you. For you yourselves know perfectly that the day of the Lord comes as a thief in the night. For when they shall say, 'Peace and safety;' then sudden destruction comes upon them, as labor pains upon a pregnant woman. And they shall not escape. But <u>YOU, brethren, are not in darkness, that THIS DAY SHOULD OVERTAKE YOU AS A THIEF."</u>*** *(I Thessalonians 5: 1 - 4).*

As ***<u>THAT DAY</u> approaches*** the unbelievers of this world won't have a clue what's about to take place. ***However, believers <u>DON'T HAVE TO BE IN THE DARK</u>*** *[ignorant],* ***either concerning what is about to happen, <u>OR WHEN it's going to happen,</u>*** *for God hasn't left us in the dark,* ***"...that this day should overtake you as a thief."*** This truth is also confirmed in Hebrews, where it says, ***"Let us hold fast the confession of our hope without wavering, for He who promised is faithful. And let us consider one another in order to stir up love and good works, not forsaking the assembling of ourselves together, as is the manner of some, but exhorting one another, <u>and so much the more AS YOU SEE THE DAY APPROACHING."</u>*** *(Hebrews 10: 23 - 25).* God made us such that when a crisis approaches, we have an increasing sense of urgency to do something. This verse tells us what we will need to do when the crisis we see approaching is the *day of the Lord*

— the day of Jesus Christ's return that will mark the end of the church age and the beginning of God's wrath against the wickedness of this world. When we see that day approaching, we who are believers will need to draw together for mutual exhortation and encouragement more than at any other time in history. That's true, because during those last days before the Lord comes, Satan will be on the earth with great wrath attacking God's children, for he also will know he has only a short time left. Revelation 12: 12 describes those days as a time of ***"Woe to the inhabitants of the earth and of the sea!"*** Hebrews 10: 25 *(above)* tells us ***what to do*** *as we see the day approaching; however,* we need to continue reading to fully understand ***why*** it will be so critically urgent to do that at that particular time.

Hebrews 10: 26 - 31 & 35 - 39 *(NKJV)*
26. For if we sin willfully after we have received the knowledge of the truth, there no longer remains a sacrifice for sins,
27. but a certain fearful expectation of judgment, and fiery indignation which will devour the adversaries.
28. Anyone who has rejected Moses' law dies without mercy on the testimony of two or three witnesses.
29. Of how much worse punishment, do you suppose, will he be thought worthy who has trampled the Son of God underfoot, counted the blood of the covenant by which he was sanctified a common thing, and insulted the Spirit of grace?
30. For we know Him who said, ***"Vengeance is Mine, I will repay,"*** says the Lord. And again, ***"The Lord will judge His people."***
31. It is a fearful thing to fall into the hands of the living God.
35. Therefore, do not cast away your confidence, which has great reward.
36. *For you have need of endurance,* so that after you have done the will of God, you may receive the promise.
37. ***"For yet a little while, and He who is coming will come and will not tarry.***
38. ***"Now the just shall live by faith; but if anyone draws back, My soul has no pleasure in him."***
39. But we are not of those who draw back to perdition, but of those who believe to the saving of the soul.

During the last days, Satan will be attacking us *(God's children)* with every means at his disposal, and he will do it in an all–out effort to cause us so much distress that we will become discouraged and tempted to give up — to ***"cast away our confidence."*** Therefore, this passage is a very solemn warning, that as we ***"see <u>THE DAY</u> approaching,"*** that will be a time of intense danger for all God's children here on earth. Jesus gave a similar warning about that future time in His prophecy concerning the time that will lead up to the end of the age. He said, ***"For false christs and false prophets will rise and show great signs and wonders to deceive, IF POSSIBLE, EVEN THE ELECT."*** *(Matthew 24: 24).* That will be a time of intense persecution of God's children, and when you add to that the fact that there will be numerous false christs and false prophets who will be using the supernatural power of Satan to deceive people into following them in Satan's path of destruction, you can begin to understand why it will be so important for believers to stand together with mutual exhortation and encouragement according to the leading of God's Holy Spirit.

Since God has given us these instructions on how to survive and overcome when that critical time comes, ***it's extremely important for us to know WHEN that day will be.*** Therefore, since God warned us to come together and exhort one another,***"and so much the more AS YOU** [WE] **SEE THE DAY APPROACHING," it is utterly absurd to think He would then make it impossible for us TO KNOW when that day is approaching.*** Yet, by the same token, it's in Satan's best interest to keep us from knowing when that day will be; *for if we don't see (recognize) when that day is approaching, we won't be on guard, and it will be much easier for him to deceive us and overcome us with discouragement by his persecution.* So what has Satan done in an effort to keep us from heeding God's warning and preparing for that critical time that will lead up to the end of the age? He simply came up with the lie ***that no one can know when Jesus will come back to earth.*** Not only did he initiate that lie, *but by his deceit he has managed to get many of the best known and most respected church leaders to teach it as though with Scriptural authority,* ***and to hold in contempt and heap scorn upon anyone who dares to teach otherwise.*** That has created an attitude within the church that discourages anyone from even going to the Lord and asking Him when He is coming again. James 4: 2 is a prophetically accurate description of the church *at this present time,* for it says, ***"Yet you do not have BECAUSE YOU DO NOT ASK."*** In one of Jesus's first promises at the beginning of His ministry, He revealed how important it is for us ***to ask,*** *and to do so persistently.*

Matthew 7: 7 - 8 *(NKJV)*
7. ***"Ask, and it will be given to you; seek, and you will find; knock, and it will be opened to you.***
8. ***"For everyone who asks receives, and he who seeks finds, and to him who knocks it will be opened"***

Have you ever prayed and asked when Jesus is going to come again? If not, could it be that you have simply accepted Satan's lie without even checking with God first? Instead of going to God in prayer, and ***asking, seeking and knocking*** in an effort to find out when Jesus is coming again, I suspect many in the church have simply accepted Satan's lie that it's just not possible for us to know when that will be. *Therefore,* ***the purpose of this book is to examine Scripture and prayerfully ASK, SEEK and KNOCK in an effort to see what God has revealed about WHEN Jesus will come back to this earth at the end of the age.***

In addition to the teaching that no one can know when Jesus is coming again, it's also generally taught that, ***One: Jesus's coming is imminent, meaning He could come at ANY TIME,*** *and* ***Two: that every prophecy has been fulfilled that's necessary in order for Him to return.*** Accordingly Chapter 1 of this book addresses these two teachings, and shows from Scripture why they cannot be true. The remainder of the book addresses the question: ***when is Jesus coming?*** It's true that there isn't a ***SINGLE specific passage of Scripture*** that definitively tells ***WHEN*** Jesus will come, *either to receive His Church in the Rapture or in the Second Coming to establish His earthly kingdom. Nevertheless, God has a schedule for the important events leading up to the return of Jesus at the end of the age, and we know He has progressively revealed that schedule through His prophets, for Amos 3: 7 says,* **"Surely the Lord God does nothing, unless He reveals His secret to His servants the prophets."** *Therefore, by a careful study of Scripture, we can learn more about* ***WHEN*** *Jesus will come* than most people dare to imagine. To accomplish this, the book is arranged in two separate parts as discussed below.

Part 1 discusses *Bible* **prophecies** that relate to *when Jesus is coming,* both in the Rapture to receive His bride the church, and in the Second Coming to establish His kingdom here on the earth. God began revealing His schedule in Exodus when He initiated His plan to deliver Israel from bondage in Egypt, and He finished revealing that schedule in the book of Revelation with the prophecy of the judgment that will take place before His throne at the end of Jesus's thousand–year–reign here on earth.

Part 2 discusses a number of *events in both the Old and New Testaments that appear to be* **prophetic examples** of the end times. By God's foreknowledge and sovereignty, He ordered the lives and events of many different people to provide examples to foreshadow things that will happen at the end of the age. Paul's letter to the Corinthians calls attention to how God used events in Israel's life as examples of things that would happen during these last days.

I Corinthians 10: 1 - 11 *(NKJV)*
1. Moreover, brethren, I do not want you to be unaware that all our fathers were under the cloud, all passed through the sea,
2. all were baptized into Moses in the cloud and in the sea,
3. all ate the same spiritual food,
4. and all drank the same spiritual drink. For they drank of that spiritual Rock that followed them, and that Rock was Christ.
5. But with most of them God was not well pleased, for their bodies were scattered in the wilderness.
6. ***Now these things became OUR EXAMPLES, to the intent that we should not lust after evil things as they also lusted.***
7. And do not become idolaters as were some of them. As it is written, ***"The people sat down to eat and drink, and rose up to play."*** *(Exodus 32: 6).*
8. Nor let us commit sexual immorality, as some of them did, and in one day twenty-three thousand fell;
9. nor let us tempt Christ, as some of them also tempted, and were destroyed by serpents;
10. nor complain, as some of them also complained, and were destroyed by the destroyer.
11. ***Now all these things happened to them as EXAMPLES, and they were written for our admonition, upon whom the ends of the ages have come.***

Prophetic examples aren't limited only to these experiences of Israel; however, God didn't specifically identify all the other events He used as such examples. Instead, He revealed the principle He used in establishing those examples. He showed us that principle when He called attention to the first such prophetic example — *that of Adam as and example of Jesus Christ.*

I Corinthians 15: 45 - 47 *(KJV)*
45. And so it is written, ***"The first man Adam, was made a living soul;"*** the last Adam was made a quickening spirit.
46. Howbeit that was not first which is spiritual, but that which is natural; and afterward that which is spiritual.
47. The first man is of the earth, earthy: the second man is the Lord from heaven.

God always provided examples in the natural realm to foreshadow similar future events that would take place in the spirit-realm. However, even though the examples took place in the natural realm, they usually involved details that catch our attention *because they are unusual and different from what we have come to expect as normal.* Therefore, when we see a natural event in Scripture for which God included details that are unusual and just don't seem to fit, or to add anything to the actual event being portrayed, we need to at least consider the possibility that God intended that event to be a prophetic example of things to come. For that reason, we need to read Scripture prayerfully, being ever mindful of the special provision God has given to us *(His children)* to help us understand His word.

I Corinthians 2: 9 - 10 & 14 *(NKJV)*
9. But as it is written: ***"Eye has not seen, nor ear heard, nor have entered into the heart of man the things which God has prepared for those who love Him."***
10. ***But God has revealed them to us through His Spirit. For the Spirit searches all things, yes, the deep things of God.***
14. ***But the natural man does not receive the things of the Spirit of God, for they are foolishness to him; nor can he know them, because they are spiritually discerned.***

Part 1

Prophecies Related To When Jesus Is Coming

And

The End Of The Age

Chapter 1

Can Jesus Come At Any Time?

Introduction. Because it is generally believed that *Jesus can come at any time,* there are very few who even bother to ask the question — ***when is He coming?*** The very existence of this book hinges on whether or not Jesus can come at any time; therefore, that subject is addressed in this first Chapter. Accordingly, we ***begin*** in Psalms, considering something God said through David that has a definite bearing on whether or not Jesus can come at any time. ***Then*** we'll look at an example involving *Israel under the law* that likewise gives a significant witness relative to that question.

The Witness from Psalms

Psalms 110: 1*(KJV)*
1. The LORD said unto my Lord, ***"Sit Thou at My right hand, UNTIL I make Thine enemies Thy footstool."***

It wasn't evident what this Psalm meant until after Jesus came and completed His earthly ministry. At that time, the Holy Spirit inspired Peter to quote that Psalm and show ***that it applied to Jesus AFTER He had been crucified and resurrected.***

Acts 2: 29 - 35 *(KJV) (This is part of Peter's sermon on the day of Pentecost.)*
29. ***"Men and brethren, let me freely speak unto you of the patriarch David, that he is both dead and buried, and his sepulcher is with us unto this day.***
30 ***"Therefore being a prophet and knowing that God had sworn with an oath to him, that of the fruit of his loins, according to the flesh, he would raise up Christ to sit on his throne,***

31. ***he seeing this before spake of the resurrection of Christ, that His soul was not left in hell, neither His flesh did see corruption.***
32. ***"This Jesus hath God raised up, whereof we all are witnesses.***
33. ***"Therefore being by the right hand of God exalted, and having received of the Father the promise of the Holy Ghost, he hath shed forth this, which ye now see and hear.***
34. ***"For David is not ascended into the heavens; but he saith himself, The LORD said unto my Lord, 'Sit Thou on My right hand,***
35. ***UNTIL I make Thy foes Thy footstool.'"***

By quoting this Psalm, Peter showed that David, *as a prophet,* had foretold what the Father was going to say to Jesus *when He ascended into heaven* ***AFTER He had been crucified, buried and resurrected***. Then, by revelation from the Holy Spirit, Peter revealed that *the outpouring of the Holy Spirit they had just experienced was* **GOD'S PROOF** ***that He had exalted Jesus to sit at His right hand in fulfillment of the prophecy in Psalms 110: 1.***

Next *we need to see* **how important this prophecy still is TODAY**. To do that, we need to consider something Joseph experienced long before when he was in prison in Egypt. At that time, Pharaoh had two dreams that troubled him greatly. In the first dream, he saw seven fat cows come up out of the river. They were followed by seven skinny cows that devoured the seven fat cows that had preceded them. Pharaoh's second dream was similar, in that he saw seven fully developed ears of grain come forth on one stalk. They were followed by seven withered and weather blasted ears on the same stalk, *and as with the cows,* the seven withered ears devoured the seven goodly ears. When Joseph told Pharaoh what the dreams meant, *he also explained* ***WHY there had been two dreams with the same message.***

Genesis 41: 32 *(NKJV)*
32. And the dream was repeated to Pharaoh twice ***it is because THE THING IS ESTABLISHED BY GOD, and God will shortly bring it to pass.***

God had given Pharaoh the dream two separate times *to* ***emphasize*** *the importance of what the dreams meant, and to show it would surely happen just as He revealed.* God used that same technique with the prophecy in Psalms 110: 1. He emphasized the importance and certainty of that prophecy; *not by repeating it twice,* ***but by repeating it SIX different times in the New Testament.*** *That means God included that prophecy a total of* **SEVEN different places in His Word** ***as follows:***

1. Psalms 110: 1
2. Matthew 22: 44
3. Mark 12: 36
4. Luke 20: 41 - 43
5. Acts 2: 30 - 35
6. Hebrews 1: 13
7. Hebrews 10: 9 - 13

Throughout Scripture, the number "***seven***" signifies Divine completion. A few examples of this are given below.

1. God established the week of ***seven*** days, as the basic division of time for mankind *(Ref: Genesis 2: 1 - 3).*
2. When Joshua fought the battle of Jericho, God required ***seven*** priests with ***seven*** trumpets to lead Israel around Jericho for ***seven*** days — once each day for the first six days — and then ***seven*** times on the ***seventh*** day *(Ref: Joshua 6: 1 - 4).*
3. God healed Naaman of leprosy by having him dip in the Jordan ***seven*** times *(Ref: I Kings 5: 10).*
4. In Revelation, God had John write to ***seven*** churches *(Ref: Rev 1: 19 - 20);* the book in God's hand was sealed with ***seven*** seals *(Ref: Rev 5: 1);* there were ***seven*** trumpets signaling ***seven*** seasons of trouble for the earth *(Ref: Rev 8: 2);* there were ***seven*** thunders revealing troubles that John was instructed not to record *(Ref: Rev 10: 4);* and last there were ***seven*** angels with ***seven*** vials which contain the completion of God's wrath against the wickedness of this earth *(Ref: Rev 15: 1).*

These examples show that the number *seven* has a special significance relative to the things of God. Therefore, by calling attention to the prophecy in Psalms 110: 1 ***seven*** *different times in Scripture,* God established that *it is* ***absolutely certain that Jesus must indeed remain seated at His (the Father's) right hand UNTIL He*** *(God the Father)* ***makes Jesus's enemies His footstool.*** As we shall see, Jesus's enemies have not yet been made to be His footstool; therefore, He will not be able to return to the earth, ***either in the Rapture for the church or at the Second Coming, UNTIL His enemies are made to be His footstool and He gets up from His seat at the right hand of the Father. That means Jesus's return cannot yet be imminent. Jesus will not be able to return UNTIL AFTER the Father fulfills the prophecy of Psalms 110: 1 by making Jesus's enemies become His footstool.***

Before we look at the witness to this truth given in the law, we need to see what it will mean for Jesus's enemies to become His footstool. It's abundantly evident that Jesus's enemies consist of Satan and the angels that have joined him in his rebellion against God. To see what it will mean for them to be made Jesus's enemies, we need to look at what God revealed in Isaiah.

Isaiah 66: 1 *(NKJV)*
1. Thus says the Lord: ***"Heaven is My throne, and earth is My footstool. Where is the house that you will build Me? And where is the place of My rest?"***

Although God cast Satan down to earth in exile when he rebelled in the far distant past, when Satan overcame Adam with sin, he regained the right to a place in heaven, and has exercised that right ever since the fall of Adam. Therefore, in order for Jesus's enemies to be made His footstool, Satan and his angels must be cast out of heaven and down to earth again, and this next time their exile will be permanent for all eternity to come. This is discussed in more detail in Chapter 5 entitled, ***"When Will God Make Jesus's Enemies His Footstool?"***

<u>The Witness from the Law.</u> The law's witness about when Jesus can come for His church is a little more involved than that above from the Psalms. However, as you shall see, the message is the same. This witness is provided by the law in the Old Testament; however, in order for us to understand it, we need to begin with something Jesus said the night before He was crucified. He knew His disciples' hearts were heavy because He had told them He was going away. Therefore, He comforted them by assuring them He would come again to get them so they would eventually be with Him.

John 14: 1 - 3 *(KJV)*
1. Let not your heart be troubled; ye believe in God, believe also in me.
2. ***In my Father's house <u>ARE</u> many mansions: if it were not so, I would have told you. <u>I GO TO PREPARE A PLACE FOR YOU.</u>***
3. ***And if I go <u>AND PREPARE A PLACE FOR YOU,</u> I will come again, and receive you unto myself; that where I am, there ye may be also.***

We understand that this promise wasn't limited to the disciples alone, but includes everyone who comes to faith in Jesus through the disciples' word. Accordingly, the very fact that *Jesus was going* ***to prepare a place for them*** *(us)* is in itself assurance that He is going to come back to get us. However, what Jesus said raises an interesting question. *Since there already*

"...ARE many mansions" *in heaven,* what was Jesus talking about when He said, ***"...I go to prepare A PLACE for you?"*** It stands to reason that ***many*** *mansions* will be required to house all those *(the church)* who come to faith in Him; ***however, He is going to prepare only "A place" — ONE SINGLE PLACE. So what can that ONE place be that Jesus is going to prepare for all those who make up the church?*** *Whatever it is, Verse 3 makes it clear that* ***He won't come again and receive us to Himself, UNTIL He has finished preparing THAT PLACE for us.*** Additionally, in Hebrews, we see that ***Jesus hasn't yet EVEN BEGUN preparing that place for us.***

Hebrews 10: 12 - 13 *(NKJV)*
12. But this man *[Jesus]*, after He had offered one sacrifice for sins forever, sat down at the right hand of God,
13. from that time waiting till His enemies are made His footstool.

After Jesus ascended into heaven, He sat down at the right hand of the Father, and was still sitting there when Hebrews was written shortly before the temple was destroyed in A. D. 70. Nothing has happened in the centuries since then that could possibly indicate Jesus's enemies have been made His footstool; therefore, we can only assume that He is still sitting at the Father's right hand. That means ***HE HASN'T YET BEGUN PREPARING THAT PLACE FOR US.*** In order to understand how Jesus will prepare that place for us, we first have to know *what that place is.* We can see that in the law in the Old Testament, but first we need to look at one more passage in the New Testament.

Hebrews 8: 1 - 5 *(NKJV)(This is discussing Jesus as the High Priest in heaven in contrast to the earthly high priests)*
1. Now this is the main point of the things we are saying: We have such a High Priest, ***who is seated at the right hand*** of the throne of the Majesty in the heavens,
2. A minister of the sanctuary, and of the true tabernacle, which the Lord erected, and not man.
3. For every high priest is appointed to offer both gifts and sacrifices. Therefore, it is necessary that this One *[Jesus, the High Priest in heaven]* also have something to offer.
4. For if He were on earth, He would not be a priest, since there are priests who offer the gifts according to the law:
5. ***who*** *[the earthly high priests]* ***serve the copy and shadow of the heavenly things,*** as Moses was divinely instructed when he was about to make the

tabernacle. For He said, ***"See, that you make all things according to the pattern shown you on the mountain."***

Israel's tabernacle/temple on earth, *and all the ministry done there,* was patterned after the temple in heaven. Therefore, everything Israel's high priest did in the earthly tabernacle/temple was an example of what Jesus will do as the great High Priest in the temple in heaven. Therefore, we'll look next at what Israel's high priest did in the Holy of Holies on the Day of Atonement; for that was an example of what Jesus had to do to make an atonement for the redeemed in heaven.

What Israel's High Priest Did on the Day of Atonement.

Leviticus 16 tells in detail what Aaron *(Israel's first high priest)* had to do to make an atonement in the earthly tabernacle.

Leviticus 16: 3, 5, 6 & 11 - 19 *(NKJV) (This is God speaking to Moses.)*
3. ***"Thus Aaron shall come into the Holy Place: with the blood of a young bull as a sin offering, and of a ram as a burnt offering.***
5. ***"And he** (the high priest) **shall take from the congregation of the children of Israel two kids of the goats as a sin offering, and one ram as a burnt offering.***
6 ***"Aaron shall offer the bull as a sin offering, which is for himself, and make atonement for himself and for his house.***
11. ***"And Aaron shall bring the bull of the sin offering, which is for himself, and shall make an atonement for himself, and for his house, and shall kill the bull of the sin offering which is for himself.***

The FIRST thing Aaron had to do was kill a bull as a sin offering, for himself and for his house. The term ***"his house,"*** referred to the others in the priestly family who served with him. Since Aaron and the other priests were all sinful men, Aaron had to kill the bull as the sin offering necessary to make the atonement *for himself and the other priests* ***before any of THEM could minister in behalf of the children of Israel.*** This was an example of Jesus, for although He personally was without sin, the Father had placed the sins of the world upon Him such that He became sin for us *(Ref: II Corinthians 5: 21).* Therefore, ***Jesus had to die, first of all to make an atonement for Himself because of OUR sins.*** Accordingly, when Jesus ascended to the Father on the morning of His resurrection *(Ref: John 20: 17),* He did that in fulfillment of the feast of the firstfruits of the wave sheaf, for the Father had to examine Him and ensure that His suffering had indeed cleansed Him of all our sins laid on Him by the Father *(Ref: Isaiah 53: 6).* Before we continue in Leviticus, we need to look in Revelation and see who Aaron's ***"house"*** represented in relation to Jesus as the High Priest in heaven.

Revelation 1: 4 - 6 *(NKJV)*
4. John, to the seven churches which are in Asia: Grace to you and peace from Him who is and who was and who is to come, and from the seven spirits who are before His throne;
5. and from Jesus Christ, the faithful witness, the firstborn from the dead, and the ruler over the kings of the earth. To Him who loved us and washed us from our sins in His own blood,
6. ***and has made us kings and PRIESTS to His God and Father,*** to Him be glory and dominion forever and ever. Amen.

Aaron's ***"house,"*** consisted of the other priests who served with him in the tabernacle; however, *as an example,* ***they represented the church of Jesus Christ, WHO WILL SERVE WITH HIM IN THE TEMPLE IN HEAVEN.*** This is confirmed in I Peter 2: 5, which was addressed to the church and says, ***"You also, as living stones, are being built up a spiritual HOUSE, A HOLY PRIESTHOOD, to offer up spiritual sacrifices acceptable to God through Jesus Christ."*** *Therefore, when Aaron killed the bull as the sin offering for himself and for his house, that was an example that foreshadowed the death of Jesus as the sin offering for our sins that were laid upon Him. Accordingly, By His own death, Jesus has fulfilled the example of the offering of the bull,* ***and has made an atonement for Himself and for His house*** *— all those who by faith make His death their personal sacrifice and* ***"sin offering."*** In Hebrews, it's confirmed that Jesus has done this in fulfillment of all the sin offerings ministered by the priests here on earth under the law.

Hebrews 10: 10 - 14
10. By that will *[God's will]* we have been sanctified through the offering of the body of Jesus Christ once for all.
11. And every priest stands ministering daily and offering, repeatedly the same sacrifices, which can never take away sins.
12. ***But this Man, after He had offered one sacrifice for sins forever, sat down at the right hand of God,***
13. ***from that time waiting till His enemies are made His footstool.***
14. ***For by one offering He has perfected forever those who are being sanctified.***

This shows that ***after*** Jesus finished making the atonement for Himself and His house *(the church) by fulfilling the example of the offering of the bull,* He sat down at the right hand of the Father. Jesus sat down at the right hand of the Father, which is the place in heaven that was represented by the Holy of Holies in the tabernacle and later in the temple. Therefore, Verses 12 & 13 *(above)* reveal that Jesus has been sitting in the Holy of Holies *(inside the veil)* of the temple in heaven ever since He ascended to heaven following His resurrection. Jesus been sitting there during all the centuries since He ascended, ***AND*** *He must remain there in the Holy of Holies in heaven* **UNTIL** *His enemies are made His footstool.* We'll see the significance of this as we continue reading in Leviticus and see *the other things* Aaron did that were also examples that must be fulfilled by Jesus in the temple in heaven.

Leviticus 16: 12 - 19 *(NKJV)* *(**After** making an atonement for himself and his house, Aaron had to do the following.)*
12. ***"THEN he shall take a censer full of burning coals of fire from the altar before the Lord, with his hands full of sweet incense beaten fine, and bring it inside the veil.***
13. ***"And he shall put the incense on the fire before the Lord, that the cloud of incense may cover the mercy seat that is on the testimony, lest he die.***
14. ***"He shall take some of the blood of the bull*** *[killed in Verse 11 above]* ***and sprinkle it with his finger on the mercy seat on the east side; and before the mercy seat he shall sprinkle some of the blood with his finger seven times.***
15. ***"Then he shall kill the goat of the sin offering, which is for the people, bring its blood inside the veil, do with that blood as he did with the blood of the bull, and sprinkle it on the mercy seat and before the mercy seat.***
16. ***"So he shall make atonement for the Holy Place, because of the uncleanness of the children of Israel, and because of their transgressions, for all their sins; and so he shall do for the tabernacle of meeting which remains among them in the midst of their uncleanness.***

After Aaron had made an atonement for himself and his house, *he also had to do all these things (verses 12 thru 16)* ***to make an atonement for the Holy Place itself.*** That was necessary because the tabernacle was located in the midst of the children of Israel, ***which meant it was defiled because it was surrounded by the children of Israel in their uncleanness.*** Therefore, these things Aaron did as the high priest on earth, *also was an example* that Jesus has to fulfill in the temple in heaven. *That means Jesus has to make an atonement for the temple in heaven,* **even including it's Holy Place — the**

very throne of God. We know this is true because of what is revealed in Hebrews 9.

Hebrews 9: 22 - 25 & 28 *(NKJV)*
22. And according to the law almost all things are purified with blood, and without shedding of blood there is no remission.
23. Therefore it was necessary that the copies of the things in the heavens should be purified with these, ***BUT THE HEAVENLY THINGS THEMSELVES WITH BETTER SACRIFICES THAN THESE.***
24. For Christ has not entered the holy places made with hands, which are copies of the true, but into heaven itself, now to appear in the presence of God for us;
25. not that He should offer Himself often, as the high priest enters in the Most Holy Place every year with the blood of another —
28. so Christ was offered once to bear the sins of many. To those who eagerly wait for Him He will appear a second time, apart from sin, for salvation.

By His death, Jesus Christ made the atonement for Himself as our sin-bearer, ***AND for us in the church — His house.*** In the same way, *He also made the **PROVISION*** necessary for the atonement *(cleansing)* of the temple and its Holy Place in heaven. But there is one important difference between the example on earth and the temple in heaven that was exemplified by Israel's tabernacle. After Aaron finished making an atonement for himself, his house, and for the people *(the children of Israel)*, he went ahead and also made the atonement for the earthly tabernacle and its Holy Place. He could do that because the atonement he had made for himself, the other priests, and for the people, had cleansed them such that their presence would not immediately defile the tabernacle again. However, that wasn't the case with Jesus as the High Priest in heaven. *He can't make the atonement to cleanse the temple and its Holy Place in heaven,* ***UNTIL His enemies are cast out and made to be His footstool.*** That's because the temple in heaven is being defiled by the presence in heaven of Satan and his angels, ***AND will continue to be defiled as long as Jesus's enemies (Satan and his angels) remain there in heaven.*** If Jesus should make the atonement necessary to cleanse the temple in heaven ***BEFORE*** Satan and his angels are cast out of heaven, ***the temple would simply be defiled all over again because of the on-going presence of Satan and his angels.*** Therefore, Jesus must wait to cleanse the temple in heaven until Satan and his angels have been cast out, and never again be able to defile heaven.

As we continue in Leviticus 16, Verse 17 gave a special restriction that had to be observed ***UNTIL* Aaron had made the atonement for the Holy Place and the tabernacle.** Because Aaron's duties were an example of what Jesus must do as the High Priest in heaven, the restriction given in Verse 17 is particularly important relative to our present study.

Leviticus 16: 17 *(ESV)*
17. ***"No one may be in the tent of meeting* from the time he** *[Aaron]* **enters to make atonement in the Holy Place until he comes out and has made atonement for himself and for his house and for all the assembly of Israel."**

Nobody else was allowed in the tabernacle of meeting UNTIL Aaron came out AFTER having completed the atonement for the Holy Place, for himself, for his house and for the people. That meant ***all the other priests*** *had to remain outside the tabernacle until Aaron had completed that part of his ministry.* That was because none of the other priests could minister in the tabernacle *until the Holy Place and the tabernacle had been cleansed. Therefore, by completing the atonement for the Holy Place and the tabernacle,* **Aaron actually prepared the tabernacle as A PLACE *for the* other priests to accomplish their ministry.** *Since that was an example of what Jesus must do as the High Priest in heaven,* **that means no other man** *[none of the priests who make up the church]* **can come into the temple in heaven UNTIL *Jesus has fulfilled that example by making an atonement for the temple and its Holy Place in heaven.*** Additionally, Jesus can't make the atonement to cleanse the temple and its Holy Place in heaven ***UNTIL* *Satan and his angels have been cast out of heaven.*** If He should cleanse heaven before Satan and his angels are cast out, *their continued presence there would simply defile it all over again.* Therefore, ***ONLY AFTER* *Satan and his angels have been cast out of heaven*** can Jesus get up from His seat next to the Father and make the atonement to cleanse heaven including its Holy Place. Until He does that, there won't be ***A PLACE*** in which the church *(the priests who will make up His house)* can minister in heaven. *That means the Rapture of the church cannot happen* **UNTIL AFTER** *Satan has been cast out of heaven and Jesus has* **PREPARED A PLACE** *of ministry for the church by cleansing heaven and its Holy Place.*

How and when God is going to accomplish that was one of His secrets; however, Amos 3: 7, says, ***"..the Lord God does nothing, unless He reveals His secret to His servants the prophets."*** God gave that promise to us through Amos, because He wants us to know that He has already revealed that secret to us through His prophets. Therefore, when we get to the appropriate place in our study, we'll see what God has revealed about both ***how*** and ***when*** He's going to make Jesus's enemies His footstool. ***But for God's revelation of that information to make sense, we need to start at the beginning of God's schedule and look at the events that will lead up to the time when He will have Satan and his angels cast out of heaven and down to the earth.***

Chapter 2

The Beginning Of God's Schedule

Introduction. Even before creation, God knew man was going to fall into sin, and He had a plan worked out to redeem man both from his sin, *and from the death that came as a result of that sin.* We know this is true because Revelation 13: 8 speaks of Jesus as ***"...the Lamb SLAIN from the foundation of the world."*** But God also has *a* ***schedule*** for all the things that make up His plan. This is apparent from what He revealed about the coming of Jesus.

Galatians 4: 4 - 5 *(NKJV)*
4. But *when the* ***fullness of the time*** *had come*, God sent forth His Son, born of a woman, born under the law,
5. to redeem those who were under the law, that we might receive the adoption as sons.

God didn't send Jesus until ***"...the fullness of the time"***— the time for Him to come according to God's schedule. The prophecies in Scripture are simply little glimpses of His schedule. We'll begin discussing God's schedule by looking in Exodus where He gave Moses instructions for the Passover. At that time, He also gave Israel a ***new calendar.***

A New Calendar for Israel.

Exodus 12: 1 - 3, 6 - 7 *(NKJV)*
1. Now the LORD spoke to Moses and Aaron in the land of Egypt, saying,
2. ***"This month shall be your beginning of months; it shall be the first month of the year to you."***

From that time on, God used this new calendar for all His dealings with Israel. The new calendar was like the old calendar in that it was divided into months *based on the moon's cycle of 29½ days.* However, the new calendar began with the month Abib, while the old calendar began with the month Tishri. Abib means ***"an ear of corn,"*** probably because that was the month when the grain harvest began. Possibly God made the new calendar begin with Abib, because that was the month in which *Jesus would rise from the dead as* ***the first-fruit of the HARVEST from the dead*** *(Ref: I Corinthians 15:20).* Tishri, *the first month of the old calendar,* simply means ***"begin."*** That may have been the month in which God accomplished the restoration of the earth in Genesis 1, which would account for its name meaning ***"begin."***

When God changed Israel's calendar, He also told Moses to begin counting off the days to establish Passover. Accordingly, He *would have given Moses those instructions* ***on the first day of that new first month Abib***. As we continue, we'll see that the first day of that new first month is prominent in God's plans for Israel. But first, as we continue in Exodus, we'll see how God's schedule for Passover related to His plan for man's redemption.

3. ***"Speak to all the congregation of Israel, saying: 'On the tenth of this monthevery man shall take a lamb, according to the house of his father, a lamb for a household.'"***
6. ***"Now you shall keep it [the lamb] until the fourteenth day of the same month*** *[Abib].* ***Then the whole assembly of the congregation of Israel shall kill it at twilight.***
7. ***"And they shall take some of the blood and put it on the two doorposts and on the lintel*** *[the top of the door frame]* ***of the houses where they eat it."***

Israel was to kill the Passover lamb in the late afternoon of the fourteenth day of the month, and eat it for the evening meal. In God's calendar, each day began with the evening meal at sundown, so Passover was ***the first meal of the fifteenth day***. The instructions for Passover applied only to Israel; however, *in God's greater plan,* that first Passover was one of His examples that foreshadowed the death of His Son as ***"...the Lamb of God who takes away the sin of the WORLD."*** *(John 1: 29).* According to that example:

- Jesus was crucified during the afternoon on the fourteenth day of Abib, ***which was the same time Israel was killing their Passover lambs***.
- When Israel sprinkled the lamb's blood on the two doorposts and the lintel, ***that formed the outline of a cross, foreshadowing how Jesus was going to die.***

- You may question this next one, but I think it fits too well to be a coincidence. Passover was *on the **15th DAY** after God gave the new calendar.* Since that first Passover took place in 1491 B. C., that means *Jesus came during the **15th CENTURY** after God gave the new calendar. So the first Passover was an example* ***that even foreshadowed WHEN Jesus would come as the Passover Lamb of God*****.** For Jesus came ***in the fullness of time, right on God's schedule*** as foreshadowed by that first Passover ***FIFTEEN centuries*** earlier in Egypt. Next we'll look at God's covenant.

Chapter 3

The Covenant

The Importance of the Covenant for Israel. God began His relationship with Israel by proving Himself as their God of deliverance and provision. He did that first by demonstrating His matchless power in delivering them from bondage in Egypt. Next, He saved them from Pharaoh's army by supernaturally providing for their escape across the Red Sea on dry ground. In the wilderness, He miraculously gave them water from the rock and manna from heaven. Then, after He had proved His dependability in their behalf, He brought them to Mount Sinai and gave them the opportunity to enter into a special covenant relationship with Himself.

Exodus 19: 3- 8 *(KJV)*
3. And Moses went up unto God, and the LORD called unto him out of the mountain, saying, ***"Thus shalt thou say to the house of Jacob, and tell the children of Israel:***
4. ***"Ye have seen what I did unto the Egyptians, and how I bare you on eagles' wings, and brought you unto Myself.***
5. ***"Now therefore, IF ye will obey My voice indeed, and keep My covenant, THEN ye shall be a peculiar treasure unto Me above all people: for all the earth is Mine:***
6. ***"And ye shall be unto Me a kingdom of priests, and an holy nation. These are the words which thou shalt speak unto the children of Israel."***
7. And Moses came and called for the elders of the people, and laid before their faces all these words which the LORD had commanded him.

Notice ***how quickly*** Israel accepted God's offer of that covenant.

8. And all the people answered together, and said, ***"All that the LORD hath spoken we will do."*** And Moses returned the words of the people unto the LORD.

Since Israel had just witnessed the miracles God had done to deliver them from bondage in Egypt, they probably thought the covenant would guarantee that God would keep on doing those same kind of miracles for them. Obviously they didn't consider what that covenant required of them. *And they certainly didn't consider what would happen* ***if they didn't keep their part of the covenant.*** Even to this day the Jews don't understand that keeping the covenant is ***ABSOLUTELY VITAL*** to their well–being as a people. In fact, ***most people*** don't give any thought to how important the covenant was, ***and still is,*** for Israel. Nevertheless, *even to this day,* everything ***either good or bad*** that happens to Israel, is a direct result of whether or not they are keeping the covenant their forefathers made with God long ago at Mt. Sinai. God warned them about this in Deuteronomy 28. The ***first 14 verses*** of that Chapter itemize how Israel would be blessed ***IF they obeyed the law according to the COVENANT. HOWEVER, the next 54 verses*** tell how they would be cursed ***IF they failed to obey the law according to their COVENANT.***

Consider this example: The Jews had been longing for their Messiah ***for centuries*** before Jesus came. Yet when He came, *in spite of all the miracles He did,* ***they not only didn't accept Him as their Messiah, but had Him crucified like a common criminal.*** **Have you ever wondered how in the world they could have done that? It was because *GOD BLINDED THEM and wouldn't let them recognize who Jesus really was!!***

Romans 11: 7 - 10, & 25 - 26 *(NKJV)*
7. What then? Israel has not obtained what it seeks; but the elect have obtained it, ***and the rest were BLINDED.***
8. Just as it is written, ***"God has given them the spirit of stupor*** *[slumber],* ***eyes that they should not see, and ears that they should not hear, to this day."***
9. And David says: ***"Let their table become a snare and a trap, a stumbling block and a recompense to them.***
10. ***"Let their eyes be darkened, so that they may not see, and bow down their back always."***

The only way Israel ***COULD*** *have recognized Jesus as their Messiah,* was if they had first acknowledged they were ***NOT*** *obeying the law according to* *their covenant, and repented, seeking God's mercy for their sin.* However, the next verse shows that one day they will finally have their eyes opened.

11. I say then, Have they stumbled that they should fall? Certainly not! But through their fall, to provoke them *[Israel]* to jealousy, salvation has come to the Gentiles.

Accordingly, Verses 25 and 26 raise a thought–provoking question.

25. For I do not desire, brethren, that you should be ignorant of this mystery, lest you should be wise in your own opinion; ***that <u>BLINDNESS IN PART</u> has happened to Israel until the fullness of the Gentiles has come in. [Note:*** *The **<u>fullness</u>** of the Gentiles is a reference to the end of the church age.]*
26. And so *[that is, at the end of the church age]* all Israel will be saved, as it is written: ***"The Deliverer will come out of Zion, and He will turn away ungodliness from Jacob*** *[Israel];*
27. ***"for this is My covenant with them, when I take away their sins."***

<u>A Point to Ponder.</u> At Jesus's **first** advent, God wouldn't let Israel recognize and accept Him as their Messiah ***<u>BECAUSE they refused to acknowledge they were not obeying the law according to their covenant, and refused to repent of their disobedience</u>***. *Therefore,* ***what must happen before Israel can recognize and accept Jesus when He returns at the Second Coming?*** *The only reasonable answer is,* ***<u>BEFORE</u> Jesus returns, <u>Israel will have to acknowledge their failure to obey God's word (the Law) according to their covenant, and repent as God requires</u>.*** As we continue in this study, it will become apparent that Israel's eventual repentance is a vital part of God's schedule for man's redemption. Next, we will look at ***<u>WHEN</u> the covenant actually began.***

<u>When the Covenant Actually Went Into Effect.</u> Although Exodus 19 *(above)* tells us *when Israel agreed to accept the covenant*, ***that wasn't when it actually went into effect.*** *To obey the law* ***according to the covenant,*** Israel had to be able to offer the sacrifices required by the law. Those sacrifices had to be offered on the altar in the tabernacle *(later replaced by the temple),* and they had to be offered by priests who had been ordained according to the law. Therefore, for about a year after Israel accepted God's covenant, they were building the tabernacle and *getting everything else ready so services could actually begin* ***according to the law.***

Only after all those necessary preparations were complete, could the covenant become fully effective. The last Chapter of Exodus tells us when *God commanded Moses to have the tabernacle set up with everything in readiness according to the law.*

Exodus 40: 1 - 3 & 33 - 35 *(KJV)*
1. Then the LORD spoke to Moses, saying:
2. ***"ON THE FIRST DAY OF THE FIRST MONTH you shall set up the tabernacle of the tent of meeting***
3. ***"And thou shalt put therein the ark of the testimony, and cover the ark with the veil.***

The verses that followed gave a detailed record of all the LORD commanded Moses to do to get ready for the covenant relationship to begin. When everything was ready, the LORD Himself moved to show that His covenant with Israel had officially begun.

33. And he *[Moses]* raised up the court all round about the tabernacle and the altar, and hung up the screen of the court gate. So Moses finished the work.
34. ***Then a cloud covered the tabernacle of meeting, and the glory of the LORD filled the tabernacle.***
35. ***And Moses was not able to enter the tabernacle of meeting, because the cloud rested above it, and the glory of the LORD filled the tabernacle.***

By God's command, Israel began their covenant relationship with Him on ***THE 1ST DAY OF THE 1ST MONTH*** *(Abib/Nisan).* Therefore, ***that became the covenant's ANNIVERSARY DATE.*** Remember, this was the same as the date when God had begun revealing His schedule by changing Israel's calendar in Exodus 12. As we continue this study, that date will come up several more times as additional important milestones in God's ongoing schedule for man's redemption.

The Covenant Broken and Set Aside. For roughly 900 years after Israel entered into the covenant, they vacillated between walking in some measure of obedience, *and outright disobedience.* The times of obedience were marked by God's blessings, but they suffered His discipline when they fell into disobedience. Unfortunately, with each repetition of that cycle, Israel became increasingly more rebellious against God. Finally, when Israel was overcome by Nebuchadnezzar of Chaldea, Ezekiel was carried away captive to Babylon. While he was there he had a vision that revealed how God was progressively and reluctantly removing His presence from Israel. This was the prelude to Israel's final destruction and captivity by Nebuchadnezzar.

Ezekiel 8: 3 - 5 *(NKJV)*
3. He *[the Lord God]* stretched out the form of a hand, and took me by a lock of my hair; and the Spirit lifted me up between the earth and heaven, and brought me in visions of God to Jerusalem, to the door of the north gate of the inner court, where the seat of the image of jealousy was, which provokes *[God]* to jealousy. *[Israel had even erected an idol in the court of the temple (Ref: Jeremiah 7: 30 & II Kings 21: 4 - 7)]*
4. *And behold,* ***the glory of the God of Israel was there*** *like the vision that I saw in the plain.*
5. Then He said to me, ***"Son of man, lift your eyes now toward the north,"*** *and there, north of the altar gate,* ***was this image of jealousy in the entrance.***

Ezekiel 9: 3 *(NKJV)*
3. Now the ***glory of the God of Israel had gone up FROM the cherub*** *[over the mercy seat],* ***where it had been, to the threshold of the temple....***

Ezekiel 10: 18 - 19 *(NKJV)*
18. ***Then the glory of the LORD departed from the threshold of the temple*** and stood over the cherubim.
19. And the cherubim lifted their wings and mounted up from the earth in my sight. When they went out, the wheels were beside them; ***and they stood at the door of the east gate of the LORD'S house, and the glory of the God of Israel was above them.***

Ezekiel 11: 22 - 23 *(NKJV)*
22. So the cherubim lifted up their wings, with the wheels beside them, and the glory of the God of Israel was high above them.
23. And ***the glory of the LORD went up from the midst of the city and stood on the mountain, which is on the east side of the city.***

Because of Israel's continued willful disobedience, God withdrew His glory, not only from the temple, which had been defiled, but also from the entire nation of Judah that had defiled it. In that way, God revealed that Israel had broken their covenant with Him, and He was removing the blessing of

His presence from them. Accordingly, in Ezekiel 12, God revealed that He would cause the nation of Judah to cease to exist. Her cities would become uninhabited and the land would become desolate. About 18 years later, in fulfillment of that prophecy, Nebuchadnezzar laid siege to Jerusalem in 587 B. C., and eventually destroyed the city and the temple, and carried the majority of the people into captivity. God had revealed through Jeremiah that this captivity was going to last seventy years *(Ref: Jeremiah 29: 10).* So the covenant relationship between God and Israel was interrupted, and the nation of Israel effectively ceased to exist for seventy years. This brings us to Daniel and his prophecy of the seventy weeks.

Chapter 4

The Prophecy of Seventy Weeks

Daniel's Prayer of Confession. Daniel was only a child when he was taken to Babylon in the mass deportation of the kingdom of Judah, but he had determined to be faithful to God and obedient to His laws and had remained obedient throughout the long years of captivity. He was aware of God's word through Jeremiah that the captivity was to last for seventy years, and when the end of those seventy years drew near, he began to pray for the restoration he believed was soon to take place.

Daniel 9: 1 - 3, & 21 - 27 *(KJV)*
1 In the first year of Darius the son of Ahasuerus, of the seed of the Medes, who was king over the realm of the Chaldeans:
2. in the first year of his reign, I Daniel understood by books the number of the years, whereof the word of the Lord came to Jeremiah the prophet, that He would accomplish seventy years in the desolation of Jerusalem.
3. And I set my face unto the Lord God, to seek by prayer and supplications, with fasting sackcloth, and ashes.

As Daniel prayed, the angel Gabriel appeared to him and revealed that God's plans were different from what Daniel had expected.

21. yea, while I was speaking in prayer, even the man Gabriel, whom I had seen in the vision at the beginning, being caused to fly swiftly, touched me about the time of the evening oblation.
22. And he informed me, and talked with me, and said, ***"O Daniel, I am now come forth to give thee skill and understanding."***

23. ***"At the beginning of thy supplications the commandment came forth, and I am come to show thee, for thou art greatly beloved: therefore, understand the matter, and consider the vision.***
24. ***"Seventy weeks are determined upon THY PEOPLE, and upon THY HOLY CITY. To finish the transgression, to make an end of sins, to make reconciliation for iniquity, to bring in everlasting righteousness, to seal up the vision and prophecy, and to anoint the Most Holy."***

God was ***NOT*** going to restore Israel and fulfill His promises for the glorious Messianic kingdom at the end of those ***seventy years*** like Daniel expected. Instead, God was setting aside seventy weeks, which are understood to be *seventy weeks–of–years,* or a total of four hundred and ninety *(490)* years.

As we consider Verse 24, it's important to see that although God was setting aside ***seventy weeks*** specifically *to accomplish His purposes upon* ***Israel and Jerusalem, the final results of what He was going to do would not be limited to Israel alone.*** By the end of those seventy weeks, God would ***"...make an end of sins,...make reconciliation for iniquity,...bring in everlasting righteousness,...seal up*** *[or fulfill]* ***the vision and prophecy, and... anoint the Most Holy."*** Anointing the ***"Most Holy"*** wasn't a reference to cleansing the Most Holy place in the temple in Jerusalem; but rather to the ultimate cleansing of the Most Holy place in the temple in heaven, which Jesus will accomplish after Satan is cast out of heaven *as briefly mentioned in Chapter 1.* This means that by the end of the seventy weeks *(490 years)* God determined to complete His plans for Israel; however, *He will also have completed His plan of redemption for the Gentiles, and will even have cleansed the temple in heaven.* Therefore, if we hope to understand what is ahead for the church and the Gentile world, we must prayerfully study what God revealed about the critical 490 years He determined for Israel and Jerusalem. Next Daniel was told when those 490 years were going to begin, and what would happen at the end of the first sixty-nine weeks *(483 years).*

When Did the Seventy-Week Prophecy Begin?

Daniel 9: 25 *(KJV)*
25. Know therefore and understand, that ***from the GOING FORTH*** of the commandment to restore and to build Jerusalem *unto the Messiah the Prince* shall be seven weeks, and threescore and two weeks *[483 years]:* the street shall be built again, and the wall, even in troublous times.

There was going to be a command to restore and build Jerusalem, *and the date that command **WENT FORTH** was when the seventy weeks (490 years) would begin.* Daniel received this prophecy in 553 B. C., so Jerusalem and the temple had already been in ruins for forty years. The command that would mark the beginning of the seventy weeks had not yet been given, so Daniel had no idea when those seventy weeks would actually begin. Neither did he realize there would be three different commands that would address the restoration of Jerusalem. The first was in 536 B. C., the second in 457 B. C., and the last in 444 B. C. That means we have the burden of determining which one of those commands established the start-date for this prophecy.

***Note:* It's extremely important to use the correct start–date for the seventy–week prophecy. If we use the wrong date, all our attempts to fully understand the prophecy will be in vain. Additionally, since this prophecy is the basis for the rest of God's schedule, if we use the wrong start–date for this prophecy, our attempts to understand the remainder of God's schedule will also be in vain.**

The Command of 536 B. C. The ***first*** *of these commands* was made by King Cyrus of Persia. He decreed that all the Jews who were willing, *could return to Jerusalem and rebuild the temple (Ref: Ezra 1: 1 - 4).* It isn't reasonable that this command was the start–date for the seventy–week prophecy because of the following:

A. Scripture doesn't give the ***PRECISE DATE the command of 536 B. C. WENT FORTH,*** and that was to be the start–date for the prophecy.

B. When we count the 69 weeks *(483 years)* from 536 B. C., it gives us 53 B. C. as the date the Messiah would have come *based on this command.* That of course was not only about *50 years* ***before*** *Jesus was actually born,* but was also *about 80 years* ***before*** *He began His ministry.*

The Command of 444 B. C. This was the ***last*** *command* related to the restoration of Jerusalem and was made by King Artaxerxes of Persia. He issued this command to rebuild Jerusalem's walls and gates. This also couldn't have been the command that marked the beginning of the seventy-week prophecy because of the following:

A. Scripture likewise doesn't give the ***PRECISE DATE this command WENT FORTH.***

B. When we count 69 weeks *(483 years)* from 444 B. C., it gives us A. D. 39 as the date when the ***Messiah should have come based on a start–date***

of 444 B. C. That, of course, was nine years <u>AFTER</u> Jesus was crucified at the <u>END</u> of His ministry.

<u>Note:</u> *Most well known prophecy teachers use the 444 B.C. date as the beginning of the seventy weeks. They do so because of the work by Sir Robert Anderson in his book entitled,* **"The Coming Prince."** *He used 444 B. C. as the start-date, and came up with April 6 of A.D. 32 as the* **end** *of the first sixty-nine weeks, which is when he said Jesus made His triumphal entry into Jerusalem. To arrive at this date, he used 360 days for each year, which he said is the number of days the Bible always uses for a prophetic year.* ***However, no such statement is made anywhere in Scripture.*** *The Bible uses the Jewish calendar to determine the length of each year, and a typical year in the Jewish calendar consists of 12* **lunar** *months. Since the lunar cycle is 29½ days, the Jewish months vary between 29 and 30 days in length, with twelve months totaling only 355 days. Since this doesn't add up to a full year, the Jewish calendar has a leap year every two to three years in which a 13th month is added. This makes the years in the Jewish calendar average out to be the same as our years of 365 days, which means* **sixty-nine weeks** *(483 years)* ***using the Jewish calendar cover <u>the same total length of time</u> as 483 years in our Gregorian calendar. Therefore,*** *as noted above,* ***if we count sixty-nine weeks (483 years) from the command of 444 B. C., it doesn't agree with the time when Jesus actually came.*** *This leaves us with the command issued by King Artaxerxes of Persia in 457 B. C.*

<u>The Command of 457 B. C.</u> King Artaxerxes of Persia issued this command in the seventh year of his reign. I believe this was the command that established the start-date for Daniel's seventy–week prophecy, ***because it's the only one of the three commands for which Scripture gives <u>the precise date when it WENT FORTH,</u>*** which is stipulated in Daniel 9: 25 *(above)*. Also, the ***<u>PRECISE DATE</u> this command went forth adds to its credibility as the command that marked the beginning of the seventy weeks.***

Ezra 7: 9 *(KJV)*

9. For ***<u>upon the first day of the first month BEGAN he to go up from Babylon,</u>*** and on the first day of the fifth month came he to Jerusalem, according to the good hand of his God upon him.

The <u>first day of the first month</u> pops up again. As already discussed, ***that was the date when God had established His covenant with Israel.*** When they broke the covenant by their disobedience and rebellion, God caused them to suffer seventy years of Babylonian captivity without His covenant-protection. Accordingly, when He was ready to restore His mercy and favor to Israel, He established *seventy* ***weeks*** during which He would complete His plans for them. However, *since the covenant was the only basis God had established for dealing with Israel,* ***when He began dealing with them again for those seventy weeks, one of the first things He had to do was restore them into the covenant relationship.*** That means it's important to see what the command of 457 B. C. actually accomplished.

What the Command of 457 B. C. Accomplished. King Artaxerxes provided silver and gold as well as everything else necessary to resume services in Israel's temple *(Ref: Ezra 7: 15 - 23).* He also decreed that those who ministered in the house of God in Jerusalem would be exempt from any ***"...toll, tribute, or custom."*** *(Ezra 7: 24). But look at what else he instructed Ezra to do.*

Ezra 7: 25 - 26 *(NKJV)*
25. And you, Ezra, according to your God–given wisdom, set magistrates and judges who may judge all the people who are in the region beyond the River, ***all such as know the laws of your God; AND TEACH THOSE WHO DO NOT KNOW THEM.***
26. Whosoever ***will NOT observe the law of thy God,*** *and the law of the king [Notice that Artaxerxes put the law of God ahead of his own law],* let judgment be executed speedily on him, whether it be death, or banishment, or confiscation of goods, or imprisonment.

By his command of 457 B.C., *King Artaxerxes* ***reestablished the law of God as THE LAW OF THE LAND in Israel.*** God had moved on Artaxerxes' heart to use his authority as king of Persia ***to REESTABLISH the law of God as the PRIMARY BASIS for government in Israel.*** Not only did God use the ***"going forth"*** *of Artaxerxes' command* to establish the beginning of the seventy-week prophecy, *but* ***He also used Artaxerxes' authority to require the children of Israel to obey the law of God.*** In that way, ***God reinstated Israel in His covenant at the beginning of the seventy-week prophecy, AND HE DID THAT ON THE ANNIVERSARY DATE OF THE COVENANT.*** *What more could God have done to show that He was using the command of 457 B. C. as the beginning of His seventy-week prophecy?* Therefore, *we'll use the command of 457 B. C. as the start–date and see if the*

Messiah actually came sixty-nine weeks later as the prophecy given through Daniel said He would.

When The Messiah Should Have Come According To Daniel 9: 25. Verse 25 says, ***"...from the GOING FORTH of the commandment to restore and to build Jerusalem unto the Messiah the Prince shall be seven weeks, and threescore and two weeks."*** Using sixty–nine weeks of ***seven years each,*** meant the Messiah was prophesied to come ***four-hundred and eighty-three (483) years after the command went forth on THE FIRST DAY OF THE FIRST MONTH IN 457 B. C.*** Accordingly, when we subtract 457 B.C. from 483 years, that leaves 26 years, which was the time that would have to pass ***in the Christian Era,*** *before the Messiah should have come based on the command of 457 B.* C. The passage of 26 years into the Christian era brings us to A. D. 27. Therefore, using command of 457 B. C. as the start–date for the sixty–nine weeks (483 years), ***the Messiah should have come on THE FIRST DAY OF THE FIRST MONTH (Abib/Nisan) in A. D. 27.*** That would have been ***EXACTLY 483 years*** after the command to rebuild Jerusalem went forth in 457 B. C.

This may *seem* to be a problem, since it's generally accepted that Jesus's ***coming as the Messiah*** *(the Christ),* occurred in A. D. 30 when He made what is called His triumphant entry into Jerusalem. However, ***is that the time God recognizes as the coming of the Messiah?*** *There's nothing in Scripture that indicates Jesus's triumphal entry into Jerusalem was what constituted His coming as the Messiah.* Also, *there's no record in Scripture that anyone began following Jesus* ***because His triumphal entry into Jerusalem CONVINCED THEM He was the Messiah.*** Quite to the contrary, within two weeks of Jesus's triumphal entry, *He was condemned to death and crucified* ***in an attempt to repudiate any claim that He might be the Messiah. Therefore, it's much more reasonable that Jesus's coming as the Messiah was at the BEGINNING of his earthly ministry, RATHER THAN AT THE END.*** Keeping that in mind, we'll consider what happened at the beginning of Jesus's ministry and see if that doesn't satisfy ***His coming as the Messiah much better than His entry into Jerusalem shortly before His crucifixion.***

When the Messiah Came According to the Gospel of John.
There are different opinions as to the actual dates of the events in Jesus's life. I'm using the information in a Bible published by Holman Company in 1942. According to that source, Jesus was baptized by John the Baptist near

the end of A. D. 26. The Gospel of John doesn't give an account of Jesus's baptism, but it does describe His ***second*** encounter with John the Baptist, which took place in the spring of A. D. 27. That occurred shortly ***AFTER*** *Jesus's temptation in the wilderness.* John's record of that second encounter is unusual, ***because he gave a day-by-day account of the events that took place for the two weeks that followed that second encounter.*** This may not seem unusual until you consider that John wrote his Gospel around A. D. 90, which was ***sixty years AFTER*** those two weeks took place. Most of us would have trouble giving a day–by–day account of a two week period that happened *six months ago,* ***much less a two week period that happened over SIXTY YEARS ago.*** So it is extremely unusual that John remembered that much detail about those particular two weeks. It's equally unusual that he would consider *such seemingly trivial information* worth including in his Gospel record. *Therefore, I believe God caused John both to remember and to include that information,* ***and I believe He did it because it's important for us to know.*** As we consider those two weeks, I think you'll see why they are important

John 1: 19 - 34 *(NKJV)*
19. Now this is the testimony of John *[the Baptist]*, when the Jews sent priests and Levites from Jerusalem to ask him, ***"Who are you?"***
20. He confessed, and did not deny, but confessed, ***"I am not the Christ*** *[Messiah].*
21. And they asked him, ***"What then? Are you Elijah?"*** He said, ***"I am not." "Are you the Prophet?"*** *(Ref: Deuteronomy 18: 18 - 19)*, And he answered, ***"No."***

Israel's religious leaders knew the time was at hand for the Messiah to come; therefore, they were alert to the appearance of anybody who might possibly have been Him. Since John the Baptist was getting so much attention the leaders in Jerusalem sent a committee to check him out. But John assured them he was not the Messiah or any of the other people they suggested.

22. Then they said to him, ***"Who are you, that we may give an answer to those who sent us: What do you say about yourself."***
23. He said: ***"'I am the voice of one crying in the wilderness: make straight the way of the Lord,' as the prophet Isaiah said."***

John the Baptist denied being the Messiah, ***but admitted being the one God had sent to prepare the way for the Messiah.*** It seems strange that God would have sent John *to prepare the way for Jesus as the Messiah* ***at***

the <u>BEGINNING</u> of His ministry, *and then not consider Him to come as the Messiah* ***<u>UNTIL THREE YEARS LATER WHEN HIS MINISTRY WAS OVER.</u>*** That would have been the case if Jesus's triumphal entry in A. D. 30 was when God considered the Messiah to have come.

24. Now those who were sent were from the Pharisees.
25. And they asked him, saying, ***"Why then do you baptize if you are not the Christ, nor Elijah, nor the Prophet?"***
26. John answered them, saying, ***"I baptize with water, but there stands One among you whom you do not know.***
27. ***"It is He who, coming after me, is preferred before me, whose sandal strap I am not worthy to loose."***
28. These things were done in Bethabara beyond the Jordan, where John was baptizing.
29. The ***next day*** John saw Jesus coming toward him, and said, ***"Behold! The Lamb of God who takes away the sin of the world!"***
30. ***"This is He of whom I said, 'After me comes a Man who is preferred before me, for He was before me.'"***
31. ***"I did not know Him: but that He should be <u>REVEALED TO ISRAEL,</u> therefore*** *[for that reason]* ***I am come baptizing with water."***
32. And John bare witness, saying, ***"I saw the Spirit descending from heaven like a dove, and He remained on Him.***
33. ***"I did not know Him, but He who sent me to baptize with water said to me, 'Upon whom you see the Spirit descending, and remaining on Him, this is He who baptizes with the Holy Spirit.'***
34. ***And I have seen and testified that <u>THIS IS THE SON OF GOD.</u>"***

In Verse 31 John made it pretty clear that God had led him to reveal Jesus to Israel as the Messiah. Then in Verses 32 & 33 John gave his testimony as to what happened when he baptized Jesus, and told how God said *he could recognize the Messiah when He came.* In verse 34, John gave his own personal testimony as to whom he believed Jesus was. ***By that personal testimony, John the Baptist revealed to Israel that <u>JESUS WAS THE LONG AWAITED MESSIAH.</u>*** I realize John didn't actually say the words — ***"<u>Jesus is the Messiah.</u>"*** But remember, he was talking ***to the priests and Levites of Israel,*** and those men knew the Old Testament prophecies concerning the Messiah. All we have to do is look at one of David's Psalms to see how clearly verse 34 ***should have shown them that Jesus was the Messiah.***

Psalms 2: 1 - 7 *(NKJV)*
1. Why do the nations rage, and the people plot a vain thing?

2. The kings of the earth set themselves, and the rulers take counsel together, **against the Lord, and against <u>HIS ANOINTED</u>** *[the Messiah]*, saying,
3. ***"Let us break Their bonds in pieces and cast away Their cords from us.***
4. He who sits in the heavens shall laugh; the Lord shall hold them in derision.
5. Then He shall speak to them in His wrath, and distress them in His deep displeasure.
6. ***"Yet I have set My King on My holy hill of Zion.***
7. ***"I will declare the decree; The Lord has said to Me, '<u>You are MY SON, today I HAVE BEGOTTEN YOU.</u>'"***

This Psalm revealed **that God's Anointed** *(the Messiah)* ***was not only <u>His King</u>, but would also be the one to whom God said, "You are <u>MY SON, TODAY I HAVE BEGOTTEN YOU</u>."*** The priests and Levites *to whom John was talking* were well aware that this was a Messianic Psalm; *therefore,* ***they knew the Messiah would also be the <u>SON OF GOD</u>*** as well as Israel's King. *So when John the Baptist identified Jesus as* ***the Son of God, <u>HE WAS IN FACT PROCLAIMING THAT JESUS WAS THE MESSIAH.</u>*** Accordingly, ***I believe the day John made that proclamation was <u>THE DAY</u> that constituted the coming of Jesus as the Messiah.*** The priests and Levites who heard John, chose to ignore what he said***, but the next day John the Baptist had a very different audience.*** At this point, we will begin counting the days in John's day-to-day account of the following two weeks.

John 1: 35 - 49 *(NKJV)*
35. Again ***the NEXT DAY***, John stood with two of his disciples, **[Day No. one]**
36. And looking at Jesus as He walked, he said, ***"Behold the Lamb of God!"***
37. The two disciples heard Him speak, and they followed Jesus.
38. Then Jesus turned, and seeing them following, said to them, ***"What do you seek?"*** They said to Him, ***"Rabbi"*** (which is to say when interpreted, Teacher), ***"where are You staying?"***
39. He said to them, ***"come and see."*** They came and saw where He was staying, and remained with Him that day (now it was about the tenth hour).
40. One of the two who heard John speak, and followed Him, was Andrew, Simon Peter's brother.

41. He first found his own brother Simon, and said to him, ***"We have found <u>THE MESSIAH</u>"*** (which is translated, the Christ).
42. And he brought him to Jesus. Now when Jesus looked at him, He said, ***"You are Simon, the son of Jonah. You shall be called Cephas"*** (which is translated, A Stone).
43. ***The following day*** Jesus wanted to go to Galilee, and He found Philip and said to him ***"Follow Me."*** **[Day No. two]**
44. Now Philip was from Bethsaida, the city of Andrew and Peter.
45. Philip found Nathanael and said to him, ***"We have found Him of whom Moses in the law, and also the prophets, wrote, – Jesus of Nazareth, the son of Joseph."***
46. And Nathanael said to him, ***"Can any good come out of Nazareth?"*** Philip said to him, ***"Come and see."***
47. Jesus saw Nathanael coming toward Him, and said to him, ***"Behold, an Israelite indeed, in whom is no deceit!"***
48. Nathanael said to Him, ***"How do You know me?"*** Jesus answered and said to him, ***"Before Philip called you, when you were under the fig tree, I saw you."***
49. Nathanael answered and said to Him, ***"Rabbi, You are THE SON OF GOD! You are THE KING OF ISRAEL!"*** *(Ref: Psalm 2: 2, & 6 - 7)*

Although the priests and Levites heard enough ***that they <u>SHOULD</u> have recognized*** Jesus as the Messiah, because their hearts were hardened, they could not receive that truth. But when Jesus's future disciples heard John's testimony, ***they immediately understood that Jesus was the Messiah and they believed and immediately began to follow Him.*** But John's account of the days continued.

John 2: 1, 12 - 16 *(NKJV)*
1. ***On the third day*** there was a wedding in Cana of Galilee, and the mother of Jesus was there.

Jesus, His mother, and His four new disciples spent the third day at the wedding in Cana. **[Day No. Three.]**

12. After this *(after the day of the wedding)* He went down to Capernaum, He, His mother, His brothers, and His disciples; and ***they did not stay there many days.***

From Cana to Capernaum is about 20 miles as a crow flies, so it would have taken at least a full day to make that trip. **[Day No. four.]** Jesus knew

He had to be at Jerusalem in time for the Passover, so they couldn't stay too long in Capernaum. Since they stayed more than one, but ***"not many days,"*** I'm assuming they spent three days in Capernaum. [**Days No. five, six, and seven.**]
13. Now the Passover of the Jews was at hand, and Jesus went up to Jerusalem.

A straight line from Capernaum to Jerusalem is *a little* ***more*** *than eighty miles*. However, because of the rough terrain, they wouldn't have walked in a straight line. The paths they had to follow would probably have added several miles to that distance. Because of the poor roads and rough terrain, it would have taken at least five full days to make the trip. [**Days No. eight, nine, ten, eleven, and twelve**]. So Jesus and His disciples would have arrived in Jerusalem late on the twelfth day ***following John's proclamation identifying Jesus as the Messiah.***
14. And He found in the temple those who sold oxen and sheep and doves, and the money changers doing business.
15. When He had made a whip of cords, He drove them all out of the temple, with the sheep and the oxen, and poured out the changers' money and overturned the tables.
16. And He said to those who sold doves, ***"Take these things away! Do not make My Father's house a house of merchandise!"***

Since they would have reached Jerusalem *late on the twelfth day*, it would have been ***the next day,*** before they went to the temple. So the day Jesus cleansed the temple would have been ***the THIRTEENTH day AFTER John's proclamation.*** That wouldn't have been the Passover itself, ***for the Passover was a Sabbath,*** which was a *high day (Ref: John 19: 31), and even as careless as the Jews had become, they wouldn't have been buying and selling on the Passover–Sabbath, which was* ***the FIFTEENTH of Abib.*** Therefore, the day Jesus cleansed the temple would have been ***the fourteenth of Abib,*** *the day of preparation.*

We've been counting the days ***FOLLOWING the day*** John the Baptist made his proclamation that identified Jesus as the Messiah. If we subtract those ***thirteen*** *days* from the actual ***date (the fourteenth)*** when He cleansed the temple, it leaves us with ***ONE***, which would have been ***the first day of the first month*** (Abib), and that was the day when John made the proclamation by which the disciples recognized Jesus was the Messiah. That means John made his proclamation identifying Jesus as the Messiah on the ***FIRST DAY OF THE FIRST MONTH in A. D. 27, which was EXACTLY sixty-nine***

weeks** (483 years)* ***after **<u>THE FIRST DAY OF THE FIRST MONTH</u>** ***in 457 B. C.,*** when Artaxerxes' command ***went forth.*** I believe this confirms that the seventy weeks of Daniel's prophecy began on the first day of the first month in 457 B. C.

This also means ***the first day of the first month in A. D. 27***, was **<u>THE BEGINNING OF THE SEVENTIETH (70th) WEEK OF DANIEL</u>**. Therefore, ***the three years of Jesus's ministry were actually the first three years of the seventieth week of Daniel, and that means <u>ONLY FOUR YEARS OF THAT SEVENTIETH WEEK STILL REMAIN TO BE SPENT AT THE END OF THE AGE.</u>*** Accordingly, the prophecies in Revelation that relate to the end of this age ***will all be fulfilled during the last <u>FOUR</u> years of this age, rather than during the last <u>SEVEN</u> years, as is commonly taught. This is because the first three years of the seventieth week of Daniel have already passed, coming to their end when Jesus was crucified.*** That's why *all of the prophecies in Revelation give a time period* ***<u>LESS THAN FOUR YEARS.</u>*** This brings us to our next question: ***what was prophesied to happen at the end of the sixty-nine weeks?***

<u>*What Was Prophesied to Happen at the End of the Sixty-nine Weeks?*</u>

Daniel 9: 25 - 26 *(KJV)*
25. Know therefore and understand, that ***from*** *the going forth of the commandment to restore and to build Jerusalem* **unto** *the Messiah the Prince* shall be seven weeks, and threescore and two weeks *[483 years]:* the street shall be built again, and the wall, even in troublous times.

We already discussed the first part of Verse 25, which was fulfilled when John the Baptist identified Jesus as the Messiah exactly sixty–nine weeks *(483 years)* ***after*** 457 B. C, when Artaxerxes's command ***WENT FORTH*** to restore and build Jerusalem. *The prophecy that the streets and wall would be built again was fulfilled by Nehemiah* ***during*** *those sixty-nine weeks, but* ***after*** *Artaxerxes's command of 445 B. C. (Ref: Nehemiah 2: 1 - 8).* This brings us to the prophesies of Verse 26.

26. And ***after*** threescore and two weeks, shall Messiah be cut off, but not for himself: and the people of the prince who is to come will destroy the city and the sanctuary *[temple].* And its end will come with a flood; even to the end there will be war; desolations are determined.

In A. D. 30, *three years **after** Jesus came as the Messiah,* He was crucified — ***"cut off;"*** not for any sins of His own, but for the sins of the world. *(Ref: I John 2: 2).* That fulfilled the first part of Verse 26. Forty years later in A. D. 70, the Romans destroyed Jerusalem and the temple. They were the people of the Roman prince Caesar, who had not yet come when Daniel received his prophecy from Gabriel. The Romans ended their 143–day siege of Jerusalem when they breeched the walls and a ***flood** of Roman soldiers* rushed into the city wreaking total destruction. That was the beginning of the desolations prophesied by Verse 26, which were to continue until the end, i.e. *the end of the age.* Accordingly, from that time until now *(almost 2000 years),* Israel has experienced constant oppression and warfare from various nations of the world. Even though the nation of Israel was reborn in 1948, they have continued living under constant threats and attempts of annihilation until this present day. And *as prophesied at the end of Verse 26,* that will continue until the Second Coming of Jesus, when Israel will finally recognize Him as their Messiah and King. This brings us to Daniel 9: 27.

Daniel 9: 27.*(KJV)*
27. And he shall confirm the covenant with many for one week: and in the midst of the week he shall cause the sacrifice and the oblation to cease, *[We'll stop here temporarily.]*

It's generally taught that this means the Anti-Christ will make a treaty with Israel for the last week *(the seventieth week of Daniel)* at the end of this age. I believe that interpretation came about because of two things.

<u>First</u>: It resulted from a mistaken idea of what was meant by the term, ***"the covenant."*** That term is used ***ninety-seven (97) times*** in the Old Testament. It appears three times in Genesis. ***Two*** are references to God's covenant not to destroy the earth again with a flood, and ***the other*** is about the covenant with Abram concerning circumcision. Ninety-three of the remaining times ***"the covenant"*** is mentioned, it's obviously a reference to ***the covenant*** *God made with Israel at Mt. Sinai.* That leaves the one remaining time in Daniel 9: 27 above. *It is inconceivable that God would use the term **"the covenant"** ninety-three times to identify His covenant with Israel, and then use that same term **one time to speak of <u>a covenant between Israel and the Anti-Christ</u>.** That becomes even more unreasonable when you consider that **<u>no such covenant with the Anti-Christ is mentioned ANYWHERE ELSE IN SCRIPTURE</u>.** Therefore, I believe the reference to **"the covenant"** in Daniel 9: 27 above, is simply another reference **<u>to God's covenant with Israel</u>.*** I also believe that when we correctly identify who the pronoun ***"he"***

is referring to in Daniel 9: 27, it will confirm that ***"the covenant"*** *is indeed God's covenant with Israel.*

<u>Second</u>: I believe the interpretation relating this prophecy to the Anti-Christ resulted from confusion about the identity of the person to whom the pronoun ***"he"*** is referring. A personal pronoun ***always refers back to someone <u>who has ALREADY BEEN IDENTIFIED.</u>*** *If you use a personal pronoun without first identifying the person to whom you're referring,* ***that pronoun is meaningless.*** Example: *If I tell you to go to a group of people and bring **"him"** to me; you would have no idea who I meant by the pronoun **"him."** But if I said, **"David is out there somewhere, please get "him" for me,"** you would know exactly who the pronoun **"him"** refers to.* Accordingly, in the preceding verses, Gabriel identified ***only two people***. In Verses 25 and 26 he spoke of ***"Messiah the Prince,"*** who was going to come at the end of sixty-nine weeks. And in Verse 26 he mentioned ***"the prince that shall come," <u>WHOSE PEOPLE were going to destroy Jerusalem and the temple</u>***. As discussed above, *since the Romans were the people who destroyed Jerusalem and the temple in A. D. 70,* it follows that ***"the prince that shall come"*** had to be a reference to the prince *(Caesar)* who ruled over the Roman people. Shortly before Jesus was born, Caesar Augustus decreed that all the world, *including Israel,* should be taxed; *however,* ***there's no record that any Caesar ever made A COVENANT with Israel.*** So when Gabriel said, ***"And he shall confirm the covenant with many for one week..."*** he must have been referring back to ***"Messiah the Prince."*** Before you reject that as a preposterous idea, look at the following prophecy in Malachi, ***which specifically relates the Messiah's ministry to God's covenant with Israel.***

Malachi 3: 1 *(KJV)*
1. Behold, I will send *my messenger*, and he shall prepare the way before ***ME***: ***and the Lord, whom ye seek, shall suddenly come to His temple, EVEN THE MESSENGER OF THE COVENANT,*** whom ye delight in: behold, He shall come, saith the Lord of hosts.

Without question, this is a prophecy about John the Baptist coming as God's messenger to prepare the way for the Lord, ***who was going to come in the person of the Messiah.*** But it also says the Messiah was going to come ***"SUDDENLY"*** to His temple, **AND** ***that He would do so as "THE MESSENGER OF THE COVENANT."*** That is exactly what Jesus did when He went suddenly to the temple and cleansed it as recorded in John 2: 13 - 16. The Messiah had no need to ***"MAKE a covenant with many,"*** *as this is rendered in some recent translations,* ***because God had <u>MADE</u> "the***

covenant" with Israel about 1500 years earlier at Mt Sinai. As we look at what Jesus actually did in His earthly ministry, keep in mind that the Hebrew word ***"gabar,"*** translated in the King James Version as ***"confirm,"*** also means ***to strengthen, or make strong.***

The Nature of Jesus's Earthly Ministry. When Jesus began His ministry, John the Baptist had already been preaching repentance to Israel for six months or better. As already discussed, the first thing Jesus did in His public ministry was go to Jerusalem during Passover and drive out those who were selling animals for sacrifices and those who were changing money. In that way, He dramatically called Israel's attention to the fact that ***they were NOT obeying God's Word with all their hearts according to the covenant.*** They *had not* ***repented*** in response to John's preaching; *therefore,* ***Jesus had to continue the same message of repentance that John had been preaching.***

Matthew 4: 17 *(KJV)(This was shortly after Jesus cleansed the temple as recorded in John 2: 13 - 16).*
17. From that time Jesus began to preach and to say, ***"REPENT, for the kingdom of heaven is at hand."***

Jesus didn't *only* tell Israel to repent; He also told them specifically what they needed to repent of. He began doing that in the ***"Sermon on the Mount,"*** which is His first recorded sermon. Much has been said about how beautiful that sermon is; however, ***it didn't sound beautiful to Israel.*** To them it was a message of conviction, *for in it,* Jesus showed Israel they needed to make radical changes in their attitude toward the law. Even the most pious of Israel's religious leaders were falling far short of the righteousness required by God.

Matthew 5: 20 - 22, 27 - 28 *(NKJV)*
20. ***"For I say to you, that unless your righteousness exceeds the righteousness of the scribes and Pharisees, YOU WILL BY NO MEANS ENTER THE KINGDOM OF HEAVEN."***
21. ***"You have heard that it was said to those of old, 'You shall not murder, and whoever murders will be in danger of the judgment.'***
22. ***"But I say to you that whoever is angry with his brother without a cause shall be in danger of the judgment. And whoever says to his brother, 'Raca!' shall be in danger of the council. But whoever says, 'You fool!' shall be in danger of hell fire."***

27. ***"You have heard that it was said to those of old, "You shall not commit adultery.'"***
28. ***"But I say to you that whoever looks at a woman to lust for her has already committed adultery with her in his heart."***

Israel thought that obeying the law related ***ONLY*** *to outward physical actions.* So they were careful ***NOT TO DO the things the law forbid****, like murder and adultery.* They were also careful ***TO DO the various rituals required by the law,*** *so they thought they were pleasing God and were righteous in His sight.* But as God's ***"messenger of the covenant,"*** Jesus revealed what God actually required by the covenant. God considered the intents of Israel's hearts ***just as important as the things they actually did or refrained from doing.*** Because Israel thought they were obeying the law according to the covenant, they were filled with the spiritual pride of self righteousness. But in God's eyes, they were actually miserably lost sinners, no better than the Gentiles they looked down on as heathens. ***So, Jesus CONFIRMED THE COVENANT, strengthening it by revealing what it meant in the eyes of God.***

That message ***was NOT*** *good news to Israel,* for it convicted them all — ***everybody from the most pious of the priests to the average man on the street*** — they were all guilty of breaking the covenant in the eyes of God. So Jesus didn't ***MAKE a covenant*** with Israel; He redefined the law they had made a covenant to obey over 1500 years before. He ***CONFIRMED that covenant,*** as prophesied in Daniel 9: 27, and He did it in the fullest sense of the meaning of the word ***"confirm."*** He made the covenant ***stronger*** than Israel had ever perceived it to be. In modern day vernacular, we would say ***Jesus put teeth in the covenant,*** that He put Israel ***'on the spot!!'*** Jesus preached this radical kind of repentance for two years, and then He told the parable of the fig tree as a powerful wake–up call for Israel.

The Parable of the Fig Tree. Jesus introduced this parable by calling attention to two tragic events that had recently happened.

Luke 13:1-5 *(KJV)*
1. There were present at that season some that told Him of the Galileans, whose blood Pilate had mingled with their sacrifices.
2. And Jesus answering said unto them, ***"Suppose ye that these Galileans were sinners above all the Galileans, because they suffered such things?***
3. ***"I tell you, Nay: but, except ye repent, ye shall all likewise perish.***

4. ***"Or those eighteen, upon whom the tower in Siloam fell, and slew them, think ye that they were sinners above all men that dwelt in Jerusalem?***
5. ***"I tell you, Nay: but, except ye repent, ye shall all likewise perish.***

Jesus used these events as object lessons *relative to Israel's situation before God.* In each case, the people involved had lost their lives in a sudden and tragic way. Jesus refuted the common notion that such things only happen because people are dreadfully wicked. He wanted Israel to understand that while they were not necessarily guilty of the obvious sins they readily recognized and condemned, ***they were guilty of equally serious matters that GOD saw <u>IN THEIR HEARTS.</u>*** In this parable, Jesus warned Israel about a terrible physical tragedy similar to those recent events they knew about. That similar tragedy would come upon them if they continued refusing to repent. With that introduction, Jesus began the parable of the fig tree.

Luke 13: 6 - 9 *(KJV)*
6. He spake also this parable; ***"A certain man had a fig tree planted in his vineyard; and he came and sought fruit thereon, and found none.***
7. Then said he unto the dresser of his vineyard, ***"Behold, these <u>THREE</u> years I come seeking fruit on this fig tree, and find none: cut it down; why cumbereth it the ground?"***
8. And he answering said unto him, ***"Lord, let it alone this year also, till I shall dig about it and dung it:***
9. ***"And if it bear fruit, well: and if not, then after that thou shalt cut it down."***

If we consider this parable in the light of Israel's disregard for the true meaning of the covenant, it isn't hard to recognize who the characters in the parable represented.

- The unfruitful fig tree ***represented the unrepentant nation of Israel.***
- The certain man who owned the fig tree ***represented God.***
- The dresser of the vineyard represented Jesus Himself.

Accordingly, this parable revealed that ***God had already come <u>THREE</u> years,*** seeking the fruit of repentance in Israel, but had found none. Since John the Baptist had begun preaching repentance before Jesus came, the ***first time*** God had sought the fruit of repentance was *at the beginning of Jesus' ministry.* Jesus had gone to the temple and found Israel had ignored John's preaching and failed to repent. When Jesus told this parable, He Himself had also been preaching that same message of repentance for two years. So for a total of three years, God had come looking for the fruit of repentance in Israel and found none. As a result, He had been ready to bring judgment against them. However, Jesus, *represented in the parable as the vine dresser,* had interceded in behalf of Israel. He had persuaded His Father to wait until He had ministered to Israel for ***one more year.*** This shows how close Israel had already come to receiving God's judgment for failing to repent. *It was only through the intercession of Jesus, that God's judgment was being delayed for an additional year.* But Jesus agreed that if Israel didn't repent at the end of that additional year, ***then God's judgment would fall.***

When Israel's Year of Grace Ended. According to the agreement, Jesus continued to preach repentance for one more year, and when that year had passed, ***He returned to Jerusalem to see if Israel had repented.***

Matthew 21:10-13 *(KJV)*
10. And when He was come into Jerusalem, all the city was moved, saying, Who is this?
11. And the multitude said, This is Jesus the prophet of Nazareth of Galilee.
12. ***And Jesus went into the temple of God, and cast out all them that sold and bought in the temple, and overthrew the tables of the moneychangers, and the seats of them that sold doves.***
13. and said unto them, ***"It is written, My house shall be called the house of prayer; but ye have made it A DEN OF THIEVES."***

Israel had wasted the additional year of God's grace. Instead of repenting, they had only grown worse. At the beginning of His ministry three years earlier, Jesus had said Israel was making the temple ***"a house of merchandise,"*** but at the end their year of grace, even though Jesus had continued urging them to repent, *they had turned the temple into* ***"...a den of thieves."*** Therefore, Jesus quickly confirmed the judgment He and the Father had agreed to the year before.

Matthew 21:18-20 *(KJV)*
18. Now in the morning as He returned into the city, He hungered.
19. And when He saw a fig tree in the way, He came to it, and found nothing thereon, but leaves only, and said unto it, ***"Let no fruit grow on thee henceforward for ever." And presently the fig tree withered away.***
20. And when the disciples saw it, they marveled, saying, ***"How soon is the fig tree withered away!"***

If we read this without considering what led up to it, it may seem like Jesus was acting irrationally — bordering on having a temper tantrum. ***However, He was simply continuing the parable of the fig tree He had begun the year before. By cursing the fig tree and causing it to quickly wither and die, He revealed that God's judgment against Israel was then certain, and would shortly come to pass.*** A few days later, Jesus confirmed the judgment He had demonstrated by cursing the fig tree. He pronounced ***"woe"*** upon Israel's religious leaders nine different times in Matthew 23, because they had led the people into disobedience, and at the end the chapter He spoke pointedly of the judgment to come.

Matthew 23: 33 - 38 *(KJV)*
33. ***"Ye serpents, ye generation of vipers, how can ye escape the damnation of hell?***
34. ***"Wherefore, behold, I send unto you prophets, and wise men, and scribes: and some of them ye shall kill and crucify; and some of them shall ye scourge in your synagogues, and persecute them from city to city:***
35. ***"that upon you may come all the righteous blood shed upon the earth, from the blood of righteous Able unto the blood of Zacharias son of Barachias, whom ye slew between the temple and the altar.***
36. ***Verily I say unto you, all these things shall come upon THIS GENERATION.***
37. ***O Jerusalem, Jerusalem, thou that killest the prophets, and stonest them which are sent unto thee, how often would I have gathered thy children together, even as a hen gathereth her chickens under her wings, and ye would not!***
38. ***"Behold, your house is left unto you desolate."***

With these words, Jesus revealed that ***because Israel had refused to repent,*** God had set the covenant aside. Therefore, instead of God's blessings and protection, Israel was faced with desolation. It was in A. D. 30, when Jesus said this, *and within the forty-year span of that generation,* His prophecy was fulfilled when the Romans under Titus utterly destroyed Jerusalem and the temple in A.D. 70. During that conflict, as many as 600,000 Jews were slaughtered, and thousands more were sent into captivity. By the end of Rome's campaign against the Jews, the nation of Israel had literally ceased to exist. ***The fig tree** [Israel] **did indeed wither and die.*** That was the beginning of almost 2000 years, during which time the Jews have been in exile among the nations of the world. During most of that time they have been under intense persecution, uncertain of their lives from one day to the next.

Ignorant and misguided people say the Jews have suffered so much throughout the church age because they are ***"Christ killers."*** But Israel's suffering hasn't been because of their part in crucifying Jesus. Rather, it's been the fulfillment of Deut. 28: 15 - 68, which foretold the curses they would experience ***IF they failed to obey God's words according to their covenant agreement.*** When Israel had Jesus crucified, that was simply the climax of their rebellion against God and failure to obey the law according to the covenant. Therefore, Israel's suffering throughout the church age is proof of the ongoing reality of God's covenant. *But when the fig tree withered and died,* **that didn't mark the actual end of Israel.**

The Parable of the Fig Tree Continues. Even as Jesus pronounced God's judgment on Israel, He also spoke of when their judgment will come to its end.

Matthew 23: 39 *(KJV)*
39. ***"For I say unto you, Ye shall not see Me henceforth, TILL ye shall say, 'Blessed is He that cometh in the name of the Lord.'"***

Israel had rejected their Messiah and He was about to go away; nevertheless, ***they are going to see Him again when He comes again at a still future date.*** However, ***that isn't going to happen UNTIL*** *they repent and come to the place of desperation longing for someone to come in the name of the Lord.* Having said this, Jesus gave His prophecy of things that would lead up to the end of the age, as recorded in Matthew 24. He ended that prophecy by ***returning to the parable of the fig tree.***

Matthew 24: 32 - 34 *(KJV)*
32. *"Now learn a parable of the fig tree; When his branch is yet tender, and putteth forth leaves, ye know that summer is nigh:*
33. ***"So likewise ye, when ye shall see all these things, know that it is near, even at the doors.***
34. ***"Verily I say unto you, 'THIS GENERATION shall not pass, till all these things be fulfilled.'"***

Just as the fig tree had withered and died, ***Israel was soon overcome by Rome and ceased to exist as a nation.*** Since A. D. 70, that has continued to be Israel's condition for almost 2000 years. However, *just as a dormant fig tree begins to show signs of life when summer approaches,* ***the dormant nation of Israel began to show signs of life again in 1948.*** The fact that

Israel was reestablished as a nation doesn't necessarily mean verse 32 has been completely fulfilled, *for God is more concerned with Israel's spiritual restoration than with her national restoration.* However, the national rebirth of Israel is a strong indication that God has again begun to move in Israel. *The fig tree has at least begun to bud, indicating that summer is near.* If nothing else, that means it's time to begin looking diligently for the other signs Jesus identified in Matthew 24. We have His assurance that *when we begin to see those signs, His coming* ***"is near, even at the doors."*** *In fact, we are assured* ***that <u>THE GENERATION</u> that sees the signs He spoke of, <u>will not pass away until all is fulfilled, including the return of Jesus for His elect, the church.</u>*** This brings us to the next prophecy in Daniel 9: 27.

Daniel 9: 27 *(KJV)*
27. And ***<u>HE</u>*** shall confirm the covenant with many for one week: ***and in the midst of the week, HE shall cause the sacrifice and the oblation to cease,...***

It's obvious that the ***"HE"*** who was to confirm the covenant is the same person as the ***"HE"*** who would cause the sacrifice and oblation to cease. Therefore, ***<u>IF</u>*** Jesus was truly the one who confirmed the covenant, *it follows that* ***He must also have caused the sacrifice and oblation to cease.*** Again, I realize it is generally taught that this was a reference to the Antichrist, ***who <u>supposedly</u>*** will make a treaty with Israel for one week *(seven years),* but will break that treaty in the middle of the week, ***and at the same time will cause the sacrifice and oblation to cease.*** That would mean this is still in the future. So next we need to consider the following question.

<u>Have The Sacrifice And Oblation Already Ceased?</u> The obvious answer is, ***YES,*** *they ceased when the Romans destroyed the Temple in A. D. 70,* ***and <u>they haven't resumed in all the centuries since then.</u>*** However, from God's point of view, the sacrifice and oblation *had actually ceased* ***well BEFORE the Romans destroyed the temple in A. D. 70.*** We can see this by looking in Hebrews, which was written ***BEFORE*** Jerusalem and the temple were destroyed in A. D. 70. We know that's true because Hebrew 8: 4, *speaking of Jesus,* says, ***"For if He were on earth, He should not be a priest, seeing that there <u>ARE</u> priests who offer gifts according to the law."*** *At the time Hebrews was written,* ***<u>priests were still offering gifts according to the law.</u>*** That wouldn't have been true if Hebrews was written ***<u>AFTER</u>*** A. D. 70. However, even though the Romans had not yet destroyed the temple, look at what else Hebrews said.

Hebrews 8: 13 & 9: 1 - 12 (KJV)
13. In that He *[God]* saith, ***"A new covenant,"*** ***He HATH MADE the FIRST OBSOLETE.*** Now that which decayeth and waxeth old is ready to vanish away.

The death of Jesus established the basis for the new covenant; *therefore,* ***when Jesus died, God made the first covenant obsolete — READY to vanish away.*** Because of that, Romans 10: 4 says, ***"...Christ is THE END OF THE LAW for righteousness to every one who believes."*** For believers, the law, *and the old covenant,* were rendered obsolete by the death and resurrection of Jesus Christ. This is confirmed in Hebrews 9: 1, which says, ***"Then indeed, even the first covenant HAD ordinances of divine service, and the earthly sanctuary."*** The word ***"sanctuary"*** applied particularly to the ***"Holy of Holies"*** in the temple or tabernacle *(Ref: Exodus 25: 8).* So *the services* performed in the ***"Holy of Holies" all applied particularly to the old covenant, which God had already made obsolete, for they are spoken of in the PAST TENSE.*** They have no bearing on our relationship with God, *which is through Jesus Christ.* Accordingly, as we continue in Hebrews, we see ***WHY*** God ***had to make*** that old covenant obsolete.

Hebrews 9: 8 *(NKJV)*
8. The Holy Ghost indicating this, ***that the way into the Holiest of all was not yet made manifest, WHILE THE FIRST TABERNACLE WAS STILL STANDING:***

The death and resurrection of Jesus Christ ***rendered the old covenant and all its services OBSOLETE. Because of that, to continue those old services of the law would have given a false testimony indicating that Jesus had not yet come and provided a NEW AND BETTER WAY into God's presence.*** This is made clear in Hebrews 10.

Hebrews 10: 18 - 22 *(NKJV)*
18. Now where there is remission of these *[our sins]*, there is no longer an offering for sin.
19. Therefore, brethren, ***having BOLDNESS to enter into the Holiest by the blood of Jesus,***
20. by a new and living way which He consecrated for us, *through the veil,* ***that is, His flesh,***
21. and having a High Priest *[Jesus Christ]* over the house of God,
22. let us draw near with a true heart, in full assurance of faith, having our

hearts sprinkled from an evil conscience, and our bodies washed with pure water.

Under the old covenant, the veil of the temple was the barrier that kept people from intruding into God's presence unprepared. Only the high priest could enter into the sanctuary of the Holy of Holies in the earthly temple. And he could go in only once a year, and had to be very careful to offer the proper sacrifices of blood. Otherwise he would be slain. But ***NOW,*** we can come ***boldly*** into God's holy presence by the new and living way Jesus prepared for us when He died, *for the veil of the temple represented Jesus's flesh.* Until Jesus died for our sins, the veil in the temple remained intact ***as a testimony that Jesus had not yet died,*** **b**ut when He died, the veil was ripped in two from top to bottom, ***and that was God's testimony that Jesus's flesh had been torn in His death, thereby providing the way for man to come into God's holy presence.*** The veil was torn from top to bottom, just as Jesus's flesh was torn, ***first*** by the crown of thorns on His head, ***next*** by the nails in His hands, ***and last*** by the nails in His feet — ***from top to bottom***.

That is why Daniel 9: 27 didn't stop saying, ***"And HE shall confirm the covenant with many for one week,"*** but went on to add, ***" and in the midst of the week HE*** *[Jesus Christ, who had confirmed the covenant]* ***SHALL CAUSE the sacrifice and oblation to cease."*** After Jesus spent three years ***confirming*** *Israel's covenant, He was crucified,* ***and by His death CAUSED the temple veil to be ripped in two from top to bottom*** *(Ref: Matthew 27: 50 - 51).* Since it was not lawful for anyone except the high priest to even look into the Holy of Holies, when that veil was ripped in two, ***that stopped the sacrifice and oblation until the veil could be repaired.*** So Jesus did indeed cause the sacrifice and oblation to cease just as prophesied in Daniel 9: 27.

However, after the veil was ripped in two, *the Jews would have repaired it as quickly as possible.* For as we've already seen, Hebrews 8: 4, *which was written* ***AFTER*** *Jesus died but* ***BEFORE*** *the temple was destroyed,* says, ***"For if He*** *[Jesus]* ***were on earth, He should not be a priest, seeing that there ARE priests who offer gifts according to the law."*** *The only way priests could have been offering gifts according to the law at the time Hebrews was written, was for the veil to have been repaired.* Nevertheless, ***Jesus had died,*** *and that meant* ***the offering of the sacrifices and gifts according to the law had become a false testimony, for their very existence testified that God's perfect sacrifice*** *(Jesus Christ)* ***had not yet come*** *(Ref: Hebrews 9: 8).* God could not permit even unbelieving Jews to continue that false testimony for very long; therefore, He caused the Romans to come against Israel and utterly destroy both the city of Jerusalem and the temple. The Romans also sent most of the remaining Jews into exile out of Israel so they were unable to rebuild the temple.

Additionally, in A. D. 687, God permitted Islam to build their sacred ***"Dome of The Rock"*** on the mountain where the temple had stood, and that oldest of Islam's shrines still stands there to this present day. In this most unusual way, *God has used Islam to prevent the Jews from rebuilding the temple and offering the sacrifices and oblations that would be a false testimony indicating that the way into the Holiest of all through Jesus Christ has not yet been provided.* So just as Daniel 9: 27 prophesied, *the Messiah did indeed cause the sacrifice and oblation to cease,* ***Jesus fulfilled that prophecy by His own death.*** However, there are other passages in Scripture that also speak of Israel's sacrifices being stopped, and it's evident they are not talking about that which Jesus caused by His death. We also need to look at those passages, which do indeed appear to be about the Antichrist.

Will the Antichrist Also Stop Israel's Sacrifice? There are three other passages ***in Daniel*** that talk about Israel's sacrifices being taken away. One of these is surely a prophecy about what will happen at the end time, for Jesus referred to it in His prophecy of things to look for as signs of His return. He gave His prophecy in answer to the disciples' question in Matthew 24: 3

Matthew 24: 3, & 15 - 20 *(KJV)*
3. And as He sat upon the mount of Olives, the disciples came unto Him privately, saying, ***"Tell us, when shall these things be? And what shall be the sign of thy coming, and of the end of the world."***

The rest of Matthew 24 is Jesus's answer to these questions. But we will look only at that part of Jesus's answer where He referred to the prophecy of Daniel.

15. ***"When ye therefore shall see the abomination of desolation, spoke of by Daniel the prophet, stand in the holy place,*** (whoso readeth, let him understand.)
16. ***"Then let them which be in Judaea flee into the mountains:***

17. ***"Let him which is on the housetop not come down to take any thing out of his house:***
18. ***"Neither let him which is in the field return back to take his clothes.***
19. ***"And woe to them that are with child, and to them that give suck in those days!***
20. ***"For then shall be great tribulation, such as was not since the beginning of the world to this time, no, nor ever shall be."***

Jesus said the setting up of the abomination of desolation spoken of in Daniel, ***will be the <u>beginning</u>*** *of the great tribulation.* So let's look at the part of Daniel to which Jesus was referring.

Daniel 12: 8 - 13 *(KJV)*
8. And I heard, but I understood not: then said I, ***"O My Lord, what shall be the end of these things?"***
9. And he said, ***"Go thy way, Daniel: <u>for the words are closed up and sealed TILL THE TIME OF THE END."</u>*** *[God didn't intend that people should understand all of Daniel's prophecies* ***<u>UNTIL</u> the time of the end. But this clearly shows that as the time of the end draws near, <u>we will be able to understand</u>.****]*
10. Many shall be purified, and made white, and tried; *[This was surely talking about the true believers in the Church.]*, but the wicked shall do wickedly: and none of the wicked shall understand: but the wise shall understand.
11. And from the time that ***the daily sacrifice shall be taken away***, and the abomination that maketh desolate set up, there shall be a thousand two hundred and ninety days.
12. Blessed is he that waiteth, and cometh to the thousand, three hundred and five and thirty days.
13. But go thou thy way till the end be: for thou shalt rest, and stand in thy lot at the end of the days.

This clearly reveals that Israel's daily sacrifice is going to be taken away twelve hundred and ninety days ***before*** *the end comes.* But it also says something called ***"the abomination of desolation"*** will be set up when the daily sacrifice is taken away. So this is definitely talking about an event that is *still in the future,* ***and which will apparently be the work of the Antichrist.*** In Revelation 13, there's a description of something that will probably be the fulfillment of this prophecy.

Revelation 13: 11 - 15 *(KJV)(This is a description of the rise of the Antichrist.)*
11. And I beheld another beast coming up out of the earth; and he had two horns like a lamb, and he spake as a dragon.
12. And he exerciseth all the power of the first beast before him *[That beast will represent the kingdom of the Antichrist]*, and causeth the earth and them which dwell therein to worship the first beast, whose deadly wound was healed.
13. And he doeth great wonders, so that he maketh fire come down from heaven on the earth in the sight of men.
14. And deceiveth them that dwell on the earth by the means of those miracles which he had power to do in the sight of the *[first]* beast; saying to them that dwell on the earth, that they should make an image to the beast, which had the wound by the sword, and did live.
15. And he had power to give life unto the image of the beast, that the image of the beast should both speak, and cause that as many as would not worship the image of the beast should be killed.

This indicates the Antichrist is going to make an image that represents his kingdom, *which will actually be the earthly manifestation of Satan's kingdom.* He will then ***take away*** Israel's daily sacrifice, and set up the image to Satan in its place. Since Israel's daily sacrifice has to be made at the altar in the temple *(or possibly a suitable tabernacle),* this means Israel must build such an edifice sometime between now and when this takes place.

What we need to see is that when Jesus's death caused the sacrifice and oblation to stop, ***they weren't replaced by the abomination of desolation.*** Rather those services had to stop as God's testimony that ***He had indeed provided a NEW way for man to come into His presence — a way that was better than the old way of the law.*** That better way replaced the old way of animal sacrifices offered by an earthly priest. In contrast, when the daily sacrifice is taken away at the end of the age, *it will be Satan who causes that to be done through the Antichrist .who will do it in an effort to cause people [primarily Israel] to stop worshiping God and start worshiping Satan.* He ***will be trying to do to Israel, what he tried to do to Jesus by tempting Him in the wilderness.***

So Jesus did indeed cause the sacrifice and oblation to cease when He died. But at the end of the age, Israel will rebuild the temple *or a suitable tabernacle*, and will resume their sacrifices and other temple services. After that, the Antichrist will cause those daily sacrifices to stop, but he will do it for a completely different reason and purpose. Since that will happen during the time God is working to bring Israel back into His favor, we need to know when that may take place.

When Is God Going to Restore Israel into His Favor?

God spoke through the prophet Hosea and revealed that He was going to forsake Israel for a long period of time. However, He also revealed that Israel eventually will repent and return to Him, and at that time He will restore them into His favor. The first clue to Israel's time of desolation is in Hosea 3.

Hosea 3: 4 - 5 *(KJV)*
4. For the children of Israel shall abide ***many days*** without a king, and without a prince, and without a sacrifice, and without an image, and without an ephod, and without teraphim:

For ***"many days,"*** *the children of Israel would essentially be* ***without ANYTHING.*** They wouldn't have a national leader or their traditional system of worshiping God. However, also during that time, they would no longer be worshiping images or have any of the trappings related to idol worship. This is an accurate description of Israel's situation throughout the centuries of the church age. They have been a people wandering among the nations, ***still claiming to know God, but with no real evidence of a relationship with Him.*** But even as God foretold Israel's time of distress, He also gave them words of hope.

5. ***Afterward shall the children of Israel return and seek the Lord their God and David their King*** *[this is a reference to Jesus as the son of David]:* ***and shall fear the Lord and His goodness in the LATTER DAYS.***

Although God was going to suspend His covenant with Israel because of her sin, by this prophecy He reassured them that eventually, ***"in the latter days,"*** they will return and seek Him and their Messiah. Therefore, the implication of this prophecy is that God will restore Israel into His favor at that time. The only reference to when that would happen is that it will be ***"in the latter days,"*** which meant it would happen ***at the end of the age***. However, God didn't leave them with only this ***hint*** of their eventual restoration, for in Chapters 5 & 6 He enlarged on the kind of distress they would experience, *and also revealed* ***WHEN their distress will come to its end and they will be restored into His favor.***

Hosea 5: 14 - 15 *(KJV)*
14. For I will be unto Ephraim *[another name for Israel]* as a lion, and as a young lion to the house of Judah: I, even I, will tear and go away; I will take away, and none shall rescue him.
15. ***I will go and return to My place, till they acknowledge their offence, and seek My face: in their affliction they will seek Me early.***

Through most of the centuries of Old Testament times, Israel enjoyed God's protection because of the covenant. But Hosea prophesied a time of desolation when God would ***go away*** *and leave Israel without the protection of the covenant.* Then, instead of being their protector, ***God would even become their enemy. He would be like a lion to wreak destruction and leave them helpless with no one to rescue them.*** Verse 15 reveals that ***God would leave them alone, and <u>return to His place</u>, and remain there <u>UNTIL</u> they wake up and acknowledge their sins.*** This began to be fulfilled at the end of Jesus' ministry, when he cried over Jerusalem saying, "...***O Jerusalem, Jerusalem, the one who kills the prophets, and stones those who are sent to her! How often I wanted to gather your children together, as a hen gathers her chicks under her wings, but you were not willing! See! Your house is left to you desolate; for I say to you, you shall see me no more till you say, 'Blessed is He who comes in the Name of the Lord!'"*** *(Matthew 23: 37 - 39).* Only a little over ***forty days*** *later,* God fulfilled His words, ***"I will go and return to My place;"*** for then, in the person of His Divine Son Jesus Christ, God returned to His place *(heaven)*, as recorded in Acts 1: 9 - 11.

That left Israel without the protection of either the Lord's presence or His covenant, and within one generation *(Ref: Matthew 23: 36),* the Romans destroyed Jerusalem, and eventually sent the Jews into the exile that began the long centuries of Israel's desolation. That long desolation is the fulfillment of the ***"..many days.."*** prophesied in Hosea 3: 4. In Hosea 3: 5, the Lord revealed that Israel's desolation would continue *until* ***"...the <u>latter</u> days.***" However, in Hosea 6, God revealed ***<u>WHEN</u> Israel will finally seek God's face again, and be restored into His favor.***

Hosea 6: 1 - 2 *(KJV)(This is a prophecy of what **<u>Israel</u>** <u>will say</u> at the end of this age, when they finally wake up to their need to return to God <u>according to the covenant</u> made by their forefathers.)*
1. Come, and let us return unto the Lord; for He hath torn, and He will heal us; He hath smitten and He will bind us up.

2. ***After TWO days will He receive us; in the THIRD day He will raise us up, and we shall live in His sight.***

After God has torn and smitten Israel for ***"two days,"*** they will finally wake up and return to Him in repentance, and He will restore them into His favor. This obviously wasn't talking about ***two normal 24–HOUR days,*** for it's already been about 1980 ***years*** since Hosea 5: 14 - 15 was fulfilled ***by the LORD returning to His place in the person of Jesus <u>when He ascended into heaven.</u>*** However, II Peter 3: 8 says, ***"..one day is with the Lord as a thousand years, and a thousand years as one day;"*** therefore, if we use this as the basis for measuring those two days, *it means* **God would smite *Israel for <u>two thousand YEARS</u>*** *before He will receive them again and heal them.* It was in A. D. 30 when God, *in the person of Jesus,* returned to His place and left Israel and her house desolate. So when you add 2000 years to A. D. 30, *you get A. D. 2030 as the time when Israel will finally return to the Lord and He will* ***receive*** *them.* At that time, the old covenant will come to its end and will be replaced with the new covenant of Jeremiah 31: 31 - 34. Therefore, during the ***"third day,"*** when God raises Israel up to live in His sight, *they will be under the new covenant.* Additionally that ***"third day"*** will be the thousand–year reign of Christ here on earth during which time He will make Israel a holy nation and a kingdom of priests according to the covenant–promise of Exodus 5 - 6. Also according to that promise, during the ***"third day"*** *(third thousand–year period),* ***Israel will serve as priests to all the other nations of the world*** *(Ref: Isaiah 61: 6).*

The next Chapter discusses when God will finally make Jesus's enemies His footstool.

Chapter 5

When Will God Make Jesus' Enemies His Footstool?

What Must Happen To Make Jesus' Enemies His Footstool?

In Chapter 1, we saw that Psalms 110: 1 is quoted six different places in the New Testament. That Psalm says, ***"The LORD said unto my Lord, 'sit Thou at My right hand, until I make Thine enemies Thy footstool.'"*** This oft–repeated verse establishes the fact that ***Jesus CAN'T RETURN,*** *either for the Rapture or the Second Coming,* ***UNTIL God makes His enemies His footstool.*** From the beginning, Satan has been man's enemy with man's destruction as his ultimate goal. He attacked Jesus more than any other man because he knew if he could overcome Jesus he would win his war against God. So Jesus' enemies, ***whom God will one day make His footstool,*** are Satan and his angels. In Isaiah, God revealed what constitutes His and Christ's footstool.

Isaiah 66: 1

1. Thus saith the LORD, ***"The heaven is My throne, and the earth is My footstool: where is the house that you build unto Me? and where is the place of My rest?"***

Therefore, to make Jesus' enemies His footstool, God will have to expel ***Satan and his angels out of heaven and send them back down to the earth.*** When Satan rebelled, God expelled him from heaven and cast him down to the earth. That's what Jesus was referring to in Luke 10: 18 where He said, ***"I beheld Satan as lightning fall from heaven."*** Because of that, *Satan and his angels were on the earth* ***in exile*** when God restored the earth as recorded in Genesis. In Hebrews, we have a description of the situation on earth after God made Adam.

Hebrews 2: 5 - 9a, & 14 - 15 *(This begins by revealing the difference between God's purpose for men and His purpose for angels.) (NKJV)*
5. For He *[God]* has not put the world to come, of which we speak, in subjection to angels.
6. But one testified in a certain place, saying: ***"What is MAN that You are mindful of him, or the son of man that You care for him?***
7. ***"You have made him*** *[man]* ***a little lower than the angels; You have crowned him with glory and honor, and set him over the works of Your hands.***
8a. ***You have put all things in subjection under his feet."*** *For in that He put all in subjection under man,* **He LEFT NOTHING that is not put under him** *[man]*....

From the beginning, God's purpose was for man to be in charge of ***"the world to come."*** Because of that, when God made man, ***He gave him authority over all the works of His hands. God put everything He made under subjection to man.*** That was the situation here on earth at the end of the first seven days of Genesis 1. At that time, ***MAN was the ruler over all the earth and every living thing on the earth.*** Since Satan and his angels were living things on the earth, ***at that time, <u>they were all under the authority MAN</u> — in subjection to him.*** However, at some undetermined time after that first week, Satan overcame man with temptation and brought him under the curse of sin and death. *It was God who ordained that the curse of death would be* **<u>MAN'S sure consequence IF he should sin, i.e. disobeyed God</u>.** But it was Satan who overcame man with temptation and caused him to sin, ***and that completely changed the situation regarding dominion and subjection here on earth.*** The last part of Verse 8 *(above)* sums that change up in one short phrase.

8b. ....But ***<u>NOW</u> we see <u>NOT YET</u>*** all things put under him *[That is under man's dominion.]*

When Satan defeated man with temptation and caused him to sin, man lost his dominion over Satan. Then, *instead of Satan being subject to man,* ***man became subject to Satan.*** Additionally, *by the law of conquest,* ***everything that had belonged to man became the possession of Satan.*** Jesus showed that this is true by telling His disciples, ***"I will no longer talk much with you, for the <u>RULER of this world</u>*** *[Satan]* ***is coming, and he has nothing in***

Me." *(John 14: 30).* This shows that when Satan defeated man by temptation to sin, ***SATAN himself became THE RULER of this world,*** and that meant that man had become subject to Satan. Even though God had created man as the ruler of this world, when Satan overcame man by temptation and sin, man lost his position of dominion, and Satan gained that position for himself. Satan then had man under bondage ***by the fear of death,*** which shows that ***Satan had gained the power of death over man.*** *(Ref: Hebrews 2: 14).*

This also explains how Satan got back into Heaven. Adam ***had been created with the right to come into God's presence and have fellowship with God.*** We see this in Genesis 2, which records how *Adam and the Lord* ***worked together*** as God brought all the earth's creatures to Adam for him to name. However, when Adam sinned, he lost his right to fellowship with God. This was revealed *when God came to the garden looking for Adam, but because he and Eve had sinned, they were afraid and hid from the Lord. (Ref: Genesis 3: 8).* It's obvious that Adam's right to come into God's presence was one of the things Satan gained by his victory over Adam, for Job 1: 6 tells about *the Lord* ***receiving*** *Satan* when he presented himself along with the other angels. Therefore, when Satan defeated man with temptation and sin, ***he won from man the right to go into God's presence, and that brought Satan's exile to an end.***

That makes it evident what must happen in order for God to be able to make Jesus's enemies His footstool? *Since Satan won the right to come back into God's presence in heaven by overcoming man with sin,* ***the only way he can lose that right is for SINFUL MEN to reverse that situation and win it back for themselves BY OVERCOMING SATAN.*** *Accordingly, before God can make Jesus's enemies His footstool,* ***SINFUL MAN will have to overcome Satan and strip him of his right to a place in heaven.*** *However, I Corinthians 15: 22 says,* ***"...in Adam ALL DIE!"*** Since all Adam's descendants died **IN HIM** when he sinned, *none of them (sinful men) were able to overcome Satan and win back the things Adam lost by sin and death.* That made man's situation seem to be hopeless; however, in Hebrews God revealed that He had an answer.

Hebrews 2: 9 - 10, & 14 - 15 *(NKJV)*
9. ***BUT WE SEE JESUS,*** who was made a little lower than the angels, for the suffering of death, crowned with glory and honor, that He, by the grace of God, might taste death for everyone.
10. For it was fitting for Him *[God]*, for whom are all things and by whom

are all things, in bringing many sons to glory, to make the captain of their salvation perfect through suffering
14. Inasmuch then as the children have partaken of flesh and blood, He Himself likewise shared in the same, that through death He might destroy him who had the power of death, that is the devil,
15. and release those ***who through fear of death were all their lifetime subject to bondage.***

Jesus is God's answer for man's seemingly hopeless situation, for ***Jesus is the ONE AND ONLY man*** who has ***NEVER*** been in bondage to Satan. The reason is ***two-fold. First: Jesus was born as the Son of God,*** *instead of being a descendant of Adam.* Therefore, He is the ***ONLY man who DID NOT die in Adam.*** That means Jesus wasn't born with death working in His being to make Him predisposed to sin. ***Second:*** Jesus lived His entire life completely free from sin. Because of these ***two UNIQUE conditions***, Jesus could truthfully say in John 14: 30 that, ***"...the prince of this world*** *[Satan]* ***is coming, AND HE HAS NOTHING IN ME."*** Satan had absolutely no claim of sin against Jesus, so ***Jesus didn't have to die.*** Jesus didn't live in fear of death like other men, and He even subjected Himself willingly to die, ***that He might taste death FOR every man as God's perfect sacrifice for sin.***

By Itself, Jesus's Personal Victory Over Satan Isn't Enough.

At this point it's important to see that *even though Jesus died for sinful men and paid the full price of death for their sin,* ***that didn't change the fact that SINFUL MAN will also have to overcome Satan BEFORE God can expel him from heaven and make him Jesus's footstool.*** This is evident from the fact that Jesus successfully paid sinful man's price of death for sin and rose to live again, and *then,* ***having finished His personal victory over Satan,*** *He has been seated at God's right hand for almost two thousand years —* ***WAITING FOR GOD TO MAKE HIS ENEMIES HIS FOOTSTOOL. During all that time, Jesus's enemies*** *(Satan and his angels),* ***HAVE KEPT THEIR RIGHT TO A PLACE IN HEAVEN.*** That shows that ***Jesus's PERSONAL victory over Satan*** *wasn't enough to enable God* ***justly*** *to expel Satan from heaven.* ***SINFUL MEN still have to overcome Satan and take back what Adam lost!*** Only after that is done, will God have Satan cast out of heaven and down to earth where he will be Jesus's footstool.

How God Will Have Satan And His Angels Cast Out of Heaven.

Revelation 12: 7 - 11 *(KJV)*
7. And there was war in heaven: Michael and his angels fought against the dragon; and the dragon fought and his angels,
8. and prevailed not; ***neither was THEIR PLACE found any more in heaven.***
9. ***And the great dragon was cast out, that old serpent called the Devil, and Satan, which deceiveth the whole world: he was cast out into the earth, and his angels were cast out with him***
10. And I heard a loud voice saying in heaven, ***"Now is come salvation, and strength, and the kingdom of our God, and the power of His Christ: FOR the accuser of OUR BRETHREN is CAST DOWN, which accused them before our God day and night."***
11. ***And THEY OVERCAME HIM by the blood of the Lamb, and by the word of their testimony; and they loved not their lives unto the death."***

A group of *redeemed sinful men* called ***"our brethren"*** are the ones who will finally overcome Satan and strip him of his right to remain in heaven. They will be in heaven before the throne of God, and Satan will accuse them day and night trying to convince God of their sin. The fact that they are called ***"OUR brethren,"*** shows they will be ***believers.*** Verse 11 reveals the ***three things*** *by which they will overcome Satan.*

FIRST: ***"Our brethren"*** will overcome him by ***the blood of the Lamb***. All men except Jesus died ***IN Adam*** *(Ref: 1 Corinthians 15: 22).* Because of that, *we're all helpless to resist sin;* ***therefore by our own sin, each of us has confirmed our own death penalty.*** Also, since Satan overcame man with sin and its curse of death, *he has the power of death over us, and keeps us in bondage all our lifetime through the fear of death.* Because of that we, *as sinful men,* can't even rise up to stand against Satan. Our sin and the constant fear of death make us all helpless to do anything in our own strength to overcome our bondage to Satan. However, Jesus is the ***ONE man*** who didn't suffer death in Adam, ***for He is the Son of God rather than a descendent of Adam.*** Not only was Jesus born without the death which all other men received from Adam, He also lived His entire life perfectly free from sin. That meant Jesus didn't have to die; ***nevertheless He did die as an act of obedience to the Father, who placed all our sins upon Him*** *(Ref: Isaiah 53: 6).* In that way Jesus accepted death as God's perfect sacrifice for our sins. He suffered the penalty of death that was due to us because of our sins. Therefore, ***when by faith*** ***<u>we MAKE the blood Jesus shed in death our personal sacrifice for sin,</u> the Father sees Jesus's seed of life in us, and we become Sons of God*** *(Ref: Isaiah 53: 10 - 11 & Galatians 4: 3 - 6). Then, because we are sons of God, we are joint-heirs with Christ, and will share with Him in the Divine eternal life* ***which is now His because He completely overcame sin and death*** *(Ref: Romans 8: 13 - 17).*

<u>NOTE:</u> Something to think about. *Romans 8: 17 says we are* ***"...HEIRS OF GOD, and joint-heirs with Christ." The only way we, along with Christ, can be heirs of God, is for God to have died, for no one can have an heir <u>UNTIL he dies</u>.*** *(Ref: Hebrews 9: 16 - 17).* ***Therefore, when*** *Jesus died, God Himself experienced death with Him. However, because Jesus experienced the fullness of death (separation from God the Father), He also suffered* ***<u>ALL</u>*** *of God's wrath against sin, that made it possible for God to raise Him back up with* ***resurrection life that stands in absolute total victory over death and Satan's power of death.*** *That means* ***the life Jesus now has, and which we will receive at His coming, is actually the <u>DIVINE LIFE OF GOD HIMSELF</u> — ETERNAL LIFE THAT GOD WON BY THE OBEDIENT SACRIFICE OF JESUS OVER SATAN, SIN AND THE POWER OF DEATH.***

Therefore, the ***first*** *means* by which ***"our brethren"*** will overcome Satan, is ***"the blood of the Lamb."*** By faith in that blood, *which represents the sacrifice of Jesus for man's sins,* they will be able to stand in God's presence, *free from the guilt of sin,* ***because Jesus's blood is manifest-proof-to-God that the penalty for their sin was fully paid by Jesus's death.*** *But we need to realize there is more involved in salvation* ***than just that which Jesus did***.

<u>SECOND,</u> "Our brethren" will also overcome Satan by, ***"the word of <u>THEIR</u> testimony."*** The fact that Jesus died for our sins ***isn't enough <u>by its self.</u>*** Each sinful person has to acknowledge his or her own guilt of sin, repent of their sin, and accept Jesus's death as the payment for their sin. *But to do that* ***acceptably to God,*** *we also have to make an open and public break from Satan and his way of living,* ***and we do that <u>by the word of our testimony.</u>*** So to overcome Satan, each of ***"our brethren"*** *must have* ***<u>his OWN personal testimony.</u>*** When I've read this verse in the past I've had a mental picture of ***"our brethren"*** *standing before the throne of God* ***giving their confession of faith.*** But recently I realized that's ***<u>NOT</u>*** what this is talking about. The testimony by which they will overcome Satan isn't something they will say ***at the throne of God***, but rather, ***it's the word of their testimony <u>by which</u>***

they openly and publically repent and confess their faith in Jesus Christ WHILE THEY ARE ALIVE HERE ON EARTH. *They won't have to confess Christ before the throne,* ***for THAT IS WHERE CHRIST WILL CONFESS THEM TO THE FATHER.***

Matthew 10: 32 - 33 *(KJV)*
32. ***Whosoever therefore shall confess Me before men, HIM WILL I CONFESS ALSO BEFORE MY FATHER WHICH IS IN HEAVEN.***
33. ***But whosoever shall deny Me before men, him will I also deny before My Father which is in heaven.***

God isn't interested in believers who are ashamed or afraid to make their faith known to other men. We're often reluctant to openly confess Jesus as our Lord and Savior because we fear the ridicule, persecution, or for some, even death that might result from a public stand for Jesus Christ. This gives new meaning to the third means by which ***"our brethren"*** will overcome Satan.

THIRD: ***"Our brethren"*** will overcome Satan by the fact that ***"...they loved not their lives unto the death."*** They will all have faced Satan's threats of persecution for making a very public confession of their faith in Jesus Christ. *And they will have overcome Satan's weapon of the fear of death,* ***by accepting death rather than renouncing their faith in Jesus.*** Since God is not interested in believers who are either ashamed or afraid to openly confess their faith to other men, the most powerful testimony a person can have is to stand firm in his faith, ***even at the price of death.*** *Not all believers have to make that ultimate stand for their faith, but if necessary, we must be willing to do so, just like these* ***"our brethren."***

Satan will diligently accuse ***"our brethren"*** of every sin they ever committed, but then God will look upon them, ***and because of what Jesus has done and their public testimony of faith, and their willingness to die rather than turn back from their faith, GOD WILL FIND THEM HOLY AND WITHOUT ANY GUILT OF SIN.*** In His perfect justice, God will find Jesus's sacrifice to be completely sufficient to cleanse them of all guilt. ***"Our brethren"*** will overcome Satan because he will not be able to find one single sin that hasn't been completely purged by the sacrifice of Jesus Christ. ***That means "our brethren" will regain man's right to be in God's presence that Satan won when he overcame Adam with sin.*** Therefore, when ***"our brethren"*** *as redeemed sinful men,* overcome Satan, they will be able to remain in God's presence in heaven, ***but Satan and his angels will lose***

their PLACE** in heaven, and Michael and his angels will finally be able to cast them down to the earth where they will become Jesus's **FOOTSTOOL. This raises the next question which is obvious.

Who Are Those People Called "Our Brethren?" They are *believers* who will be caught up ***TO HEAVEN BEFORE*** *Satan is cast down to the earth.* That means *they will* **also be in heaven BEFORE the Church is caught up, because Jesus won't be able to stand up from His seat next to the Father and come for the Church UNTIL AFTER Satan is made to be His footstool.** Therefore, we need to see what Scripture says *about* **who "our brethren" are,** *and* **how they will get into heaven BEFORE the Church is caught up in the Rapture.** It shouldn't be a surprise that *this same 12th Chapter of Revelation begins by identifying* **just such a group**.

Revelation 12: 1 - 4 *(KJV)*
1. And there appeared a great wonder in heaven; a woman clothed with the sun, and the moon under her feet, and upon her head a crown of twelve stars:
2. And she being with child cried, travailing in birth, and pained to be delivered.
3. And there appeared another wonder in heaven; and behold a great red dragon, having seven heads and ten horns, and seven crowns upon his heads.
4. And his tail drew the third part of the stars of heaven, and did cast them to the earth: and the dragon stood before the woman which was ready to be delivered, for to devour her child as soon as it was born.

This description shows that John didn't see an ***actual woman.*** Rather, *he saw a vision of something that* **looked like** *a woman.* His description gives a good clue about what the vision represented. She was ***"...clothed with the sun, and the moon under her feet, and upon her head a crown of twelve stars."*** This is remarkably similar to what Joseph had seen in a dream many centuries before.

Genesis 17: 9 - 10 *(KJV)*
9. And he *[Joseph]* dreamed yet another dream, and told it to his brethren, and said, ***"Behold, I dreamed a dream more; and, behold, the sun and moon and the eleven stars made obeisance to me."***
10. And he told it to his father, and to his brethren; and his father rebuked him, and said unto him, ***"What is this dream that thou hast dreamed?***

Shall I AND THY MOTHER AND THY BRETHREN indeed come to bow down ourselves to thee to the earth?"

Jacob immediately recognized that Joseph's dream represented his family — ***the children of Israel.*** *(Note: Joseph would have been the 12th star, but he wasn't included because he was the one to whom the others were bowing down.)* From this, it's apparent that the woman in John's vision also represented *the children of Israel.* But this doesn't tell us who was represented by the ***"man child."*** It's been suggested that the ***"man child"*** represented Jesus, since he was born as a Jew *in the nation of Israel, and was caught up to heaven after being crucified and resurrected.* However, that answer doesn't agree with what John heard at the beginning of his vision.

Revelation 4: 1 *(KJV)(This was at the beginning of the strictly* ***prophetic*** *portion of John's vision.)*
1. After this I looked, and, behold, a door was opened in heaven: and the first voice which I heard was as it were of a trumpet talking with me; which said, ***"Come up hither, and I will shew thee THINGS which must be HEREAFTER."***

This established the fact that John was about to see ***things that were going to happen AFTER THAT POINT IN TIME.*** *Since John received his vision about A. D. 90,* ***everything he was about to see would happen AFTER A. D. 90.*** Jesus had been born, crucified, resurrected and caught up to heaven at least 60 years before John received the Revelation; therefore, since the ***"man child"*** was going to be born sometime ***AFTER*** John received his vision in A. D. 90, it's obvious the ***"man child"*** couldn't represent Jesus. ***The "man child" represented someone who will be a vital part of the end-time events.*** Since the ***"man child"*** isn't mentioned anywhere else in Revelation, we have to look elsewhere in Scripture for a clue to it's identity. The only other place such a person is mentioned is in Isaiah.

Isaiah 66: 7 - 8 *(KJV)*
7. ***Before she travailed,*** *she brought forth;* ***before her pain came,*** *she was delivered of a* ***man child.***
8. Who hath heard such a thing? Who hath seen such things? Shall the earth be made to bring forth in one day? For as soon as Zion travailed, she brought forth ***her children.***

This sounds like a riddle. Verse 7 describes something that's completely contrary to the natural sequence of events in a birth. Everybody knows that

the travail *(labor pains)* ***always comes BEFORE the delivery.*** Yet the "***man child***" will be delivered ***BEFORE*** *the labor pains.* Verse 8 acknowledges that such a thing is unheard of; ***nevertheless, it confirms that when Zion*** *(Israel)* ***brings forth her children, her travail will come AFTER the delivery.*** *We'll discuss this later, but first,* this verse also shows that Israel's "***man child" will be MORE THAN JUST ONE PERSON. Israel's "man child" will actually be "her CHILDREN."*** Also, since this is talking about the ***NATION of Israel*** *bringing forth children, it obviously* ***WON'T be a birth in the normal sense of BABIES being born.*** Isaiah 66 also explains what it means for Israel *to bring forth* "***her children,*** who are also known as the "***man child.***"

Who Will The Man Child Actually Be?

Isaiah 66: 1 - 8 *(KJV)*
1. Thus saith the LORD, "***The heaven is my throne, and the earth is my footstool; WHERE IS THE HOUSE THAT YE BUILD UNTO ME? AND WHERE IS THE PLACE OF MY REST ?***"
2a. "***For all those things*** *[the heaven and earth]* ***hath Mine hand made, and all those things have been,***" saith the Lord:...

God was pointing out how ridiculous it was for Israel to think they could build a house or temple that could serve as a resting place for Him — ***Jehovah God.*** To understand what God wanted Israel to see, we need to look at what Solomon said when he dedicated the temple he had built.

I Kings 8: 27
27. ***But will God indeed dwell on the earth? Behold, the heaven and heaven of heavens cannot contain thee; how much less this house that I have builded?***

Solomon understood that man could never build a house great enough to contain God. Earlier, in Verse 20, he confessed that he had only "***...built an house for the NAME of the Lord God of Israel.***" So in Isaiah 66 when God asked the question, "***WHERE IS THE HOUSE THAT YE BUILD UNTO ME," He had already answered that question by saying, "The heaven is My throne, and the earth is My FOOTSTOOL.*** No matter how great a house Israel might build for God, it would still be ***only an insignificant building located on God's FOOTSTOOL.*** After showing how futile it would be for Israel to try an build a house for Him, God gave a hint about ***the kind of house He was going to build for Himself.***

Isaiah 66: 2b *(KJV)*
2b. ***"but to this MAN will I look, even to him that is poor and of a contrite spirit, and trembleth at My word."***

This doesn't ***seem*** to be related to God's opening comments about a resting place for Himself, and most likely nobody in Israel understood what He was talking about. However, ***AFTER Jesus came and was rejected by Israel,*** God revealed how that last part of Verse 2 relates to *the place of rest* ***He was going to provide for Himself.***

II Corinthians 6: 16 *(KJV)*
16. ***"And what agreement hath the temple of God with idols? FOR YE ARE THE TEMPLE OF THE LIVING GOD: as God hath said, 'I will dwell in them, and walk in them; and I will be their God, and they shall be my people.'"***

God is building His Own temple, and it will consist of the people who make up the Church. Israel's temple was simply one of God's examples that foreshadowed the Church. Since God is the source of all life, *the only kind of temple that could be suitable for Him is* ***a LIVING temple.*** *In I Peter we see how God is building that kind of temple.*

I Peter 2: 4 - 6 *(NKJV)(This is speaking of Jesus and of our salvation.)*
4. Coming to Him as ***to a living stone***, rejected indeed by men, but chosen by God and precious,
5. *you also,* ***as LIVING STONES, are being built up a spiritual house,*** a holy priesthood, to offer up spiritual sacrifices acceptable to God through Jesus Christ.
6. Therefore it is contained in the Scripture, ***"Behold, I lay in Zion a chief cornerstone, elect, precious, and he who believes on Him will by no means be put to shame."***

God is building a ***LIVING temple with living stones*** *and He's building it on the* ***LIVING CORNERSTONE of Jesus Christ.*** In Isaiah 66: 2, when God said, ***"but to this MAN will I look, even to him that is poor and of a contrite spirit, and trembleth at My word;"*** *He was talking about the* ***kind*** *of people He was going to use* ***as the RAW MATERIAL for His temple.*** He then went on to show how He felt about those self–righteous Jews who, *even in Isaiah's day,* were only going through the rituals that were prescribed by the law, while in their hearts they were disobedient and rebellious against Him. To depend on those rituals alone was a terrible offense to God.

Isaiah 66: 3 - 4 *(KJV)*
3. He that killeth an ox *[for a sacrifice] is as if he slew a man;* he that sacrificeth a lamb, *as if he cut off a dog's neck;* he that offereth an oblation, *as if he offered swine's blood;* he that burneth incense, *as if he blessed an idol.* Yea, they have chosen their own ways, and their soul delighteth in their abominations.
4. I also will choose their delusions, and will bring their fears upon them; because when I called, none did answer, when I spake, they did not hear; but they did evil in Mine eyes, and chose that in which I delighted not.

The majority in Israel had lost sight of the fact that ***they had to offer sacrifices <u>BECAUSE</u> of their sins.*** They believed they were pleasing God simply because they were going through the proper motions of religion. When Jesus came about seven centuries later, that same mistaken attitude still prevailed in Israel, and Jesus spent the three years of His ministry exhorting Israel to acknowledge their sins and repent. But instead of repenting, they had Him crucified. Then, because Israel had persisted in their disobedience and rebellion, God turned to the Gentiles and blinded Israel, giving them a spirit of slumber that they might not see *(Ref: Romans 11: 7 - 8).* As a result of that blindness, the majority of Jews have rejected Jesus and His message of repentance *throughout the Church age.* ***However, a small but steady flow of Jews have trembled at God's word, and have come to Him with a poor and contrite spirit. God has been pleased to open their eyes to see the truth about Jesus, and seeing, they have repented.*** Verse 5 was an important prophecy about how the majority of Jews were going to treat those Jews who trembled at God's word, repented, and came to faith in Jesus Christ.

5. Hear the word of the LORD, ***YE that tremble at His word*** *[speaking prophetically to those who would repent and believe in Jesus Christ.]* ***"Your brethren that hated you, that cast you out for My name's sake, said, 'Let the LORD be glorified:' but He shall appear to your joy, and they shall be ashamed."***

Throughout the Church age, many Jews who became Christians were so hated by their family and Jewish friends, that they were cast out — *completely* ***ostracized.*** In some cases they have been counted as dead, and it has been forbidden to mention their names anymore. In other cases they've even been put to death for believing in Jesus Christ. This began at the end of Jesus's earthly ministry and has continued throughout the Church age. Stephen is *the first person mentioned in Scripture* who had to pay ***the ultimate price of death*** because of his belief in Jesus. The irony is that the rebellious majority have thought *they were glorifying God by casting out their believing relatives and friends.* But referring to Christ's coming at the end of the age, Verse 5 said, when ***"...He*** *[the Lord] shall appear...," it will bring joy to the ostracized Jewish believers, but those who banished them will be overcome with shame and regret.* Verse 6 reveals how strong God's attitude is against those self-righteous unbelieving Jews.

6. A voice of noise from the city, a voice from the temple, ***a voice of the LORD that rendereth recompense to his enemies.***

Those who *think* they are glorifying God by casting out their believing relatives and friends are actually *storing up wrath against themselves as the enemies of God.* So God began Isaiah 66 by prophesying that the majority in Israel were going to cast out their brothers who came to the repentance and faith in Jesus that God desires. Then God gave a most unusual example to illustrate that situation that would divide so many families and friends in Israel. In His example, He pictured the nation of Israel travailing in child--birth and delivering a ***man child, but the labor pains were going to FOLLOW the birth rather than PRECEDE it.***

7. Before she travailed, she brought forth; before her pain came, she was delivered of a ***man child.***
8. Who hath heard such a thing? Who hath seen such things? Shall the earth be made to bring forth in one day? *For as soon as Zion [Israil] travailed, she brought forth* ***her children.***

Verse 8 reveals that *the man child will actually be an* ***unspecified number of CHILDREN.*** Those children will be the Jews who would be cast out by their brethren, because they repented as God required and came to faith in Jesus Christ. As mentioned above, that ***man child*** has been developing throughout the Church age which has been the equivalent of a gestation period. For the birth of a natural baby, the gestation period is about nine months, but for Israel's ***man child*** the gestation period will be about two–thousand years. With this background from Isaiah, we must turn back to Revelation 12 to see what will happen to the ***man child*** when it will be delivered at the end of its prolonged gestation period.

Revelation 12: 1 - 4 *(KJV)*
1. And there appeared a great wonder in heaven; a woman clothed with the sun, and the moon under her feet, and upon her head a crown of twelve stars:

2. And she being with child cried, travailing in birth, and pained to be delivered.
3. And there appeared another wonder in heaven; and behold a great red dragon, having seven heads and ten horns, and seven crowns upon his heads.
4. And his tail drew the third part of the stars of heaven, and did cast them to the earth: *and the dragon stood before the woman which was ready to be delivered, **for to devour her child as soon as it was born.***

It's obvious that the delivery of the ***man child*** won't be anything like the delivery of a normal baby, for the ***man child's*** delivery will involve many people, *all of whom will have already experienced **natural** **birth,** and also will have died — **apparently having been put to death.** **So what will the delivery of the man child consist of?*** We can answer this question by looking at the behavior of the dragon *(Satan)* as the time of the ***man child's*** delivery draws near. Verse 4 says he will be standing before the woman waiting ***"...to DEVOUR her child as soon as it is born."*** *Notice that Satan won't be concerned about the **man child** **as long as it HASN'T BEEN DELIVERED**.* But as soon as it's delivered, he will do all he can to devour it. To understand why this will be true, we have to recall that the ***man child*** *will be made up of people **who have already been put to DEATH.*** They will have died one-by-one down through the centuries of the Church age, ***and they will all REMAIN dead while they're waiting to be delivered as the man child.*** *Although they will have died separately, **they will all be delivered at the same time as the man child.***

When they died, they all came under the power of Satan, because Hebrews 2: 14 identifies Satan as the one who has ***the power of death***. Therefore, as long as the ***man child*** hasn't yet been delivered, Satan will have nothing to worry about, *because he will have all those who make up the **man child** **under his own power** — **the power of death.*** The fact that Satan is waiting, *poised to devour them as soon as the **man child** is delivered, **shows us that the man child's DELIVERY will actually consist of the RESURRECTION of all those who make up the man child.***

For them to be raised from the dead will pose the most serious threat to Satan since the resurrection of Jesus. Jesus's resurrection demonstrated the proof that His death and suffering in hell *was sufficient to cleanse Him **personally** from all our sins that the Father had laid upon Him according to Isaiah 53: 6*. However, Jesus's resurrection ***DIDN'T PROVE*** that His death had also been effective vicariously — ***that it was the perfect substitute for***

everybody who by faith makes Him their sacrifice for sin. In contrast, the resurrection of those who make up the man child will be God's testimony to the effect that Jesus's death did in fact pay the debt of death that we believers owe because of our sin. *Therefore, when Verse 4 says Satan will attempt to devour the* **man child** *when it's delivered, that means* **he will try** ***to convince God that those who make up the man child still have their guilt of sin, and therefore must remain dead. Satan will argue that they cannot justly be resurrected to live in God's presence in heaven.*** Verse 5 is where Satan will be given his chance to devour the resurrected ***man child.***

5. And *she brought forth* a man child, who was to rule all nations with a rod of iron: ***and her child was caught up unto God, and to HIS THRONE.***

This special group of people are identified as the ***"man child"*** **ONLY** *during the time God is calling them out* **here on earth** *to make up the body that will be "brought forth" (delivered) according to Verse 5 (above).* Their identity as **the *woman's*** *(Israel's)* ***man child,*** shows that they are *exclusively Jews* who came to faith in Jesus in spite of Israel's strong and even violent objection. They will have paid the dreadful price Jesus spoke of in Matthew 10: 21 - 22 which says, ***"And the brother shall deliver up the brother to death, and the father the child: and the children shall rise up against their parents, and shall cause them to be put to death. And ye shall be hated of all for My name's sake: but he that endureth to the end shall be saved."***

After the man child is delivered and caught up to God *(Ref: Verse 5 above), they will be identified as* ***"our brethren."*** That new identity shows that they will be a part of the Church, for it will be in their capacity *as believers* that Satan will accuse them before the throne of God. As ***"our brethren,"*** they will overcome Satan at the throne of God in heaven as previously discussed. Then, when Satan is cast out of heaven down to the earth, it will be necessary for the woman *(Israel)* to flee into the wilderness to escape the wrath of Satan. This is first mentioned in Revelation 12: 6, and is repeated with more detail at the end of the chapter.

Revelation 12: 6, & 12 - 17 *(KJV)*
6. And the woman fled into the wilderness, where she hath a place prepared of God, that they may feed her there a thousand two hundred and three-score days.
12. Therefore rejoice, ye heaven, and ye that dwell in them. Woe to the inhabitants of the earth and of the sea! for the devil is come down unto you, having great wrath, because he knoweth that he hath but a short time.

13. *And when the dragon saw that he was cast unto the earth,* ***he persecuted the woman which brought forth the man child.***
14. And to the woman were given two wings of a great eagle, that she might fly into the wilderness, into her place, where she is nourished for a time, and times, and half a time, from the face of the serpent.
15. And the serpent cast out of his mouth water as a flood after the woman, that he might cause her to be carried away of the flood.
16. And the earth helped the woman, and the earth opened her mouth, and swallowed up the flood which the dragon cast out of his mouth.
17. And the dragon was wroth with the woman, and went to make war with the remnant of her seed, which keep the commandments of God, and have the testimony of Jesus Christ.

Satan will be filled with wrath because of being cast down to the earth, and although he'll bring ***woe upon the entire earth,*** the woman *[Israel]* will be the primary target of his wrath. Verse 6 says she will flee into the wilderness and be fed for 1260 days. Verse 14 essentially repeats Verse 6, but speaks of her time in the wilderness as ***"a time, and times and half a time."*** The time in each of these verses equates to *three and a half years,* which will be the time Satan will have left on earth before the angel of Revelation 20: 1 - 3 casts him into the bottomless pit. Since the woman represents Israel, this shows that Satan will use the last 3½ years of this age in an attempt to destroy Israel. He began his attempt to destroy Israel long ago in the days of Moses when they were in Egypt.

The reason Satan has so persistently tried to destroy Israel relates to the promise God made to Abram as part of the *covenant of circumcision (Ref: Genesis 17: 7 - 10).* By that everlasting covenant, God promised ***to give all the land of Canaan to Abram and his seed as an EVERLASTING possession.*** That gave Satan the incentive to do everything he could to destroy Israel, ***for if he could do away with them as a separate identifiable people, it would render God unable to keep His covenant, and that would mean Satan had overcome God.*** In Jeremiah, God promised to do something else for Israel at the end of the age that will give Satan one last incentive to try to destroy them in an effort to prevent God from being able to keep His word in their behalf.

Jeremiah 30: 3 - 7 *(KJV)(In these verses God is declaring what He's going to do for Israel at the end of the age.)*
3. ***"For, lo, the days come,"*** saith the Lord, ***"That I will bring again the captivity of my people Israel and Judah,"*** saith the Lord: ***"and I will cause***

them to return to the land that I gave to their fathers, and they shall possess it."
4. And these are the words that the Lord spake concerning Israel and concerning Judah.
5. For thus saith the Lord; ***"We have heard a voice of trembling, of fear and not of peace."***
6. ***"Ask ye now, and see whether a man doth travail with child? Wherefore do I see every man with his hands on his loins, as a woman in travail, and all faces turned into paleness?"***
7. ***"Alas! For that day is great, so that none is like it: IT IS EVEN THE TIME OF JACOB'S TROUBLE; BUT HE SHALL BE SAVED OUT OF IT."***

This shows that the *great tribulation* at the end of this age will be directed primarily against Israel, for it will be ***" the time of JACOB'S** [Israel's]* ***trouble."*** But even as God revealed this truth about Israel's trouble, ***He gave His word that "...he** [Israel]* ***will be saved out of it."*** In an attempt to break this promise of God for Israel, Satan will do everything he possibly can to annihilate Israel during those last 3½ years before he is cast into the bottomless pit.

Revelation 12 *(above)* closes with the prophecy that Satan, *in his wrath,* will make war against those who are left in Israel, as well as against everyone else who remains true to God and Jesus Christ. Although Revelation 13 isn't a part of this study, as a matter of interest, it picks up where Revelation 12 ends, and gives a description of the unusual beast that symbolically represents the Antichrist's kingdom which Satan will use to exercise his wrath against God's people here on earth during the last few years of this age. Next we'll look at the last part ***"our brethren"*** will have in God's plan.

The Last Part "Our Brethren" Will Have In God's Plan.

The last part ***"our brethren"*** have in God's plan is important to this study *about* ***when*** *Jesus is coming,* ***and is an extremely important part of God's plan for man's redemption.*** We last saw ***"our brethren"*** in Revelation 12 standing before the throne of God where they will overcome Satan so he and his angels can be cast out of heaven. By their victory, ***"our brethren"*** will not only strip Satan of his right to a place in heaven, ***but they will also win that right FOR THEMSELVES.*** Therefore, Revelation 14 opens with a vision of ***"our brethren"*** enjoying their place in heaven after overcoming Satan as discussed in Revelation 12.

The Hundred And Forty-Four Thousand Of Revelation 14.

This part of John's vision provides some additional important information about ***"our brethren"*** who will then be identified as the hundred and forty-four thousand.

Revelation 14: 1 - 5 *(KJV)*
1. And I looked, and, lo, a Lamb stood on the mount Sion, and with Him an hundred and forty and four thousand, having his Father's name written in their foreheads.
2. And I heard a voice from heaven, as the voice of a great thunder: and I heard the voice of harpers harping their harps:
3. And they sung as it were a new song before the throne, and before the four beasts, and the elders: and no man could learn that song but the hundred and forty and four thousand, which were redeemed from the earth.
4. These are they which were not defiled with women; for they are virgins. These are they which follow the Lamb whithersoever He goeth. These were redeemed from among men, being the firstfruits unto God and to the Lamb.
5. And in their mouth was found no guile: for they are without fault before the throne of God.

The first thing we notice in this passage is they are no longer identified as ***"our brethren."*** Nevertheless, we know that's who the hundred and forty-four thousand are. That's because ***as "our brethren," they will be THE FIRST AND ONLY ONES to overcome Satan before the throne of God,*** and this group of a hundred and forty-four thousand are spoken of as, ***"...REDEEMED from among men, being the FIRSTFRUITS unto God and the Lamb."*** These two distinctions could not accurately apply to two ***DIFFERENT groups of people***. Revelation 14 *(above)* reveals some things about this special group of people that's important for all of us in the church.

- ***Verse 1:*** *Each of them will have the name of the* ***Lamb's Father*** *written on the forehead.* Having God's name on their forehead will show beyond dispute that they belong to the Father *(God), and that means nobody will ever again be able to lay a hand on them to harm them.*
- ***Verse 2:*** John heard them singing a song that nobody other than they themselves can learn or sing. That song must be ***their own UNIQUE testimony*** about the part *they* have in God's plan of redemption. Since

they have a unique part in God's plan, nobody else can ever learn and sing that same testimony put to song.

- ***Verse 4:*** *They will all be* ***virgins*** *— not defiled by women.* This implies that ***they will all be MEN.*** But it also raises an interesting question. God Himself created male and female and commanded them to be fruitful, which means God was the one who blessed the *physical union* between a man and his wife. So why is their being celibate spoken of as having merit before God? It's because man's situation changed when sin entered mankind. ***Before*** man sinned, God's command to mankind was ***to be fruitful, and multiply and replenish the earth, and to subdue it*** *(Ref: Genesis 1: 27 - 28).* However, when man sinned, God worked out His plan for redemption, and gave believers the new commandment ***to be witnesses of that salvation to all the world*** *(Ref: Acts 1: 8).* That new commandment to be witnesses doesn't impose any restrictions ***against*** men marrying and having children; ***HOWEVER, being married can result in tension between the responsibilities to God under that new commandment, and the responsibilities that go along with having a wife and family.*** The fact that these men are all virgins, implies that they chose not to marry, choosing instead ***to live their lives fully dedicated to serving God.*** That would mean they were free from any responsibilities to a wife and family. This is addressed in I Corinthians.

I Corinthians 7: 32 - 34a (UNAS)
32. But I want you to be free from concern *[things that distract one from the priority of pleasing God]. One who is* ***unmarried*** is concerned about the things of the Lord, how he may please the Lord;
33. But *one who is* ***married*** is concerned about the things of the world, how he may please his wife,
34. and his interests are divided.

- ***Verse 4 (contd):*** ***"They follow the Lamb whithersoever He goeth."*** This shows that they will be part of the Church, for I Thessalonians 4: 17 *speaks of Christ coming for the Church* and says, ***"Then we which are alive and remain shall be caught together with them*** *[those resurrected from the dead]* ***in the clouds to meet the Lord in the air, and so shall we ever be with the Lord."*** Since the Raptured Church will ***"ever be WITH THE LORD,"*** it follows that those who ***"...will follow the Lamb whithersoever He goeth,"*** *must also be a part of the Church.*
- ***Verse 4 (contd):*** They will be ***"...redeemed from among men, being the FIRSTFRUITS unto God and to the Lamb."*** Their identity as the

FIRSTFRUITS** unto God and to the Lamb,* relates to ***the UNIQUE part God has for them to play in His plan of redemption. This is discussed in detail below.

- ***Verse 5:*** They will be ***"...without fault before the throne of God."*** This will be God's verdict after Satan has accused them by reminding God of all the sins they committed when they were alive here on earth. Because of their faith in the sacrifice of Jesus for their sins, all of their sins will have been completely obliterated, and God will look upon them and see them just as holy and pure as He Himself.

The Firstfruits Unto God And To The Lamb. After the ***man child*** is complete, *has been delivered and caught up to heaven, and* as ***our brethren*** have won the victory over Satan before God's throne, they'll be identified in a different way. From then on they will be the ***"FIRSTFRUITS** (of redeemed men)* ***Unto God And To The Lamb."*** This new name will forever set them apart from all the other redeemed, for there can be only one firstfruits, and all that follow will be the main harvest. This is significant because their designation as the firstfruits indicates they will fulfill the example provided by Israel's fourth annual feast — the feast of firstfruits of the wave loaves. God required Israel to observe ***eight** different feasts*, and each one of them was an example that foreshadowed a different major aspect of God's plan for man's redemption. We'll look briefly at the first five feasts to show how they are examples.

The ***first*** of these feasts was the Sabbath which Israel had to observe on the last *(seventh)* day of every week *(Ref: Leviticus 23: 3).* As you know, the Sabbath began with a special meal, and was to be kept as ***a day of rest — all work was forbidden for the entire day.*** Therefore, *as an example,* the Sabbath foreshadowed the rest that believers find in Jesus Christ — ***rest from the works-of-the-law to be righteous before God***. In Matthew 11: 28 - 30 Jesus showed that He is the fulfillment of the Sabbath for those who believe in Him, for He said, ***"Come unto Me, all ye that labor and are heavy laden, and I will give you REST. Take My yoke upon you, and learn of Me; for I am meek and lowly in heart: and ye shall find rest unto your SOULS. For My yoke is easy, and My burden is light."***

Israel's ***first ANNUAL feast*** was ***Passover*** *(Ref: Leviticus 23: 5).* Although it commemorated the first Passover by which God delivered Israel from bondage in Egypt, that first Passover in Egypt was actually God's example ***of the death of His Son to provide for man's deliverance from the bondage***

of sin. Therefore, the example of killing Passover lamb was fulfilled by the death of Jesus Christ.

The **second** ***ANNUAL feast*** was ***the feast of unleavened bread.*** *(Ref: Leviticus 23: 6 - 8).* That feast began on the fifteenth day of the first month, and lasted seven days. During those seven days Israel was to eat only unleavened bread, and also observe the first and last days as days of rest. That feast was an example that foreshadowed ***the life those who believe in Jesus are supposed to live.*** Resting on the first and seventh days foreshadowed the fact that our righteousness through faith in Jesus, both begins and ends with rest in His righteousness. Since leaven was an example of sin, eating only ***unleavened*** *bread* for the full seven days of the feast, *foreshadowed the fact all believers are supposed to live the rest of their lives in repentance* ***— doing all they can to keep their lives free from sin.***

The ***third ANNUAL feast*** was ***the feast of the firstfruits of the Wave Sheaf*** *(Ref: Leviticus 23: 10 - 14).* On the day following the first Sabbath after the grain harvest began, the priest was to wave a sheaf of freshly cut grain before the Lord as the firstfruits of the harvest. This was an example that foreshadowed Jesus presenting Himself for the Father's inspection after He was resurrected. That was necessary to ensure that His suffering of death and God's wrath had indeed purged away ***ALL of the sins of mankind that God had placed upon Him before He died*** *(Ref: Isaiah 53: 6).* ***If God had found any sin still upon Him, that would have meant His suffering had not been sufficient to remove our sins and that would have meant He could not have been our Savior.*** Jesus fulfilled ***the feast of the firstfruit of the Wave Sheave*** the morning after His resurrection. You recall that He appeared to Mary and told her that ***He had to go to the Father*** *(Ref: John 20: 14 - 17).* We know that God found Jesus to be pure and without sin, because that night He appeared to the disciples and ***imparted to them the Holy Spirit as the assurance of their salvation.***

The ***fourth ANNUAL feast*** was ***the feast of the firstfruits of the Wave Loaves*** *(Ref: Leviticus 23: 15 - 21).* On *the* **FIFTIETH** ***day*** *after* offering ***the firstfruits of the Wave Sheaf,*** the priest was to offer ***the firstfruits of the Wave Loaves.*** He was to take two loaves of bread made from that year's harvest, and wave them before the Lord. That feast was different from the feast of the *Wave* ***Sheaf*** in several significant ways. ***First,*** the *wave* ***sheaf*** was just *one small handful of freshly cut grain* that was still in the husk. As a single *sheaf,* it represented just *one person.* In contrast, the two *loaves* were made from two tenth deals of flour, which was equal to about a gallon. So each of the two *loaves* were about the same size as a regular loaf of bread. The gallon of flour used for those two *loaves* would require grain from a great many sheaves; *therefore, the two* ***loaves*** *were an example representing* ***a significant number of people. Second,*** since the grain of *the Wave* ***Sheaf*** was still in the husk, it was *completely free from leaven*, and since God used leaven to represent sin, *the Wave* ***Sheaf*** *was an accurate example of Jesus who lived perfectly free from sin.* In contrast, the two *Wave* **Loaves** had to be ***baked <u>WITH LEAVEN,</u>*** *which meant* ***they represented people who were <u>sinners.</u>*** *But the* ***loaves were <u>BAKED,</u>*** which meant the leaven was no longer active. Therefore, *even though the people represented by the* ***loaves*** *had been sinners, since the loaves were baked, that indicated that sin was no longer active in their lives —* ***the Wave <u>Loaves</u> represented <u>REDEEMED sinners.</u>*** Additionally, since the ***loaves*** were ***the <u>FIRSTFRUITS</u> of the harvest, they represented the <u>FIRST REDEEMED PEOPLE</u> who would be presented to God.*** Therefore, *since the hundred and forty-four thousand of Revelation 14 are identified as* ***"the firstfruits*** *[of redeemed men]* ***unto God and the lamb,"*** *they are the ones who will fulfill the example presented by the feast of the Wave Loaves.*

There's one other aspect of the feast of the first fruits of the Wave Loaves that is easy to overlook. The high priest waved the two Wave Loaves before the Lord for His approval. The reason for this is that when the Lord approved the firstfruits, that meant the entire harvest they represented was also acceptable. This is an extremely important aspect of the feast of the Wave Loaves in regard to its example being fulfilled by the church. God didn't address this in the Revelation, for He had already revealed it through the Apostle Paul.

<u>The Importance Of The Firstfruits of the Redeemed to the Rest of the Church.</u> The importance of the ***<u>Firstfruits</u> of the redeemed*** relates to a subject that's rarely, *if ever*, discussed. That is the fact that ***at this present time, <u>believers have ONLY God's PROMISE of Salvation. SALVATION ITSELF hasn't yet become an established fact.</u>*** This is made clear in Peter's first epistle.

I Peter 1: 3 - 6

3. Blessed be the God and Father of our Lord Jesus Christ, *which according to His abundant mercy* ***hath begotten us again unto a lively*** *[living]* ***<u>HOPE</u> by the resurrection of Jesus Christ from the dead,***

4. ***to an inheritance incorruptible, and undefiled, and that fadeth not away, <u>RESERVED</u> in heaven for you,***

5. ***who are kept by the power of God through faith unto salvation <u>READY TO BE REVEALED IN THE LAST TIME.</u>***

This same truth is confirmed in Ephesians.

Ephesians 1: 13 - 14
13. In Him *[Christ]* you also trusted, after you heard the word of truth, the gospel of your salvation; in whom also, ***having believed, you were sealed with the Holy Spirit of promise.***
14. ***Who is the guarantee of our inheritance <u>UNTIL the redemption of the purchased possession</u>***, unto the praise of His glory.

This has been true for believers throughout the centuries of the Church age. ***No one has yet actually <u>RECEIVED SALVATION.</u>*** Instead, Jesus gives us the Holy Spirit as the guarantee *(or earnest)* of our purchased possession. In that capacity, the Holy Spirit dwells within each believer giving us God's ***<u>TESTIMONY</u>*** that one day we are going to experience the fullness of salvation. When Jesus went to the Father on resurrection morning, He was found to be completely cleansed from our sins that the Father had placed upon Him while He was on the cross. Because Jesus's suffering had purged away those sins, ***He Himself*** was able to be resurrected and live again in God's presence, **<u>AND</u>** ***could grant <u>God's PROMISE of salvation</u>*** *to everybody who repents and by faith accepts that Jesus paid their debt for sin.* ***But there was nothing about Jesus's examination by the Father that <u>PROVED</u> His suffering had ALSO been effective for us who believe in Him. Additionally, <u>until this day</u>, there is still nothing that has happened to prove that what Jesus suffered <u>WAS ALSO EFFECTIVE FOR US.</u>*** But in Romans *God revealed something that is going to happen* ***that will prove Jesus's suffering for sin was <u>ALSO EFFECTIVE TO PROVIDE SALVATION TO ALL WHO REPENT AND BELIEVE IN HIM.</u>***

Romans 11: 11 - 16 (NKJV) *(In this passage, Paul revealed that God's plan for Israel will be worked out shortly before the return of Christ.)*
11. I say then, have they *[Israel]* stumbled that they should fall? Certainly not! But through their fall, to provoke them to jealousy, salvation has come to the Gentiles.
12. Now if their fall is riches for the world, and their failure riches for the Gentiles, how much more their fullness
13. For I speak to you Gentiles; inasmuch as I am an apostle to the Gentiles, I magnify my ministry.

14. If by any means I may provoke to jealousy those who are my flesh and save some of them.
15. For if their being cast away is the reconciling of the world, ***what will their acceptance be but life from the dead?***

When God restores Israel to His favor, *that will prove to be* ***life from the dead for the entire church.*** The next verse reveals why this will be true.

16. ***For if the FIRSTFRUIT is holy, the LUMP IS ALSO HOLY; and if the ROOT is holy, so are the BRANCHES.***

Verse 16 is looking beyond Israel's actual feast and is speaking of its fulfillment in redeemed men. Therefore, just as the Lord's approval of the Wave Loaves means the entire grain harvest is acceptable, *in fulfillment of that example, when the Lord examines* **"our brethren"** *(the hundred and forty-four thousand),* **and finds them completely free from all sin, *THAT WILL MEAN THE ENTIRE CHURCH IS ALSO COMPLETELY FREE FROM SIN.*** Accordingly, ***at that time, salvation will no longer be ONLY God's promise, and WILL BECOME A PROVEN FACT.***

Everything up to this point in Chapter 5 has been the background necessary to substantiate the answer to the chapter's basic question: ***When will God make Jesus's enemies His footstool?*** Now, based on the background provided, it's time to address that question.

When Will God Make Jesus's Enemies His Footstool? In Revelation 12, verses 6 and 14 both speak of the woman *(Israel)* having to flee into the wilderness to escape the wrath of the dragon *(Satan)* when he is cast out of heaven.

Revelation 12: 6 & 14 *(NKJV)*
6. Then the woman *[Israel]* fled into the wilderness, where she has a place prepared by God, that they should feed her there one thousand two hundred and sixty days.
14. But the woman was given two wings of a great eagle, that she might fly into the wilderness to her place, where she is nourished for a time and times and half a time, from the presence of the serpent.

As mentioned earlier in this chapter, since the *time span* given in each of these verses is the equivalent of three and a half *(3 ½)* years, it's apparent that Satan and his angels will be cast out of heaven ***at the <u>BEGINNING</u>*** of the last three and a half years of this age *(the church age).* Also in Chapter 4, in the paragraph entitled, "*When Is God Going to Restore Israel into His Favor?*" it was determined that God should restore Israel into His favor in A. D. 2030, which should also be ***the <u>END</u> of this age*** *(the church age).* Therefore, Satan and his angels should be cast out of heaven in A. D. 2026, which will be three and a half years prior to the end of the age in A. D. 2030.

Additionally, as discussed above, ***"our brethren"*** will be examined at the throne of God in fulfillment of the example provided by *the feast of* ***Firstfruits of the Wave Loaves***, which is now better known as Pentecost. *Therefore, they should be examined on the actual date of Pentecost in keeping with the precedent set when Jesus was crucified in fulfillment of the example of Passover* ***<u>on the actual date of Passover.</u>*** Accordingly, ***"our brethren"*** should be examined at the throne of God in fulfillment of *the feast of* ***Firstfruits of the Wave Loaves*** on the day of Pentecost in A. D. 2026, which will begin at sundown on May 22 of that year, and will mark the beginning of the last three and a half (3 ½) years of this age. ***That means God should make Jesus's enemies His footstool either <u>on or shortly after May 22, 2026.</u>*** As we consider the possibility of the end of the age being so close, we need to face the following question.

<u>Has the Last Generation of this Age Already Begun?</u> In relation to this question, consider something that occurred in the spring of 1990. I had been interested in prophecy for many years prior to 1990, but had only recently become aware of the importance of *the first day of the first month (Abib/Nisan)* as the anniversary of Israel's covenant with God. That spring I was looking through a copy of the *Jerusalem Post*, and because these things were fresh on my mind, one of the articles in that issue of the Post caught my attention. Israel was in the midst of a political struggle, with its two major political parties trying to gain the majority necessary to lead the government. Since neither party had a majority, they were courting the minority parties trying to form a working coalition. One of the minority parties that was thrust into the spotlight by this struggle, was an ultra orthodox religious party led by a Rabbi named Eliezer Shach, who was about 90 years old. In an effort to gain his cooperation, one of the major parties offered him the opportunity to address the entire nation of Israel on national TV. The Post noted that he took advantage of that rare opportunity, ***and declared to Israel on national T.V. that, "<u>YOU SHOULD</u>***

BE KEEPING THE TORAH.*"** In this way, Rabbi Shach served notice to ***ALL Israel, that they should be obeying the law according to the covenant. It's doubtful that such a message had been given ***to the entire nation of Israel*** since the days of Joshua, when he gathered all the tribes to Shechem and told them, ***"Choose for yourselves this day whom you will serve,...... But as for me and my house, we will serve the Lord."*** *(Joshua 24: 15).* Because of the following reasons, Rabbi Shach's imperative call for Israel to return to obedience of the law was ***extremely important.***

- That command was made by one of the most prominent leaders of orthodox Judaism in Israel. Therefore it should have been recognized by the Jews as an authoritative call to return to the covenant their forefathers made with God long ago at Mt Sinai.
- It was in perfect agreement with the prophetic words of both Moses and Malachi, that had been addressed to Israel ***specifically for the LATTER days.***

Deuteronomy 30: 1 - 3 *(NKJV) (This is the Lord speaking to Israel through Moses.)*

1. ***"And it shall come to pass, when all these things come upon you, the blessing and the curse, which I have set before you, and you call them to mind among all the nations where the Lord your God drives you*** *[this clearly is speaking of the time of the end],*
2. ***and you return to the Lord your God, and obey His voice according to all that I command you today, you and your children, with all your heart, and with all your soul,***
3. ***that the Lord your God will bring you back from captivity, and have compassion on you, and gather you again from all the nations where the Lord your God has scattered you."***

Malachi 4: 4 - 6 *(NKJV)*

4. ***"Remember the law of Moses My servant, which I commanded him in Horeb for all Israel, with the statutes and judgments.***
5. ***Behold I will send you Elijah the prophet before the coming of the great and dreadful day of the Lord.***
6. ***And he will turn the hearts of the fathers to the children, and the hearts of the children to their fathers, lest I come and strike the earth with a curse."***

Both of these prophecies were directed ***specifically to Israel***, and both gave essentially the same message, namely, *that as the end of the age draws near,*

Israel must return to strict and careful obedience of the law as required by their covenant with God. *It was because of Israel's failure to obey the law according to the covenant, that God wouldn't permit them to* ***recognize Jesus as their Messiah and Lord when He came the first time.*** Isaiah had prophesied this saying, ***"For the Lord has poured out on you THE SPIRIT OF DEEP SLEEP, AND HAS CLOSED YOUR EYES...."*** *(Isaiah 29: 10).* Paul quoted from this passage in Romans and revealed that Israel's ***God–imposed blindness*** would continue until the end of the Church age.

Romans 11: 8 & 25 *(KJV)*
8. (According as it is written, ***"God hath given them*** *[Israel]* ***the spirit of slumber, eyes that they should not see, and ears that they should not hear:"***) unto this day. *[This was written in A. D. 60, 30 years after the crucifixion of Jesus.]*
25. For I would not, brethren *[addressing the Church]*, that ye should be ignorant of this mystery *[the mystery of Israel's inability to recognize and accept Jesus as their Messiah and Lord]*, lest ye should be wise in your own conceits; ***that blindness in part is happened to Israel, UNTIL the fullness of the Gentiles be come in.***

The only way Israel can be restored to God's favor, is ***to WAKE UP SPIRITUALLY and return to Him by obeying His law according to their covenant.*** When Rabbi Eliezer Shach made his declaration to Israel in 1990, he was actually repeating these messages given by Moses and Malachi *(above).* But there's something else about Rabbi Shach's declaration that adds particular significance to its importance. ***His declaration had an even greater urgency than what Moses and Malachi said, because of WHEN HE MADE IT!*** According to the dates given in the Jerusalem Post, *Rabbi Shach made his declaration to Israel on the* ***first day of the first month*** *(Abib/Nisan),* ***in the year 1990, which was EXACTLY FORTY YEARS*** *(the span of one generation)* ***BEFORE the first day of the first month*** *(Abib/Nisan)* ***of A.D. 2030. As discussed in this Chapter, AND in the discussion of Hosea 5 & 6 in Chapter 4, A. D. 2030 is when this present age*** *(the Church age)* ***should come to its end. Therefore, it seems that Rabbi Shach's declaration was God's warning that THE LAST GENERATION of this present age HAD BEGUN ON THAT DAY. If this is correct, it means that NOW, less than twenty years remain before the end of that generation which Jesus said will not pass until all is fulfilled that He prophesied in Matthew 24.*** Accordingly, we must face the fact, that as Jesus said, ***"...it*** *(His return)* ***is near, EVEN AT THE DOORS."***

We need to take one last look at the victory of ***"our brethren"*** over Satan at God's throne. After that victory is won and Satan and his angels have been cast out of heaven, a loud voice from heaven is going to ***proclaim that four things have THEN come.*** Those four things will effect both believers and all who come in contact with believers, and will do so in ways that are without precedent throughout the centuries of the church age. Those four things and their effects are discussed in the next chapter.

Chapter 6

Four Things That Are Yet To Come

Introduction.

Revelation 12: 10 *(KJV)*
10. And I heard a loud voice saying in heaven, ***"NOW is come SALVATION, and STRENGTH, and the KINGDOM OF OUR GOD, and the POWER OF HIS CHRIST: for the accuser of our brethren is cast down, which accused them before our God day and night."***

These four things, ***Salvation, Strength,*** the ***Kingdom of our God,*** and the ***Power of His Christ*** won't *come in their fullness,* ***UNTIL Satan is cast out of heaven.*** As we consider each of these things in detail, hopefully we'll begin to understand ***WHY*** that is true.

Now Is Come SALVATION ! The proclamation in Revelation 12: 10 *(above)* that will come from heaven after Satan is cast down to the earth confirms the truth discussed in Chapter 5 in the paragraph entitled *"The Importance Of The Firstfruits of the Redeemed to the Rest of the Church."* In that paragraph, we saw that throughout the church age salvation has only been *God's* **PROMISE** *for those who repent and come to God by faith in Jesus.* However, when the firstfruits of the redeemed stand before God and have Satan accuse them of all the sins they ever committed, because they have repented and by faith trusted in Jesus as their sacrifice for sin, God in His perfect justice will find them holy and without sin. Therefore ***at that time,*** God's promise of salvation will have been demonstrated to be a proven fact. Additionally, that proof of God's promise of salvation won't be limited only to those who are the firstfruit. Since they will represent all true believers, God's promise of salvation will then become a proven reality for the entire church of Jesus Christ. Just as God revealed through Paul, "*...if the firstfruit be holy, the lump is also holy: and if the root be holy, so are the branches." (Romans 11: 16).*

As we continue in Revelation 12, we see that this will bring about an interesting situation. *When Satan is cast out of heaven and down to the earth for the last three and a half (3 ½) years of this age,* ***the church will also be here on the earth.***

Revelation 12: 12 & 17 *(KJV)*
12. Therefore rejoice, ye heavens, and ye that dwell in them. Woe to the inhabitants of the earth and of the sea! For the Devil is come down unto you, having great wrath, because he knoweth that he hath but a short time.
17. And the dragon was wroth with the woman, and went to make war with the remnant of her seed, *which keep the commandments of God,* ***and have the testimony of Jesus Christ.***

The rest of the church will still be on the earth, ***AND*** will continue to be ***targets of Satan*** right up to the end of the last *three and a half years of this age.* Although this may be a disturbing thought, we should be encouraged by the fact that during those last three and a half years, the situation of believers will be different from what it has been at any other time during the Church age. We believers will continue to have the Holy Spirit dwelling within us; however, His testimony will then be that *we have salvation that is a proven reality — no longer just God's promise.* That new testimony can't help but provide an inner strength like believers have never experienced before. Only time will tell how that will effect our Christian walk, *and as we consider that along with the other three things that will then come, it should fill us with a sense of eager anticipation.*

Now Is Come STRENGTH! The second thing that will come is ***"strength."*** This will be different from ***"the power of His Christ,"*** which is the fourth thing that will come. ***Strength*** relates to the ***physical ability*** that resides in us by virtue of our own ***natural being.*** In contrast, as used in Scripture, ***power*** relates to ***authority*** *that must be submitted to and obeyed.* God has ***ALL*** *power,* and He gives it to others in different measures depending on His sovereign will and purpose. We see this in Romans 13: 1 which says, ***"Let every soul be subject unto the higher powers. For THERE***

IS NO POWER but of God: the powers that be are ordained of God." To understand what it will mean for ***strength to <u>COME,</u>*** we need to recognize one of God's purposes for His angels.

Hebrews 1: 13 - 14 *(KJV)(This chapter discusses how God has exalted the position of His Son, compared to the position of angels.)*
13. But to which of the angels said He at any time, ***"Sit on My right hand, until I make Thine enemies Thy footstool?"***
14. Are they *[the angels]* not all ministering spirits, *sent forth* ***to minister for them who shall be heirs of salvation?***

God's purpose for angels is that they should minister ***"for them <u>who shall be heirs of salvation,</u>" i.e., for Christians <u>HERE ON EARTH.</u> After we are caught up to heaven and have received our inheritance of salvation, we will no longer have the need for angels to minister for us.*** However, this passage in Hebrews raises an interesting question. Since God's purpose for the angels is for them to minister to believers, ***how is it that strength will come, <u>ONLY</u> at that time in the future at the beginning of the last three and a half years of this age?*** One of Daniel's experiences will help us answer this question

Daniel 10: 2 - 5, 8 - 14 & 18 - 19 *(NKJV)*
2. In those days I Daniel was mourning three full weeks.
3. I ate no pleasant food, no meat or wine came into my mouth, nor did I anoint myself at all, till three whole weeks were fulfilled.
4. And on the twenty-fourth day of the first month, as I was by the side of the great river, that is the Tigris,
5. I lifted my eyes, and looked, and behold, a certain man clothed in linen, whose waist was girded with gold of Uphaz:

When this happened there was a great quaking which frightened everybody around Daniel and they all ran off and hid.

8. Therefore I was left alone when I saw this great vision, ***and no strength remained in me; for my vigor was turned to frailty in me, and <u>I retained no STRENGTH.</u>***
9. Yet I heard the sound of his words, and while I heard the sound of his words I was in a deep sleep on my face, with my face to the ground.
10. Suddenly, a hand touched me, which made me tremble on my knees and on the palms of my hands.

11. And he said unto me, ***"O Daniel, a man greatly beloved, understand the words that I speak to you, and stand upright, for I have been sent to you."*** While he was speaking this word to me, I stood trembling.
12. Then said he to me, ***"Do not fear, Daniel, for from the first day you set your heart to understand, and to humble yourself before your God, your words were heard, and I have come because of thy words."***
13. ***"But the prince of the kingdom of Persia withstood me twenty-one days: and behold, Michael, one of the chief princes, came to help me; for I had been left alone there with the prince of Persia."***
14. ***"Now I have come to make you understand what will happen to your people in the later days, for the vision refers to many days yet to come."***

Daniel had prayed for a total of twenty-four days with no answer, ***even though God had sent an angel with the answer on the very first day.*** The delay was caused by *interference* from the prince of Persia, who apparently was the *demon prince* who ruled for Satan over the earthly kingdom of Persia. The Archangel Michael went to assist the angel who had Daniel's answer, but it still wasn't until the ***twenty-fourth day*** that he managed to get through to Daniel with the answer. *Even with Michael's help, it took **three more days** for God's angel to get through to Daniel. The demon prince of Persia was able to do this, **because he, along with Satan, <u>had a right to be in heaven because of Satan's victory over Adam.</u>*** Since they were in heaven, Satan was able to send one of his most powerful demons to hinder God's angel from *even getting out of heaven* to deliver God's answer to Daniel. But when God's angel finally got through to Daniel, *he did more than just deliver God's answer to Daniel's prayer.*

18. Then again, the one having the likeness of a man *[God's angel]* touched me ***and <u>STRENGTHENED</u> me.***
19. And he said, ***"O man greatly beloved, fear not! Peace be to you; <u>BE STRONG</u>, yes, <u>BE STRONG</u>!"*** So when he spoke to me ***I was strengthened,*** and said, ***"Let my lord speak, for you have <u>STRENGTHENED</u> me."***

After praying and observing at least a partial fast for twenty-four days, Daniel was physically and emotionally drained when the angel finally got to him. The angel recognized this, *and supernaturally strengthened Daniel before delivering God's answer to his prayer.* God is well aware of our ***physical*** *limitations;* therefore, a major part of His angels' ministry is to strengthen us when we reach the limit of our own strength. That ministry has been available to God's children throughout the ages; however, *Daniel's experience reveals that **since** Satan and his angels have access to heaven, it's* *been possible for them to interfere with God's angels and hinder them from freely accomplishing what God sends them to do.* In Daniel's case, God's angel was delayed for a total of twenty-four days, *and in all likelihood, Daniel's persistence in prayer played a major part in God's angel finally getting through,* **both to deliver God's answer AND to <u>STRENGTHEN</u> Daniel.** We can better understand the importance of this supernatural strengthening by angels, ***when we see that even Jesus needed it.***

Matthew 4: 8 - 11 *(KJV)(This was when Jesus was in the wilderness, after He had fasted for forty days and had been tempted by Satan.)*
8. Again, the devil taketh Him up into an exceeding high mountain, and sheweth Him all the kingdoms of the world, and the glory of them:
9. And saith unto Him, ***"All these things will I give Thee, if Thou wilt fall down and worship me."***
10. Then saith Jesus unto him, ***"Get thee hence, Satan: for it is written, 'Thou shalt worship the Lord thy God, and Him only shalt thou serve.'"***
11. Then the devil leaveth Him, ***and, behold <u>angels came and ministered unto Him</u>***.

After forty days without food, Jesus was weak to the point that He probably didn't have the strength to get back to civilization. Therefore, God sent angels to minister to Him and give Him the strength He needed. This same situation occurred again later, but under very different conditions. When Jesus was in the garden the night before His crucifixion, He faced the most intense temptation of His life. He was faced with the choice of accepting our sin and all of the penalty for that sin. He understood that accepting our sin would separate Him from the Father and break the perfect fellowship that had been His in the Trinity from eternity past.

Luke 22: 41 - 44 *(KJV)*
41. And He was withdrawn from them about a stone's cast, and kneeled down and prayed,
42. saying, ***"Father, if Thou be willing, remove this cup from Me: nevertheless not My will but Thine be done."***
43. ***And there appeared an angel unto Him from heaven, <u>STRENGTHENING</u> Him.***
44. And being in an agony He prayed more earnestly: and His sweat was as it were great drops of blood falling down to the ground.

At that moment, Jesus confronted the enormity of what He was facing. Having to make that final dreadful choice *put Him under such an unimaginable strain that* ***in the weakness of His humanity,*** He was completely drained of His natural strength. Therefore, the Father sent an angel to strengthen Him so He would be ***physically able*** to stand the ordeal of the trial and crucifixion. Daniel's experience shows that God's provision to supernaturally strengthen His children by means of the angels wasn't limited only to Jesus. It's available to all of God's children; however, few of us have actually experienced supernatural strengthening *like Daniel did. Could that be because Satan's demons have hindered God's angels from getting through to us,* ***and we haven't prayed enough to help them get through?***

Satan and his angels are able to interfere with God's angels, because Satan regained access to heaven when he overcame Adam with sin and death. From that position of advantage, they know when God sends His angels to minister to us, and can intercept them and hinder them. However, when Satan and his angels are cast out of heaven, that situation is going to change. They will no longer be in a position ***to know*** what God's angels are doing, and they will no longer be able to hinder them. The result for us, will be that ***strength*** *(supernatural strength from God)* ***will come*** without delay whenever we need it. When that finally happens, the angels of God will rejoice, because they will finally be free to accomplish God's purposes for them without the constant interference by Satan and his angels.

Revelation 12: 12 *(NKJV)*
12. Therefore, rejoice, O heavens, and you who dwell in them! Woe to the inhabitants of the earth and the sea! For the devil has come down to you, having great wrath, because he knows that he has a short time.

We see from this, that strength is going to come at the point in time when we, as God's children, will need it more than ever before in history. The next thing that will come is the kingdom of our God.

<u>Now Is Come the Kingdom of Our God.</u> The fact that the kingdom of our God is going to come *at this* ***future*** *date*, may be confusing to us, because most of us have thought the kingdom of God has always existed. But when Jesus taught us how to pray, *the first thing* He said we should pray is ***"...Thy kingdom <u>COME.</u>"*** *(Ref: Matthew 6: 9 - 13). Obviously, He wouldn't tell us to pray for something* ***to come, <u>IF IT WAS ALREADY HERE!</u>*** *To understand why the kingdom of God* ***still needs to come***, we need to see what Scripture says *actually constitutes the kingdom of God*. Our first thought may be that it simply consists of the heavens and earth, ***i.e., all of creation,*** but the creation had existed for eons of time ***before*** Jesus said we should pray for God's kingdom to come. Therefore, the kingdom of God must be different from simply ***all of creation.*** On another occasion, Jesus revealed what that ***difference*** actually is

Luke 11: 20 *(NKJV)*
20 ***"But if I cast out demons with the finger of God, surely THE KINGDOM OF GOD HAS COME upon you."***

The kingdom of God exists ***<u>ONLY</u> where God isn't being opposed by enemies who are challenging His right to rule.*** Therefore, the kingdom of God hasn't existed in its fullness since Satan and his angels rebelled against God in the far distant past. In fact, throughout the centuries since Adam sinned and Satan gained the right to be in heaven, ***the kingdom of God hasn't even existed IN HEAVEN, for Satan has been there challenging God and opposing His right to reign.*** Therefore, *when Satan is overcome* ***and cast out of heaven, the kingdom of God will finally be restored to heaven.*** *Nevertheless, since Satan and his demons will* **then** *be opposing God and persecuting God's people here on earth,* ***the kingdom of God will not yet have been restored <u>TO THE EARTH.</u>*** In I Corinthians we see what must happen before the kingdom of our God will finally be completely restored according to God's plan.

I Corinthians 15: 24 - 28 *(KJV)*
24. ***THEN*** *cometh the end,* when He *[Jesus]* shall have ***delivered up the kingdom to God,*** even the Father; ***<u>WHEN HE SHALL HAVE PUT DOWN ALL RULE AND ALL AUTHORITY AND POWER.</u>***
25. ***For He*** *[Jesus]* ***must reign, till He hath put ALL ENEMIES under His feet.***
26. The last enemy that shall be destroyed is death
27. For He *[the Father]* hath put all things under His *[Jesus's]* feet. But when He *[the Father]* saith all things are put under Him *[Jesus]*, it is manifest that He *[the Father]* is excepted, which did put all things under Him *[Jesus]*.
28. And when ***ALL THINGS*** shall be subdued unto Him *[Jesus]*, then shall the Son also Himself be subject unto Him *[the Father]* that put all things under Him *[Jesus]*, that God may be all in all.

This shows that the Father sent His Son to the earth to do more than just provide the means for man's redemption. That was simply one important part of the greater task of restoring the kingdom of God to its complete fullness. We've already seen *that as the end of this age draws near,* Satan will be overcome before the throne by ***our brethren. Then,*** *Satan and his angels will be cast out of heaven and down to the earth,* ***and that means <u>the kingdom of God will THEN BE RESTORED TO HEAVEN.</u>*** That will be the beginning of the end for Satan's challenge to God's right to reign over His kingdom. Therefore, when the kingdom of God is restored to heaven, the voice in heaven will announce the resurgence of God's kingdom by proclaiming, ***"<u>Now</u> is come.... the kingdom of our God."*** *(Revelation 12: 10).* That will be true ***for heaven;*** however, one more thing will still need to come before the kingdom of God can be restored on earth as well as in heaven.

<u>NOW Is Come the Power of His Christ!</u>

Revelation 12: 10 *(KJV)*
10. And I heard a loud voice saying in heaven, ***"Now is come salvation, and strength, and the kingdom of our God, AND the Power of His Christ: for the accuser of our brethren is cast down, which accused them before our God day and night."***

Since ***"the Power of His Christ"*** is not going to come ***<u>UNTIL</u>*** that time in the future when Satan is finally cast out of heaven, *that means* ***<u>IT HASN'T COME YET,</u>*** *which raises two questions.*

<u>First:</u> Shortly before Jesus ascended into heaven, He told His disciples, ***"... All power is given unto me in heaven and in earth."****(Matthew 28: 18).* He said that in A. D. 30 almost 2000 years ago; therefore, how can it be that ***"<u>the power of His Christ</u>"*** is ***<u>NOT going to come UNTIL</u> Satan is cast out of heaven <u>shortly before the end of this age?</u>*** To understand the answer to this question, we first have to remember that *the word **"Christ"** is not actually **<u>PART</u> of Jesus's <u>NAME.</u>*** The word ***"Christ"*** is English for the Greek word ***"Christos"*** which means ***"anointed."*** In many places in Scripture, the Hebrew word for ***"Messiah"*** was translated simply as ***"Christ,"*** which was not completely correct, for the word ***"Messiah"*** means ***"anointed one,"*** referring to the ***"anointed one of God."*** But the word ***"Christ/Christos"*** *only* means ***"anointed."*** Do you see the difference? Many things in Scripture were ***"anointed,"*** but there is only one Messiah ***(the anointed one of God),*** and that is ***<u>Jesus.</u>*** If that's not confusing enough, it doesn't stop here. The descriptive title ***"Messiah"*** isn't limited ***<u>ONLY</u> to the man Jesus***. The full scope of the word ***"Messiah"*** is revealed in I Corinthians.

I Corinthians 12: 27 *(KJV)*
27. Now ***YOU*** *[speaking to the Church]* are the body of Christ *[more correctly **Messiah, (the anointed one)]***, and members in particular.

Jesus will be complete as God's ***Messiah*** *(the anointed one)*, only when He is united with His body the church. So when Jesus said ***"All power is given unto Me..,"*** He was speaking *only of **Himself**,* who is the head of the body of Christ. But that leads us to our second question.

<u>Second:</u> Shortly after Jesus said ***all power*** *had been given to Him,* He also told His followers ***they were going to receive power.***

Acts 1: 8 *(KJV)*
8. ***"But ye shall receive power, after that the Holy Ghost is come upon you, and ye shall be witnesses unto Me both in Jerusalem, and in all Judaea, and in Samaria, and unto the uttermost part of the earth."***

This was fulfilled ten days later, when that little band of a hundred and twenty believers were baptized with the Holy Ghost and power on the day of Pentecost. *(Ref: Acts 2: 1 - 4)*. Therefore, it would seem that ***" the power of His Christ"*** actually came almost two thousand years ago at Pentecost. However, *if we're honest,* we have to admit that since the day of Pentecost, there have been countless believers who haven't received the Holy Ghost and power *like the believers did at Pentecost.* It is because of this very real condition, that Revelation 12: 10 prophesies that at some day in the future, ***the power of His Christ is going to <u>COME.</u>*** The answer to this problem is given in James.

James 5: 7 - 8 *(KJV)*
7. Be patient therefore, brethren, unto the coming of the Lord. Behold, the husbandman waits for the precious fruit of the earth, and hath long patience for it, until he receives the early and latter rain.
8. Be ye also patient; establish your hearts; for the coming of the Lord draws near.

The Church has been anticipating Jesus's return ever since He ascended into heaven. The early believers expected Him to return at any time. However, as time passed, it became apparent He wasn't going to return as soon as they thought. Scripture doesn't clearly say ***when*** *Jesus will return*, but it does give some clues as to when His return will be ***<u>ABOUT</u> to happen***. This passage in James gives one of those clues. James began by admonishing us ***to be***

patient** in waiting for the Lord's return.* That showed Jesus's return wasn't going to happen as soon as the early Church thought. He then gave an example related to a farmer raising grain ***in Israel. He began his example by saying, ***"Behold,"*** which is a command that means ***to pay attention to what follows.*** *What followed was the fact that the husbandman (or farmer)* ***waits with <u>LONG PATIENCE</u> for the precious fruit of the earth.*** Since the ***"fruit of the earth"*** is described as ***"precious,"*** it obviously ***represents something <u>MORE</u>*** *than just the ordinary harvest of grain raised by farmers in Israel.* The Greek word translated as ***"precious"*** means ***"of great price, esteemed, especially dear."*** Therefore, it's apparent the husbandman is an example of Jesus, who is waiting with ***"<u>LONG PATIENCE</u>"*** *until He receives the Church,* ***which is His "...precious fruit of the earth."*** Therefore, this example's message is that ***Jesus*** is waiting with ***"long patience"*** for the harvest of the Church, that will result from the seed of the Gospel that's been planted throughout the Church age. Verse 7 then focuses our attention on ***two*** events the farmer had to wait for before he could get the harvest. ***"Behold, the husbandman waiteth for the precious fruit of the earth, and hath long patience for it, <u>UNTIL</u> he receive the <u>EARLY</u> and <u>LATTER</u> rain."*** In Israel ***there had to be <u>TWO</u> separate seasons of rain <u>BEFORE</u> receiving a harvest.*** In their *"ENCYCLOPEDIA OF BIBLE LIFE," Madeleine S. & J. Lane Miller* described the weather conditions necessary ***to plant and harvest*** grain crops in Israel, as follows:

"All summer long the spent fields of Palestine and Syria lie parched and resting. Looking at their rock-mud clods, we wonder if they will ever again open up to produce. But late in September and early October come the "former" rains. Plowing becomes possible. Winter continues wet with occasional snowfall as far south as Bethlehem's gardens and grazing fields...." "...In March and April come the "latter" or abundant showers, filling empty cisterns and soaking cracked fields to ensure harvest from seed sown in December." [1]

The grain harvest in Israel ***requires <u>BOTH</u> the <u>FORMER</u> and the <u>LATTER</u> rains;*** so God used the Israeli farmer as an example to show that Israel's ***"former"*** and "***latter"*** rains ***represent*** *two things* ***<u>in the spirit-realm</u>*** that are just as necessary for the harvest of the Church, as the ***"former"*** and ***"latter"*** rains are necessary ***in the natural realm*** for Israel's grain-harvest. So what are those two things that must come in ***the spirit realm, <u>BEFORE</u> the Lord can come and harvest His Church?*** Just before Jesus ascended into heaven, *He revealed* ***what had to come before the gospel could be <u>PLANTED.</u>***

Luke 24: 45 - 49 *(NKJV)*
45. And He opened their understanding, that they might comprehend the Scriptures.
46. Then He said to them, ***"Thus it is written, and thus it was necessary for Christ to suffer and to rise from the dead the third day,***
47. ***and that repentance and remission of sins should be preached in His name to all nations, beginning at Jerusalem."***
48. ***"And you are witnesses of these things."***
49. ***"Behold, I send the promise of My Father upon you; but tarry in the city of Jerusalem UNTIL YOU ARE ENDUED WITH POWER FROM ON HIGH."***

For three years, Jesus had taught the disciples and they witnessed the miracles He had done. Then, they saw Him crucified, and buried in the tomb. After three days, He rose from the dead, appeared to them, and showed them the wounds in His hands, feet, and side as assurance that it was truly Him and that He had indeed been resurrected. They continued to see Him for forty days after He arose, and then witnessed Him ascend up to heaven. *Therefore,* ***of all people****, the disciples would seem to have been eminently qualified to give an effective testimony about the Gospel of salvation through Jesus Christ.* ***HOWEVER, one of the last things He did before He ascended, was COMMAND them to WAIT — not to do anything, "…. UNTIL YOU ARE ENDUED WITH POWER FROM ON HIGH."*** After waiting ***ten more days***, they were baptized with the Holy Ghost and with power on the day of Pentecost, and ***immediately after that****, Peter preached a simple sermon and about three thousand souls were saved.*

Therefore, when James 5: 7 said the husbandman *(farmer)* ***"...waiteth for the precious fruit of the earth, and hath long patience for it, UNTIL he receives the EARLY and LATTER rain,"*** *it's obvious that the* ***"EARLY" rain*** *was an example referring to* **the Holy Ghost and power that came down at Pentecost.** However, ***in the example,*** although the ***"EARLY"*** rain was necessary to prepare the hard dry soil before seed could be planted, ***the LATTER rain was just as necessary to bring the grain to maturity before it could be harvested****. Accordingly, since the* ***EARLY*** *rain was an example of the outpouring of the Holy Spirit and power at Pentecost,* ***the LATTER rain must be an example of ANOTHER SIMILAR OUTPOURING OF THE HOLY SPIRIT AND POWER that must come at the end of the age to bring the Church to maturity — ready for the harvest when Jesus comes.*** *However, before we discuss the* ***LATTER rain*** *that's still in the future, there's something else we need to recognize about the* ***EARLY rain*** *that began at*

Pentecost. Shortly after Pentecost, Philip went down to a city of Samaria and preached the Gospel with tremendous results. Many people were both healed and saved. But look at what happened next.

Acts 8: 14 - 17 *(KJV)*
14. Now when the apostles which were at Jerusalem heard that Samaria had received the word of God, they sent unto them Peter and John:
15. who, when they were come down, prayed for them, that they might receive the Holy Ghost:
16. (For as yet He was fallen upon none of them: only they were baptized in the name of the Lord Jesus.)
17. Then laid they their hands on them, and they received the Holy Ghost.

After what happened at Pentecost, *the apostles believed people should **automatically** receive the Holy Ghost and power **at the time they believed**.* But that didn't happen to the believers in Samaria, so they sent Peter and John down to set things in order. Nevertheless, *what happened in Samaria revealed that **people <u>DON'T</u> automatically** receive the baptism in the Holy Spirit **when they believe**. What's more, we know from almost two thousand years of church history that what happened in that town in Samaria **has been the <u>RULE</u> rather than the <u>EXCEPTION</u>** for believers **throughout** the Church age. How many believers do you think are baptized in the Holy Spirit at the time they believe in today's Baptist, Methodist, and Presbyterian churches? **How many <u>of you</u> were baptized with the Holy Spirit <u>LIKE WHAT HAPPENED AT PENTECOST,</u> when you believed?*** You see, the experience of that city of Samaria has continued throughout the church age, ***and there haven't been any apostles to go around and correct the situation***. The ***<u>EARLY</u> rain*** of the Holy Spirit that began at Pentecost served God's purpose to get the Church firmly established. Also, on-going showers of that ***<u>EARLY</u> rain*** *of the Holy Spirit* have continued sporadically during the church age *as needed to accomplish God's purpose in the Church.* However, the ***<u>EARLY</u> rain*** was still *only **moderate*** in nature, for the dramatic results it had at Pentecost haven't continued throughout the centuries of the Church age. If we're honest, we have to acknowledge that relatively few believers have experienced the power of the Holy Spirit like those believers at Pentecost. That's not something we can control; ***therefore, it's apparent that God simply hasn't continued pouring out His Holy Spirit throughout the church age with <u>the same intensity</u> that He did at Pentecost.*** In light of that, there's something else we need to see about the ***<u>LATTER</u> rain*** spoken of in James 5 above. In that example the husbandman *(who represented Jesus Christ)*, had to have *long patience until he received both the early and latter rain;* however, as we saw above in the quote from the *ENCYCLOPEDIA OF BIBLE LIFE*, ***"In March and April come the latter or ABUNDANT showers."*** [2] Israel's ***LATTER rains*** that are necessary to ensure the harvest *are noticeably* ***more abundant*** *than the* ***EARLY rains*** that come at the beginning of the planting season. *That indicates the outpouring of the Holy Spirit at the end of the age will be greater than what happened at Pentecost, and that raises the question —* ***WHY?***

Why Will the Latter Rain of the Holy Spirit Be Greater than That at Pentecost. This question is answered in Revelation 12: 10. John heard a loud voice say, ***"Now is come salvation, and strength, and the kingdom of our God, and the power of HIS CHRIST." When that power comes, WHO do you think will receive it?*** Since it's identified as the ***"...Power of His CHRIST,"*** *that means* **it will BELONG TO His (God's) CHRIST!** Therefore, it follows ***that when it COMES, it will come to the one to whom it BELONGS, which will be CHRIST!!*** Since Jesus is the head of ***CHRIST,*** and the Church is the body of ***CHRIST,*** when the ***"...power of His CHRIST,"*** comes, it must necessarily come to the Church, for Jesus received *His power* when He was resurrected *(Ref: Matthew 28: 18)*. ***This means all true believers who are still on earth at the beginning of the last three and a half years of this age, are going to receive the baptism of the Holy Spirit and Power like those hundred and twenty believers received it at Pentecost.***

Therefore, consider this. About 30 years after those hundred and twenty believers received the Holy Spirit and power at Pentecost, Paul and Silas went to Thessalonica. Listen to how the enemies of the Church expressed their concern. ***"These THAT HAVE TURNED THE WORLD UPSIDE DOWN are come here also!"*** *(Acts 17: 6)*. Since that was the result of the ***EARLY rain*** coming upon *only those hundred and twenty believers*, there's no way to even imagine what it will be like when the ***LATTER rain*** of the Holy Spirit and power comes on millions of believers all over the entire world. As you consider how that ***latter rain*** of the Holy Ghost will enable the Church to stand against Satan when he's cast down to the earth, you can understand why he has worked so hard throughout the Church age to confuse God's children about the baptism of the Holy Spirit. Satan has deceived many believers into thinking any outward manifestation of the Holy Spirit's presence is something to be ridiculed and made fun of. ***Satan knows by His own experience just how much of a threat Spirit-filled***

believers are to him. *If the Church fully appreciated the importance of that precious and unique gift from God, we would be seeking it with all our hearts.*

Why Will We Need That Greater Power? The Church has survived and grown for almost two thousand years with the measure of the Holy Spirit and power that God sent down on the day of Pentecost. So why will it be necessary for Him to send down a more abundant measure of that same Holy Spirit and power as the end of the age approaches? The obvious answer is that we'll need it because Satan and all his demons will be on earth during those last three and a half years. Because he will be so actively persecuting Christians through the Antichrist during that time, *we may be tempted to believe we'll need the greater power of the Holy Spirit* ***just to survive.*** But God intends for His children to do much more than merely survive. As previously discussed, God gave ***MAN*** the responsibility for subduing *(overcoming)* Satan. Accordingly, just as *redeemed* ***men*** *(our brethren of Revelation 12)* will be the ones who overcome Satan ***in heaven, so he can be cast down to the earth,*** **AFTER** he is cast down to earth, ***redeemed MEN must then overcome Satan here on earth BEFORE he can be cast down into the pit of hell.***

Revelation 20: 1 - 3a *(KJV)*
1. And I saw an angel come down from heaven, having the key of the bottomless pit and a great chain in his hand.
2. And he laid hold on the dragon, that old serpent, which is the Devil, and Satan, and bound him a thousand years,
3. and cast him into the bottomless pit.

During the last three and a half years of the church age, redeemed men on earth are going to overcome Satan so completely, *that one single angel will be able to bind him in chains and cast him into the pit.* The only way we will be able to do that will be by means of the Holy Spirit, who is ***"...the power of His Christ*** *[the church].*" Therefore, instead of concentrating on the persecution Satan will inflict on us during the coming tribulation, *we need to think of what God wants us to do in the midst of that tribulation* ***to overcome Satan and strip him of his right even to be on the earth.*** Since Jesus is God's perfect example for us to follow, we need to consider how the Father equipped Jesus to accomplish the purpose ordained for Him.

Acts 11: 13 *(KJV)(In this passage, Peter told Cornelius about Jesus, and revealed how Jesus was able to do all the mighty things the Father had ordained for Him to accomplish. Notice Peter didn't call attention to Jesus as the Devine Son of God, but rather as the **MAN, Jesus of Nazareth.**)*
13. How ***God anointed Jesus of Nazareth with the Holy Ghost and with power,*** who went about doing good and healing all who were oppressed by the devil, *for God was with Him.*

Jesus didn't do ***ANYTHING simply because He was the Devine Son of God!*** He confessed this in John 5: 19 where He said, ***"Verily, verily, I say unto you, 'The Son can do nothing of Himself, but what He seeth the Father do; for what things He doeth, these also doeth the Son likewise.'"*** *Everything Jesus did,* ***He did by the power of the Holy Ghost who came upon Him when He was baptized by John the Baptist.*** *However, that special provision of the Holy Spirit didn't stop with Jesus;* for after He was crucified and resurrected, He told His disciples, ***"...as My Father hath sent Me, EVEN SO SEND I YOU!"*** *(John 20: 21).* God's plan was for believers to spread the Gospel of salvation *using the same provision of power that Jesus used to make that salvation available* — ***through the power of the Holy Ghost Who was sent down as the EARLY rain on the day of Pentecost.*** Therefore, when Satan is cast down to the earth at the end of the age, ***God is going to give His children ANOTHER ANOINTING of the Holy Spirit to equip them, not just to STAND AGAINST Satan in that time of great tribulation, but also to completely overcome him*** *so the single angel of Revelation 20: 1 - 3 (above) can cast him into the pit.*

From the above discussions, it's evident that these four things *(Salvation, Strength, the Kingdom of our God and the Power of His Christ)* that are yet to come will be tremendously important to the church. Therefore, it's in order to consider when we can expect them to actually come.

When Can We Expect These Four Things (Salvation, Strength, the Kingdom of our God, and the Power of His Christ) to Come? It is apparent from Revelation 12: 10 that these four things will all come essentially at the same time, when Satan is cast out of heaven and down to the earth. However from the discussion above, it is also apparent that the coming of the Power of His Christ as the ***LATTER rain*** of the Holy Spirit will likely have the most prominent manifestation of the four when it comes. Therefore, as we consider when these four things might come, we will direct out attention particularly to that last one – ***the Power of His Christ.***

When the Church age approaches its end, God is going to send ***the Power of His Christ*** as the ***LATTER rain*** of the Holy Spirit to bring the Church to full maturity in preparation for its harvest in the Rapture. Since the Holy Spirit came as the ***EARLY rain*** on ***the day of Pentecost*** following Jesus's death and resurrection, it is reasonable to expect that the ***LATTER rain of the Holy Spirit will also come on day of Pentecost.*** This likelihood is increased by the fact that the ***LATTER rain*** will come as a result of ***our brethren*** winning their victory over Satan in heaven. That is because, *as already discussed,* our brethren are identified in Revelation 14: 4 as the ***"...redeemed from among men, being the FIRSTFRUITS unto God and to the Lamb."*** Accordingly, when the ***FIRSTFRUITS of redeemed men*** appear before God and the Lamb in heaven, *they will be the fulfillment of the example presented by Israel's* ***feast of the Firstfruits of the Wave Loaves.*** Since that feast is now more commonly known as Pentecost, it would be in order for the fulfillment of the example presented by that feast to also take place on the actual date for Pentecost. In Chapter 5, in the paragraph entitled, ***"When Will God Make Jesus's Enemies His Footstool",*** it was shown that the feast of the wave loaves should be fulfilled on the day of Pentecost in the year A. D. 2026. ***Therefore, that is date when the Power of His Christ (the greater Pentecost of the LATER rain) should begin. Since all four of the things that are yet to come will come at essentially the same time, that means they should all come on, or very shortly after the day of Pentecost in A. D. 2026. In that year, the day of Pentecost should come on May 22.***

END NOTES

1. Madeleine S. and J. Lane Miller, *ENCYCLOPEDIA OF BIBLE LIFE,* (Harper & Row, Publishers, 1955), p 2 & 3
2. Madeleine S. and J. Lane Miller, *ENCYCLOPEDIA OF BIBLE LIFE,* (Harper & Row, Publishers, 1955), p 3

Chapter 7

When Is HE Coming?

Introduction. It's generally taught that nobody can know when Jesus is going to come, ***either for His church, or in His Second Coming.*** However, Scripture addresses both of these events in a way that gives a very good idea when each of them will take place. This chapter discusses what Scripture says about when these two events are going to take place.

Jesus' Prophecy about the End of the Age. Matthew 24 contains Jesus's prophecy about the events that will lead up to the end of the age. As we read what He said, we need to remember that He was answering specific questions the disciples had asked as recorded at the beginning of that chapter. He and His disciples had just left the temple and the disciples were admiring it, but Jesus surprised them by saying it was going to be destroyed with not one stone left on another. The disciples naturally asked when it was going to happen.

Matthew 24: 3 *(NKJV)*
3. Now as He sat on the Mount of Olives, the disciples came to Him privately, saying, ***"Tell us, when will these things be. And what will be the SIGN of Your coming, and of the end of the age?"***

Jesus first told them a number of things that would happen before the end of the age. Then He told what will *mark the* ***beginning*** of the great tribulation that will immediately precede the end of the age.

Matthew 24: 15 - 22 *(NKJV)*
15. ***"Therefore when you see the '<u>abomination of desolation,</u>' spoken of by Daniel the prophet, standing in the holy place"*** *(whoever reads, let him understand),*
16. ***"then let those who are in Judea flee to the mountains.***
17. ***"Let him who is on the housetop not go down to take anything out of his house.***
18. ***"And let him who is in the field not go back to get his clothes.***
19. ***"But woe to those who are pregnant and to those who are nursing babies in those days!***
20. ***"And pray that your flight may not be in winter or on the Sabbath.***
21. ***"For then there will be great tribulation, such as has not been since the beginning of the world until this time, no, nor ever shall be.***
22. ***"And unless those days were shortened, no flesh would be saved; but for the elect's sake those days will be shortened."***

Satan will cause this tribulation when he's cast out of heaven. *(Ref: Revelation 12: 9, & 12 - 13).* Revelation 12: 14 says that tribulation will last, ***"..a time, times, and a half a time,"*** which is another way of saying, ***three and a half years.*** Verses 29 - 31 give Jesus's answer to the disciples' question, ***"What will be the <u>SIGN</u> of Your coming?"***

Matthew 24: 29 - 31
29. ***"Immediately <u>after</u> the tribulation of those days the sun will be darkened, and the moon will not give its light; the stars will fall from heaven, and the powers of the heavens will be shaken.***

Immediately ***<u>AFTER</u> the tribulation*** the heavens will seem to be out of control, because the very power that keeps the heavens in order will be interrupted. The next verse explains why that's going to happen.

30. ***"Then the <u>SIGN</u> of the Son of Man will appear in heaven, and all the tribes of the earth will mourn, and they will see the Son of Man coming on the clouds of heaven with power and great glory.***
31. ***"<u>And He will send His angels with a great sound of a trumpet, and they will gather together HIS ELECT from the four winds, from one end of heaven to the other.</u>"***

When Jesus appears in power and glory, all the heavens will be shaken. Jesus said this in answer to the disciples' question,***"What will be the <u>SIGN</u> of Your coming."*** *When they asked that question,* they didn't know there was going to be a *Church,* ***much less that Jesus will come to receive His church in what we now call the Rapture.*** They had asked about *a* **SIGN** *that will show when His* **Second Coming** *is near, because that was the only* ***coming they knew about.*** Therefore, in Verses 30 & 31, He identified ***the SIGN that will indicate His Second Coming is near.*** Accordingly, ***when Jesus comes in the clouds of heaven with power and great glory, and with a great sound of a trumpet, sends His angels to gather His*** *(Christ's)* ***elect from the four winds of the earth AND from heaven itself, that will be the SIGN that His SECOND COMING is very near.*** As we read this, it sounds just like the gathering described in I Thessalonians 4: 15 - 16 and I Corinthians 15: 51 - 52; therefore, since I Corinthians 15: 52 specifically says the dead in Christ will rise at the ***LAST*** trumpet, that must necessarily be the same trumpet as the one Jesus said will take place ***AFTER*** the tribulation when His angels will gather His elect *(the church)* from the four winds *(of the earth)* and even from one end of heaven to the other. From this, we must conclude that there will be only one gathering of the church, and that it will take place ***AFTER*** the tribulation just as Jesus said. Also, it will take place at the sounding of the ***LAST*** trumpet which must be the seventh trumpet of Revelation 11 since that's the last trumpet mentioned in God's word.

As Jesus continued to answer His disciples' questions, He made another reference to His Second Coming that has also been widely misunderstood.

Matthew 24: 32 - 36
32. ***"Now learn this parable from the fig tree: When its branch has already become tender and puts forth leaves, you know that summer is near.***
33. ***"So you also, when you see all these things, know that it*** *[His Second Coming]* ***is near — at the doors!***
34. ***"Assuredly, I say to you, this generation will by no means pass away till all these things take place.***
35. ***"Heaven and earth will pass away, but My words will by no means pass away.***
36. ***"But of that day and hour no one knows, not even the angels of heaven*** *[Mark 13: 32 adds, "neither the Son"],* ***but My Father only."***

When Jesus said no one knows the day or the hour of His coming, ***He was still answering the disciples' question about His Second Coming.*** So when Verse 36 is used to support the idea that *we* ***can't know*** *when Jesus is coming* ***in the Rapture, it's being used completely out of context,*** *for Jesus had just* *told them **<u>when</u>** the Rapture is going to come as a **sign*** indicating that His Second Coming is very near. As we continue considering Jesus's coming for His church in connection to the last trump, we'll see what Revelation says is going to happen when the last trumpet sounds.

<u>What Will Happen When the Last Trumpet Sounds?</u>

Revelation 10 reveals that something very special is going to happen when the angel begins to blow the seventh trumpet, ***which will also be the <u>LAST</u> trumpet.***

Revelation 10: 5 - 7*(NKJV)*
5. The angel whom I saw standing on the sea and on the earth raised up his hand to heaven
6. and swore by Him who lives forever and ever, who created heaven and the things that are in it, the earth and the things that are in it, and the sea and the things that are in it, ***that there should be delay no longer:***
7. ***but in the days of the sounding of the seventh angel, when he is about to sound, <u>the mystery of God</u> would be finished, as He declared to His servants the prophets.***

God has a mystery that He's going ***to <u>FINISH</u>*** when the seventh trumpet angel begins to blow his trumpet. To understand what that means, we need to know what ***"the mystery of God"*** is. There are a number of mysteries mentioned in Scripture, but in Ephesians Paul expressed wonder that God had given him the revelation of *one particular mystery* that's related directly to God.

Ephesians 3: 1 - 10 *(NKJV)*
1. For this reason I, Paul, the prisoner of Christ Jesus for you Gentiles
2. if indeed you have heard of the dispensation of the grace of God which is given to me for you,
3. how that by revelation He made known unto me the ***mystery*** (as I have briefly written already *(Ref: Ephesians 1: 9 - 10)*
4. by which, when you read, you may understand my knowledge in the mystery of Christ),
5. which in other ages was not made known to the sons of men, as it has now been revealed by the Spirit to His holy apostles and prophets:
6. *[this is the mystery]* ***that the Gentiles should be fellow heirs, of the same body, and partakers of His promise in Christ through the Gospel,***

7. of which I became a minister according to the gift of the grace of God given to me by the effective working of His power.
8. To me, who am less than the least of all saints, this grace was given, that I should preach among the Gentiles the unsearchable riches of Christ,
9. and to make all see what is the fellowship of ***the MYSTERY, which from the beginning of the ages has been hidden IN GOD*** ***who created all things through Jesus Christ.***

Paul also shared this truth about the mystery of God in Colossians.

Colossians 1: 24 - 26 *(NKJV)*
24. I now rejoice in my sufferings for you, and fill up in my flesh what is lacking in the afflictions of Christ, for the sake of His body, which is the church,
25. of which I became a minister according to the stewardship from God which was given to me for you, to fulfill the word of God,
26. ***THE MYSTERY*** which has been hidden from ages and from generations, but now has been revealed to His saints.
27. ***To them God willed to make known what are the riches of the glory of this mystery among the Gentiles: which is CHRIST IN YOU THE HOPE OF GLORY.***

The ***"mystery of God" is THE CHURCH. The knowledge of the Church, comprised mostly of Gentiles, is God's mystery that He kept hidden within Himself from the beginning of the ages.*** Therefore, in Revelation 10: 6b - 7a, when the angel said, ***"... there should be delay no longer; but in the days of the sounding of the seventh angel, when he is about to sound, the MYSTERY OF GOD would be finished;"*** *that simply means* ***the CHURCH*** *will be finished (or completed) when the seventh trumpet of Revelation sounds. Since the Church will be finished* ***ONLY when Jesus comes and takes it out of the world in what we call the Rapture,*** *it's apparent that the Rapture will take place when the* **seventh (LAST)** *trumpet is blown, which is what* I Corinthians says.

I Corinthians 15: 51 - 52 *(KJV)*
51. Behold, I show you a mystery: we shall not all sleep, but we shall all be changed.
52. In a moment, in the twinkling of an eye, ***at the LAST TRUMP: for the trumpet shall sound, and the dead shall be raised incorruptible, and we shall be changed.***

53. For this corruptible must put on incorruption, and this mortal must put on immortality.

Since the ***SEVENTH*** *trumpet* of Revelation is ***the <u>LAST</u> trumpet,*** that means ***Jesus will come for His Church when the <u>SEVENTH</u> (last) trumpet is blown.*** That brings us to the question: Does the Revelation account of the ***<u>LAST</u> trumpet*** confirm that will be the signal for the Rapture to occur?

<u>The Loud Voices In Heaven.</u>

Revelation 11: 15 *(NKJV)*
15. Then the seventh angel sounded: And there were loud voices in heaven, saying, ***"The kingdoms of this world have become the kingdoms of our Lord, and of His Christ: and He shall reign for ever and ever!"***

When those voices announce that ***"Tthe kingdoms of this world have become the kingdoms of our Lord and of His Christ,"*** that will mean this world will finally have been restored to the kingdom of God. It will also mean that ***<u>MAN</u> will have fulfilled his God-given responsibility to overcome Satan.*** The redeemed of the Church will accomplish that during the last three-and-a-half years of this age. During that time, Satan will use the persecution of the tribulation in an effort to make believers on earth renounce their faith. ***But they will stand firm in their faith, <u>and Satan will lose, JUST LIKE HE LOST WITH JOB.</u> You see, the patience of Job was actually God's example of how the Church will endure all of Satan's persecution during those last three-and-a-half years, and will stand firm in their faith ,<u>JUST LIKE JOB DID!</u>*** In that way, the redeemed men and women of the Church will overcome Satan on earth and strip him of his position as the prince of this world. They will ***also*** take away his right to be on earth, such that the ***<u>ONE</u>*** *angel* of Revelation 20: 1 - 3 will be able to bind him and cast him into the bottomless pit. The position as prince of this world will then belong to Christ, ***which will consist of Jesus as the head, and the Church as the body.*** Jesus will be the rightful owner of that position, because He overcame Satan *as the* ***<u>MAN</u>*** *who lived completely free from sin,* ***<u>AND</u>*** *who overcame Satan's power of death by rising from the dead after He willingly died for* ***<u>OUR</u>*** *sins. However* His body, the Church, will share with Him in that position, because it will consist of ***sinful <u>MEN,</u> who will have overcome Satan by repenting — turning from Satan and the pleasures of sin — and by choice, living in obedience to Jesus, trusting in His sacrificial death as the payment for their sins.*** During the last three-

and-a-half years of this age when Satan has been cast down to the earth, *the Church will overcome Satan here on the earth, just like* ***"our brethren,"*** *the firstfruit of redeemed men, will overcome him in heaven (Ref: Revelation 12: 10 - 11).* Therefore, both the firstfruit and the full Church will overcome Satan in the same way — ***by the blood of the Lamb and by the word of their testimony, and by the fact that they loved not their lives to the death.***

<u>The Testimony of the Twenty-four Elders.</u> After John heard the loud voices from heaven make their declaration, the twenty-four elders gave their testimony about what will happen when the last *(seventh)* trumpet is blown.

Revelation 11: 16 - 18 *(NKJV)*
16. And the twenty-four elders, who sat before God on their thrones fell upon their faces, and worshiped God,
17. saying, ***"We give You thanks, O Lord God Almighty, the One who is and who was and who is to come, because You have taken Your great power and reigned.***
18a. ***"The nations were angry...,"***

After giving thanks to God for exercising His power to reign, the twenty-four elders will reveal that *when the earth is restored into God's kingdom* ***the nations will be angry****. That's because there will no longer be any doubt that God is real,* ***<u>and that He is an all powerful and perfectly HOLY God.</u>*** The nations will be angry because that will be the end of the power they enjoyed while Satan was the prince of this world. That realization will make them cooperate with the Anti-Christ when he assembles the armies of the world in a desperate effort to overcome Israel, who ***<u>AFTER</u> the rapture will be the only people of God left on the earth.*** We're not going into detail about that part of the end-time events, because right now our concern is about what else will happen when the seventh *(last)* trumpet sounds. Verse 18b continues with that information.

18b. "***...and Your <u>WRATH</u> has come, and the time of the dead that they should be judged, and that You should reward Your servants the prophets and the saints, and those who fear Your name, small and great, and should destroy those who destroy the earth."***

This identifies ***four other primary things*** *that will happen when the seventh trumpet sounds.*

A. ***When the Seventh Trumpet sounds, God's WRATH will come.*** The last trumpet will mark the beginning of God's wrath, but the seven vials actually define what it will consist of, and that's in Revelation 15

Revelation 15: 1 - 4 *(NKJV)*
1. And I saw another sign in heaven, great and marvelous: seven angels having the seven last plagues, ***for in them THE WRATH OF GOD is complete.***
2. And I saw something like a sea of glass mingled with fire, ***and those who have the victory over the beast, over his image and over his mark and over the number of his name, standing on the sea of glass, having the harps of God.***
3. They sing the song of Moses, the servant of God, and the song of the Lamb, saying, ***"Great and marvelous are Your works, Lord God Almighty! Just and true are Your ways, O King of the saints.***
4. ***"Who shall not fear You, O Lord, and glorify Your name? For all nations shall come and worship before You, for Your judgments have been manifested."***

Note: Verse 2 shows that before God's wrath actually comes, ***all the saints will be in heaven.*** That is because the Rapture will be one of the last things that happens before God pours out His wrath. This is in agreement with God's promise to His children in I Thessalonians.

I Thessalonians 5: 4 & 8 - 9 *(NKJV)(Spoken to the Church concerning Jesus's return.)*
4. But you brethren, are not in darkness, so that this Day should overtake you as a thief.
8. But let us who are of the day be sober, putting on the breastplate of faith and love, and as a helmet the hope of salvation.
9. ***For God did not appoint us to WRATH,*** but to obtain salvation through our Lord Jesus Christ.

B. ***When the Seventh Trumpet sounds, it will be the time of the dead, when they should be judged.*** This is not a reference to the judgment before the great white throne in Revelation 20: 11 - 15. Instead, it is referring to the fact that when the Rapture takes place, ***that will be the judgment that defines who is included in the Church.*** That's why Revelation 10: 7 says the mystery of God, *which is the church,* will be finished when the seventh trumpet begins to blow. ***No one will be added to the Church AFTER the rapture!***

C. ***When the Seventh Trumpet Sounds, it will be time for God to reward all those who are His people.*** When the Rapture takes place at the seventh trumpet, that will mark the beginning of God's reward for His adopted children. This is confirmed in Revelation 22: 12 - 13, which says, ***"And behold, I am coming quickly, and My REWARD is with Me, to give to every one according to his work. I am the Alpha and the Omega, the Beginning and the End, the First and the Last."***

D. ***When the Seventh Trumpet sounds, it will be time for God to destroy those who destroy the earth.*** If you recall, Genesis 1: 1 says, ***"In the beginning God created the heaven and the earth,"*** but Verse 2 says, ***"The earth was without form, and void; and darkness was on the face of the deep. And the Spirit of God was hovering over the face of the waters."*** It's inconceivable that God created the earth in the sorry state described in Verse 2. Therefore, that miserable uninhabitable state obviously came about in the far distant past when Satan rebelled and was cast down to earth. Revelation 9: 11 gives one of Satan's names as ***"Abaddon"*** which in the Greek is ***"Apollyon"*** and means ***"A destroyer."*** By that very name, we know that when Lucifer was cast out of heaven for rebelling against God, he set out to destroy everything God had created here on the earth. Accordingly, after God restored the earth and created man, His first command to man was, ***"Be fruitful and multiply; fill the earth and subdue it;...."*** God created man in a position of authority over Satan and all other created beings, and since Satan was still on the earth with his vindictive and destructive nature, part of man's God–given task was to subdue Satan. However, instead of doing that, man let Satan overcome him with sin, and came under his (Satan's) destructive power of death. Therefore, when the seventh trumpet sounds, it will be time for God to destroy those who destroy the earth. That means the time will finally have come when God will destroy Satan and all those who have given themselves over to his destructive nature. This will be possible because men who have been redeemed by repentance and faith in Jesus Christ, will finally have overcome Satan, not only in heaven *by our brethren before the throne,* but also on earth *by the church who will stand firm in their faith in spite of the horrors of the tribulation instigated by Satan through the Antichrist.* God will begin that destruction by the seven vials of His wrath. They will end with the seventh vial, which will usher in the Second Coming of Christ, and the battle of Armageddon. Lest you think the battle of Armageddon will be confined just to the valley of Megiddo in Israel, look at what God revealed through Jeremiah.

Jeremiah 25: 31 - 33 *(This reveals the world-wide extent of the destruction that will have Armageddon as its focal point, at the time of the Second Coming.) (NKJV)*
31. A noise shall come to the ends of the earth — for the Lord has a controversy with the nations; He will plead His case with all flesh. He will give those who are wicked to the sword, says the Lord.
32. Thus says the Lord of hosts: ***"Behold, disaster shall go forth from nation to nation, and a great whirlwind shall be raised up from the farthest parts of the earth.***
33. ***"And at that day <u>THE SLAIN OF THE LORD shall be from one end of the earth even to the other end of the earth</u>. They shall not be lamented, or gathered, or buried; they shall become refuse on the ground.***

Note:
This destruction will occur at the Second Coming of Jesus. The ***"slain of the Lord"*** in Verse 33 will be the same as those called the ***"goats"*** in Matthew 25: 41 - 46. Those who are left alive after this destruction will be those called the ***"sheep"*** in Matthew 25: 33 - 40. Since the sounding of the last *(seventh)* trumpet is when the Church will be caught up to be with Jesus, and will also be when God begins to pour out His wrath to purge the wicked out of this world in preparation for the kingdom age; however, this destruction will not be totally complete until the judgment before the great white throne which will take place after the thousand--year reign of Christ (the kingdom age).

Next we need to seen when Scripture indicates the seventh trump will be sounded.

<u>When Will The Seventh Trumpet Sound?</u> As we've already seen, Scripture makes it clear that the Rapture is going to take place when the seventh *(last)* trumpet of Revelation 11 is blown. Therefore, our next question is, ***can we know ahead of time when that seventh trumpet will be blown?*** Although Scripture doesn't give a specific date when it will be blown, it does give enough information for us to know well ahead of time when it's going to happen. The first part of Revelation 11 describes a very recognizable set of circumstances *that will lead up to the blowing of the seventh (last) trumpet.*

Revelation 11: 1 - 2 *(NKJV)*
1. Then I was given a reed like a measuring rod. And the angel stood, saying, ***"Rise and measure the temple of God, the altar, and those who worship there.***

2. ***"But leave out the court which is outside the temple, and do not measure it, for it has been given to the Gentiles. And they will tread the holy city underfoot for forty-two months."***

At the beginning of the ***seventieth week of Daniel***, Jesus began His ministry by going to the temple on Passover to see if Israel had repented in response to the preaching of John the Baptist. Instead of finding worship with reverence that indicated repentance, He found they had turned His Father's house into a house of merchandise. Therefore, ***for the next three years*** He preached the same message of repentance that John had been preaching. But then, instead of repenting, Israel rejected both Jesus and His message, and had Him crucified. Because of that, God suspended His covenant with Israel, *and interrupted the seventieth week of Daniel with four years still remaining.* Therefore, at the end of the age, God is going to reinstate Israel under the old covenant ***to complete those last four years*** *of Daniel's seventieth week,* and since the first day of the first month is the anniversary date for the covenant, it is extremely likely that He will reinstate Israel under the old covenant on the first day of the first month in A. D. 2026, which will be four years prior to A. D. 2030, which we've already established as the likely time for the end of this age. Accordingly, John was given a reed like a measuring rod to measure the temple, its altar, and those who worship there. That shows that when God reinstates Israel under the covenant for those last four years, He will once again determine if they are obeying His word according to their covenant. This will be necessary, because Israel ***<u>MUST</u> repent and begin obeying God according to their covenant*** before He will permit them to recognize Jesus as their Messiah when He returns at the Second Coming. We know that at least an acceptable remnant out of Israel will be found acceptable to God, for both Jeremiah 31 and Hebrews 8 say that God is going to make a new covenant with Israel and Judah at the end of the age. Nevertheless, Verse 2 above reveals that for the last forty--two months *(three and a half years)* both the temple and Jerusalem will be given over to the Gentiles. That is an indication that the Anti-Christ will be in authority over Jerusalem during the last three and a half years of the age. Verse 3 then begins a prophecy that is very important to our question concerning *when the seventh trumpet is going to be blown.*

Revelation 11: 3 - 15 *(NKJV)*
3. ***"And I will give power to My two witnesses, and they will prophesy one thousand two hundred and sixty days, clothed in sackcloth."***

During those last three and a half years, two men will give a powerful witness for God in Israel, and He will give them special power to oppose the forces of evil and keep them from doing as much harm as they would like to do.

4. These are the two olive trees and the two lamp stands standing before the God of the earth.
5. And if anyone wants to harm them, fire proceeds from their mouth and devours their enemies. And if anyone wants to harm them, he must be killed in this manner.
6. These have power to shut heaven, so that no rain falls in the days of their prophecy; and they have power over waters to turn them to blood, and to strike the earth with all plagues, as often as they desire.
7. When they finish their testimony, the beast that ascends out of the bottomless pit will make war against them, overcome them, and kill them.

When the time allotted to them is over, they will be killed by the beast who's going to ascend out of the bottomless pit. Since he'll come out of the bottomless pit, it's apparent he will be a *demon (fallen angel).* He is also spoken of in Revelation 17, where John saw the great harlot sitting on him, and Revelation 17: 8 describes him saying, ***"The beast that you saw was, and is not, and will ascend out of the bottomless pit and go into perdition."*** So apparently, he is the ***demon prince*** who will rule for Satan over the kingdom of the Antichrist. The fact that he ***"..was and is not,"*** simply means he had ruled over an earthly kingdom ***prior to that time*** *(the time John was writing),* but was ***then*** in the bottomless pit and was no longer ruling. However, he ***"..will ascend out of the bottomless pit;"*** meaning he's going to come back out of the pit at the end of the age when he will rule over the Antichrist's kingdom. But after that, he will be overcome ***"...and go into perdition,"*** which means ***destruction.*** After the two witnesses are killed, the Antichrist and his people will think they have won, but they will soon learn how wrong they are.

8. And their dead bodies will lie in the street of the great city which spiritually is called Sodom and Egypt, where also our Lord was crucified.
9. Then those from the peoples, tribes, tongues, and nations will see their dead bodies three-and-a-half days, and not allow their dead bodies to be put into graves.
10. And those who dwell on the earth will rejoice over them, make merry, and send gifts to one another, because these two prophets tormented those who dwell on the earth.
11. Now after the three-and-a-half days the breath of life from God entered them, and they stood on their feet, and great fear fell on those who saw them.

12. And they heard a loud voice from heaven saying to them, ***"Come up here."*** And they ascended to heaven in a cloud, and their enemies saw them.
13. In the same hour there was a great earthquake, and a tenth of the city fell. In the earthquake, seven thousand people were killed, and the rest were afraid and gave glory to the God of heaven.
14. The second woe is past. Behold, the third woe is coming quickly.
15. ***<u>THEN</u> the seventh angel sounded:*** And there were loud voices in heaven, saying, ***"The kingdoms of this world have become the kingdoms of our Lord and of His Christ, and He shall reign forever and ever!"***

One day in the future, the top story on the ***Six O'clock News*** will be that two men have been killed and their bodies have been left lying in the streets of Jerusalem for three and a half days. But the really big news will ***be when they came back to life, <u>AND ARE ACTUALLY SEEN AS THEY ASCEND INTO HEAVEN.</u>*** *When you see that news report,* ***you can know that the Rapture is going to take place within the <u>NEXT VERY FEW DAYS.</u>*** However, even before that happens, those two witnesses will be unusual enough to get our attention simply because of their ministry. Although Scripture doesn't say when they will begin their ministry, we will consider that question in detail in Chapter 10 in the paragraph entitled ***"Noah's Age As An Example."***

<u>The Second Coming.</u> Although Scripture doesn't tell when the Second Coming will be, the book of Daniel gives the best information about when it will be. We'll begin where Daniel first began to receive prophecies about the end of the age. That was when Nebuchadnezzar had a dream that troubled him. He sensed the dream had a special meaning, *but he couldn't even remember the dream.* God revealed that dream to Daniel, and also gave him its interpretation. When Daniel interpreted the dream he began by telling Nebuchadnezzar *when the dream was going to be fulfilled.*

Daniel 2: 27 - 28 *(NKJV)*
27. Daniel answered in the presence of the king, and said, ***"The secret which the king has demanded, the wise men, the astrologers, the magicians, and the soothsayers cannot declare to the king.***
28. ***"But there is a God in heaven who reveals secrets, and He has made known to King Nebuchadnezzar what <u>will be in the LATTER DAYS.</u> Your dream, and the visions of your head upon your bed, were these:***

This prophecy set the tone for all the other prophecies in Daniel by showing that they relate to things that will happen in ***"the latter days" — that short period of time that will immediately precede the end of the age.*** The last chapter of Daniel is the conclusion of the prophecies given to him. It begins with an ***extremely brief summary*** of what's going to happen during the last four years of this age.

Daniel 12: 1 - 4 *(NKJV)(This is the angel speaking.)*
1. ***"At that time Michael shall stand up, the great prince who stands watch over the sons of your people; and there shall be a time of trouble, such as never was since there was a nation, even to that time. And at that time your people shall be delivered, every one who is found written in the book.***

This is referring to when Michael will lead his angels in war against Satan and his angels and will cast them out of heaven *(Ref: Revelation 12: 7 - 9).* Realizing he will have only a short time left, Satan will have great wrath and cause unprecedented tribulation for the last three and a half years of this age *(Ref: Revelation 12: 12 - 17).* The reference to Daniel's people being delivered is talking about the end of those last four years, when Jesus will come in the Second Coming, and bring an end to that ***"...time of trouble..."*** by delivering all those in Israel who will have repented according to Deuteronomy 30: 1 - 10. They will survive that time of trouble to see and recognize Jesus when He comes again.

2. ***"And many of those who sleep in the dust of the earth shall awake, some to everlasting life, some to shame and everlasting contempt.***
3. ***"Those who are wise shall shine like the brightness of the firmament, and those who turn many to righteousness like the stars forever and ever.***

These verses show that the end of the age will also be marked by resurrection of the dead. This doesn't give enough detail to identify the various different resurrections, but simply shows that both the righteous and the unrighteous will be raised at the end of the age. In Verse 4 the angel showed Daniel he was at the end of the prophecies God had for him. But it also gives a brief, yet revealing revelation about certain conditions that will characterize the end of the age.

4. ***"But you, Daniel, shut up the words, and seal the book until the time of the end; many shall run to and fro, and knowledge shall increase."***

The prophecies given to Daniel were sealed until the time of the end, which meant they wouldn't be fully understood until the time was near for them to be fulfilled. But the angel revealed two interesting things that would characterize the time of the end. ***First:*** Many people would rush to and fro. For thousands of years after the angel told Daniel that, it was true that no one knew what that prophecy meant. ***But now WE know!!*** Just within our life time, we've seen that prophecy fulfilled beyond anything that could have been imagined *even a hundred years ago, much less twenty-five-hundred years ago when the angel told this to Daniel.* When I was born, commercial airlines didn't even exist. But now thousands of airplanes are carrying hundreds of thousands of passengers all over the world every day. A hundred years ago, the automobile was just beginning to become more than a novelty, for the Model T was first made in 1909. Except for the rail roads, people still traveled primarily by horse and buggy. Sixty years ago, when I was in high school, U. S. Highway 41 was known in Atlanta as ***"the four-lane,"*** *because it was the only four–lane highway going out of the city.* Now, sixty years later, ***Atlanta is part of the interstate highway system*** that covers the entire nation, and literally millions of cars and trucks constantly rush back and forth at speeds that were unbelievable a century ago. And even this can't compare with the fact that we have now traveled to and from the moon. ***Second:*** When I was at Georgia Tech in the 1950's, the ***slide rule*** was the latest technology available as an aid for students in math. Today, students at Tech don't even know what a slide rule is. They now have pocket-sized calculators that can instantaneously do more than we even dreamed of doing with those antiquated slide rules. Technology has literally gone out of sight in the forty some–odd years since I graduated from Tech. And we could go on and on talking about the increased knowledge in medicine and every other area of scientific endeavor.

That angel knew what he was talking about when he said knowledge would increase. However, I believe he was also talking about knowledge and understanding of God's word. Although we can't deny there's been an increase in the knowledge of God's Word, that increase can't yet compare with the advances in knowledge in the natural realm. I believe we're only ***at the beginning*** of the time when the knowledge of God's word will increase comparably with that of the natural world around us. Remember I Corinthians 15: 46 says, ***"However, the spiritual is not first, but the natural, and AFTERWARD the spiritual."*** We need to pray for God's grace that we may be included in *the explosion of* ***SPIRITUAL knowledge*** *that is just as sure to come as the increase in knowledge of natural things touched on above.*

<u>Daniel's Question about the End of Israel's Time of Trouble.</u>

Considering the likelihood of an increase in ***spiritual*** *knowledge*, we need to pay particular attention to what Daniel heard next.

Daniel 12: 5 - 13 *(NKJV)*
5. Then I, Daniel, looked; and there stood two others, one on this riverbank and the other on that riverbank.
6. And one said to the man clothed in linen, who was above the waters of the river, ***"How long shall the fulfillment of these wonders be?"***
7. Then I heard the man clothed in linen, who was above the waters of the river, when he held up his right hand and his left hand to heaven, and swore by Him who lives forever ***that there shall be for a time, times, and half a time; and when the power of the holy people has been completely scattered, all these things shall be finished.***

<u>Note:</u>
Daniel wasn't ***the <u>FIRST</u> one to ask <u>WHEN</u> those prophecies would be fulfilled.*** He didn't ask ***his*** question until ***<u>AFTER</u>*** one of the angels initiated that line of questioning. Through that angel, God led Daniel to ask the question in Verse 8.

8. Although I heard, I did not understand. Then I said, ***"My lord, what shall be the end of these things?"***

I believe this was God's way of showing that it's ***His will for us to seek and pray for understanding about <u>WHEN</u> and how His plans for the end of the age are going to take place. <u>AFTER</u>*** Daniel asked his question, *God provided him* ***a very detailed answer as to <u>WHEN</u> those things will both <u>begin and end.</u>***

9. And he said, ***"Go your way, Daniel, for the words are closed up, and sealed <u>TILL THE TIME OF THE END.</u>***
10. ***"Many shall be purified, made white, and refined, but the wicked shall do wickedly: and none of the wicked shall understand, but the wise shall understand.***
11. ***"And from the time that the daily sacrifice is taken away, and the abomination of desolation is set up, there shall be one thousand two hundred and ninety days.***
12. ***"Blessed is he who waits, and comes to the one thousand three hundred and thirty-five days.***

13. ***"But you, go your way till the end; for you shall rest, and will arise to your inheritance at the end of days."***

Daniel was given two separate periods of time in answer to his question. The first one, *the* ***twelve hundred and ninety days*** *from when the abomination of desolation is set up in the holy place,* was obviously the answer to Daniel's question — ***"what shall be the END of these things?"*** For ***"these things"*** related to the tribulation that will begin when *the abomination of desolation* is set up. So Israel's time of *great tribulation* will begin when the abomination of desolation is set up in the holy place, ***and it will end twelve hundred and ninety days later. But what will cause that time of great tribulation to END?*** Zechariah 14 tells what's going to happen at the end of the age to bring an end to Israel's tribulation that will result from Satan's wrath.

Zechariah 14: 1 - 3 *(NKJV)(This is God speaking to Israel though Zechariah.)*
1. ***"Behold, the day of the Lord is coming, and your spoil will be divided in your midst.***
2. ***"And I will gather all the nations to battle against Jerusalem; the city shall be taken, the houses rifled, and the women ravished. Half the city shall go into captivity, but the remnant of the people shall not be cut off from the city.***

This army that comes against Jerusalem will be the fulfillment of Revelation 16: 12 - 14, which is a prophecy of how Satan and the Anti–Christ will convince the nations of the world to come against Israel and attempt to destroy them.

3. ***"Then the Lord will go forth and fight against those nations, as He fights in the day of battle.***
4. ***"And in that day His feet will stand on the Mount of Olives, which faces Jerusalem on the east. And the Mount of Olives shall be split in two, from east to west, making a very large valley; half of the mountain shall move to the north and half of it to the south.***

This will be the ***Second Coming***, when all those who come against Israel will be completely destroyed. The day Jesus comes back in power and glory will mark the end of the twelve hundred and ninety days of Israel's trouble at the hands of Satan and those who submit themselves to him through the Anti–Christ. However, the blessing will come only to him who waits, "***... and comes to the thousand three hundred and thirty-five days.***" *(Daniel*

12: 12 above). ***What will happen during those additional forty-five days*** *(a month and a half)***, that will result in a blessing for those who wait?** To answer this question, we need to go back to what will happen when the seventh angel blows his trumpet. At that time, John heard loud voices from heaven say the following: ***"...The kingdoms of this world are become the kingdoms of our Lord and of His Christ, and He shall reign for ever and ever."*** *(Revelation 11: 15.)* ***At the Rapture,*** *the kingdoms of this world become the kingdoms of Christ,* and His first order of business will be to purge His new kingdom *(the kingdoms of this world),* of all the enemies of God — ***those who are wilfully in rebellion against Him.*** In Revelation, God revealed how Jesus Christ is going to accomplish that at His Second Coming.

Revelation 19: 19 - 21
19. And I saw the beast, the kings of the earth, and their armies, gathered together to make war against Him who sat on the horse *(Jesus, Verses 11 - 13)* and against His army.
20. Then the beast *(the demonic prince from the abyss)* was captured, and with him the false prophet *[the Anti-Christ]* who worked signs in his presence, by which he deceived those who received the mark of the beast and those who worshiped his image. These two were cast alive into the lake of fire burning with brimstone.
21. ***And the rest were killed with the sword*** *[the Word of God]* ***which proceeded from the mouth of Him who sat on the horse.*** And all the birds were filled with their flesh.

The armies that come against Israel will be totally destroyed there in Israel; ***however, that destruction won't be limited only to the ones who actually make up the armies that come against Israel.*** As we've already seen, Jeremiah 25: 33 *(ESV)* shows that many more will die, for it says, ***"And those pierced by the Lord on that day*** *[the Second Coming]* ***shall extend from one end of the earth to the other. They shall not be lamented, or gathered, or buried, they shall be dung on the surface of the ground."*** When Jesus comes at His Second Coming, He is going to purge His kingdom *(the entire world)* of all those who are the enemies of God. *In Matthew 25, Jesus identified those people as the goats — the ones who will cooperate with Satan in his efforts against the people of God* ***(Israel and the Church).*** That destruction apparently will be completed ***in just one day — the actual day of the Second Coming at the end of the twelve hundred and ninety days.***

However, when Jesus comes at His Second Coming, ***it's unlikely that <u>ALL of Israel</u>*** *will have repented and returned to obedience according to the covenant.* Therefore, since a blessing is pronounced ***<u>ONLY</u> upon those who wait and come to the end of the additional forty-five days,*** the Lord will most likely use that additional period of time to render judgment against the ***<u>JEWS</u> who have still made no effort to keep the covenant.*** Those additional forty-five days will bring Israel's time under the old covenant to its end. Therefore, at that same time — *the end of the additional forty-five days —when the old covenant ends, the new covenant of Jeremiah 31: 31 - 34 will begin,* ***<u>AND</u>****. Jesus's thousand-year reign on earth will begin. That means those forty-five days should end* ***on the anniversary date of the covenant,*** *which will be* ***the first day of the first month in A. D. 2030.*** This is in agreement with the discussion in Chapter 4 under the paragraph entitled ***"When Is God Going to Restore Israel Into His Favor?"*** *But is there a second witness that gives added confirmation that this is a correct interpretation?* In answer, we need to consider the following question.

<u>Will the Second Coming Fulfill One of Israel's Annual Feast Days?</u> God established a pattern of using major events in His plan for man's redemption, to fulfill the examples presented by various ones of Israel's annual feast days. Jesus was crucified on Passover, ***fulfilling the feast of Passover.*** Likewise, He arose and went to be examined by the Father on the day of the feast of the wave sheaf, ***fulfilling the feast of the wave sheaf.*** We've also seen how our brethren will also be examined before the throne of God on the day of Pentecost *(the feast of the wave loaves),* ***to fulfill the feast of the wave loaves.*** Therefore, it's reasonable to expect the Second Coming to fulfill the example provided by *another* of Israel's feasts, ***<u>AND</u> to take place on the actual date for that feast. The question is: <u>WHICH FEAST?</u>***

Because of what's going to happen at the Second Coming, it's likely that the feast of Purim is the feast that foreshadows both *<u>WHAT</u> will happen at the Second Coming, and <u>WHEN</u> it will happen.* The feast of Purim was established while Israel was subject to the Persian empire, and shortly after Esther, a Jewish maiden, became the queen. The book of Esther tells how that feast came into being. The king of Persia, Ahasuerus, had promoted a man named Haman as the chief prince in the Persian government. That filled Haman with pride and he enjoyed having all of the king's other servants bow down to him when he passed by. But Esther's uncle Mordecai didn't bow down and that filled Haman with wrath. He decided it wasn't enough to punish only Mordecai, and since Mordecai was a Jew, Haman decided to destroy all the Jews in the kingdom of Persia. He deceived King Ahasuerus into agreeing with his plot by telling him the Jews were a rebellious people who should be destroyed because they refused to obey the king's laws. So with the king's permission, Haman established the thirteenth day of the twelfth month *(Adar)* as the date when the citizens of Persia should rise up against the Jews and slaughter them. Haman worked out his plans in the first month, so he had ten months to have everything ready when the twelfth month arrived. But Ahasuerus found out the truth about Haman's plot, and had Haman hanged. He also granted that on the day appointed to slaughter the Jews, ***they could defend themselves against their enemies.*** Therefore, on the thirteenth day of Adar, the Jews rose up against their enemies and won a great victory. Since the victory wasn't completed on that day, they were permitted to continue fighting on the fourteenth also. The result of their victory is recorded in the 9th chapter of Esther.

Esther 9: 20 - 22 *(KJV)*
20. And Mordecai wrote these things, and sent letters unto all the Jews near and far, who were in all the provinces of King Ahasuerus,
21. to establish among them ***that they should celebrate yearly the fourteenth and fifteenth days of the month of Adar,***
22. ***as the days on which THE JEWS HAD REST FROM THEIR ENEMIES***, as the month which was turned from sorrow to joy for them, and from mourning to a holiday; that they should make them days of feasting and joy, of sending presents to one another and gifts to the poor. ***(Note: Verse 26 tells us those two days would be called Purim.)***

On the feast of Purim, *the Jews* ***celebrate FINDING REST FROM THEIR ENEMIES who had determined to destroy them long ago in Persia.*** *Therefore, what could be more fitting* ***than for that feast to be fulfilled by the Second Coming of Jesus who, as Israel's Messiah, will deliver them from the Antichrist AND ALL THEIR ENEMIES THROUGHOUT THE WHOLE WORLD.***

Earlier, we noted that ***since*** *the blessing is promised to those who wait and come to the end of the thousand, three hundred and thirty-five days, that should also mark the beginning of the kingdom age when Israel will reign with their Messiah under the new covenant of Jeremiah 31: 31 - 34.* In Chapter 5, in the paragraph entitled "***When Is God Going to Restore Israel into His Favor?,***" we saw that the new covenant should begin on the first day of the first month *(Abib/Nisan)* in A. D. 2030. Therefore, ***IF it's true** that the Second Coming is going to take place on the feast of Purim twelve hundred and ninety days after the abomination of desolation is set up, that means there will have to be forty-five days between the feast of Purim and the first day of the first month (Abib/Nisan)* **in A. D. 2030** *when the new covenant should begin for the thousand years of Christ's kingdom here on earth.*

Accordingly, Adar is the twelfth month in Israel's calendar and normally has 29 days. However, A. D. 2030 is a Jewish leap year in which Adar has thirty days, and a thirteenth month *(Adar II)* is added which has twenty nine days. Therefore, if the Second Coming should take place on the first day of Purim *(the 14th day of Adar as suggested above)*; consider the following. Since Adar will have thirty *(30)* days in A. D. 2030, that will leave sixteen *(16)* days before the beginning of Adar II. When we add those sixteen *(16)* days to the twenty-nine *(29)* days of Adar II, it gives forty-five *(45)* days as the time between the first day of the feast of Purim, and the first day of the first month Abib/Nisan. Therefore, if the twelve hundred and ninety *(1290)* days of Daniel 12: 12 ends with the Second Coming on Adar 14, *the first day of Purim in A. D. 2030,* then the forty-five additional days will fulfill the thousand, three hundred and thirty-five *(1335)* days of Daniel 12: 12 and will bring you to the first day of the first month of A. D. 2030. This confirms that the first day of the first month of A. D. 2030 should be the beginning of God's new covenant with Israel. Accordingly, *all Jews who are still alive on that day* **will indeed be blessed** *to enter into their Messiah's kingdom and do so under the new covenant.* ***This makes a pretty good case for the Second Coming taking place in A. D. 2030 on the 14th of Adar I, which will be the first day of the feast of Purim, and will be the 18th of February in our Gregorian calendar.***

Chapter 8

The Two Witnesses

Introduction. The 11th Chapter of Revelation introduces the two witnesses who will play an important part in events in Israel during the last three and a half years of this age. Since there's been quite a bit of speculation as to who those two witnesses will be, in this chapter we'll consider what Scripture says about their identity.

Who Will The Two Witnesses Be? There's good evidence in Malachi that Elijah will be one of the two witnesses.

Malachi 4: 5 *(KJV)*
5. Behold, I will send you Elijah the prophet before the coming of the great and dreadful day of the Lord:
6. And he shall turn the heart of the fathers to the children, and the heart of the children to their fathers, lest I come and smite the earth with a curse.

Based on this Scripture, people in Jesus's day believed Elijah was going to come back to the earth *before* the coming of the Messiah. Therefore, the disciples believed the appearance of Moses and Elijah on the Mount of Transfiguration was the fulfillment of the prophecy in Malachi above. Jesus corrected them, but confirmed that Elijah was indeed going to come.

Matthew 17: 9 - 13 *(NKJV)*
9. Now as they came down from the mountain, Jesus commanded them, saying, ***"Tell the vision to no one until the Son of Man is risen from the dead."***

10. And His disciples asked Him, saying, ***"Why then do the scribes say that Elijah must come first?"***
11. Jesus answered and said to them, ***"Indeed, Elijah is coming first and will restore all things.***
12. ***"But I say to you that Elijah has come already, and they did not know him but did to him whatever they wished. Likewise the Son of Man is also about to suffer at their hands."***
13. Then the disciples understood *that He spoke to them of* ***John the Baptist.***

This relationship between John the Baptist and Elijah was in keeping with what the angel said when he told Zacharias that John the Baptist was going to be born to him and his wife Elizabeth.

Luke 1: 17 *(NKJV)(The angel speaking to Zacharias about his son, John the Baptist)*
17. ***"He*** *[John the Baptist]* ***will also go before Him*** *[the Lord]* ***in the spirit and power of Elijah, '<u>to turn the hearts of the fathers to the children,</u>' and the disobedient to the wisdom of the just, to make ready a people prepared for the Lord"***

On another occasion, Jesus again spoke of the unusual relationship between John the Baptist and Elijah.

Matthew 11: 14
14. ***"And if you are willing to receive it, he*** *[John the Baptist]* ***is Elijah <u>WHO IS TO COME.</u>"***

God sent John the Baptist ***"...in the spirit and power of Elijah,"*** *to prepare the way for Jesus* ***in His <u>FIRST</u> coming.*** In that capacity, ***John the Baptist was an example of Elijah*** *whom God is going to send back to earth* ***in person*** *to prepare the way for Jesus* ***in His <u>SECOND</u> Coming.*** Since Elijah was carried into heaven ***<u>without dying,</u>*** it has been assumed that the second witness will also be someone who has been carried to heaven without dying, and Enoch is the only one who seems to satisfy that condition. But is it really going to be Enoch? There's a passage in Hebrews that indicates otherwise.

Hebrews 11: 5
5. By faith Enoch was translated ***that he should not see death;*** and was not found, because God had translated him: for before his translation he had this testimony, that he pleased God.

Since Enoch was translated so ***"...he should not see death,"*** *that eliminates him from being the second witness,* ***because both witnesses are going to be killed at the end of their testimony.*** That leaves us with the question, ***who will the second witness be?*** There is one other person whom Scripture rather strongly suggests might be that second witness, and *that is* ***the Apostle John.*** Both the Gospel of John and the book of Revelation strongly indicate that John might be the second witness. Jesus gave the first hint about this after His resurrection at the end of His ministry.

John 21: 20 - 23 *(RSV)*
20. Peter, turning around, saw the disciple whom Jesus loved *(John)* following them; The one who also had leaned back on His breast at supper, and said, ***"Lord, who is the one who betrays You?"***
21. Peter therefore seeing him said to Jesus, ***"Lord, and what about this man?"***
22. Jesus said to him, ***"If I want him to remain until I come, what is that to you? You follow Me!"***
23. *This saying therefore went out among the brethren that that disciple would not die; yet Jesus did not say to him that he would not die, but only,* ***"If I want him to remain until I come, what is that to you?"***

Jesus didn't speak foolishly saying things that had no meaning. In fact in John 8: 28, He confessed that He only spoke those things that His Father taught him. Therefore, we have to conclude that He spoke of *John remaining until He returned* because His Father led Him to say it. So Jesus wasn't posing a meaningless hypothetical question. He was beginning to reveal what God had planned for the Apostle John. Obviously the disciples took what Jesus said seriously, because as a result of Jesus saying that, the early believers generally believed that John wasn't going to die. But John was careful to note that Jesus didn't say *he wasn't going to die,* but rather; ***"If I want him to remain UNTIL I come, what is that to you?"*** But notice that Jesus *was careful to leave the possibility open for* ***John not to die UNTIL He comes again.*** Accordingly, if John should come back as the second witness and die ***after*** he finishes his testimony in that capacity, it would fulfill what Jesus said about him tarrying until He comes. But that could only happen ***IF John hasn't already died.***

Has John Died? In light of what Jesus said, it's interesting to note that according to *"Fox's Book of Martyrs,"* all the apostles died as martyrs, ***with the exception of John.*** Fox's book of martyrs says the following about John.

"The 'beloved disciple,' was brother to James the Great. The churches of Smyrna, Pergamos, Sardis, Philadelphia, Laodicea, and Thyatira, were founded by him. From Ephesus he was ordered to be sent to Rome, where it is affirmed he was cast into a cauldron of boiling oil. He escaped by miracles, without injury. Domitian afterwards banished him to the Isle of Patmos, where he wrote the Book of Revelation. Nerva, the successor of Domitian, recalled him. He was the only apostle who escaped a violent death."

There is no record ***or tradition*** of John's having died. Therefore, after John received the Revelation, it's possible that God may have quietly taken him to heaven in a manner similar to Enoch, *and that he's remained there* **ALIVE,** *waiting until it's time for him to return as the second witness at the end of the age.*

Further Evidence That John Might Be The Second Witness.

In addition to what Jesus said to Peter, there's also evidence in Revelation that John might be the second witness.

Revelation 10: 1 - 4 *(NKJV)*
1. I saw still another mighty angel coming down from heaven, clothed with a cloud. And a rainbow was on his head, his face was like the sun and his feet like pillars of fire.
2 He had a little book open in his hand. And he set his right foot on the sea and his left foot on the land,
3. and cried with a loud voice, as when a lion roars. When he cried out, seven thunders uttered their voices
4. And when the seven thunders uttered their voices, I was about to write; but I heard a voice from heaven saying to me, ***"seal up those things which the seven thunders uttered, and do not write them."***

It's obvious that the seven thunders also revealed troubles that are going to come on the earth, but John was instructed not to write them. Therefore they are not included in Revelation. *That means John is the only man who knows what the seven thunders said.* **There could be no purpose for God to reveal those judgments ONLY to John.** Therefore, it follows that *God must have had another ministry for John beyond just recording the Revelation that we now have,* ***for there is no other way he could reveal what the seven thunders said.*** Next, the angel told John that the mystery of God would be finished when the seventh angel blows his trumpet. But look at what he said after that.

Revelation 10: 8 - 11 *(NKJV)*
8. Then the voice which I heard from heaven, spoke to me again and said, ***"Go, take the little book which is open in the hand of the angel who stands on the sea and on the earth."***
9. So I went to the angel, and said to him, ***"Give me the little book."*** And he said unto me, ***"Take and eat it; and it will be as sweet as honey in your mouth."***
10. Then I took the little book out of the angel's hand and ate it, and it was as sweet as honey in my mouth. But when I had eaten it, my stomach became bitter.

The little book evidently contained information that applied to John personally. He didn't reveal what the information was, but he told how it effected him when he received it. *At first, It was* ***sweet as honey, but became bitter as it reached his stomach.*** His first response was to be very pleased by the information in the little book, but when he understood its full meaning, it was distressing. What the angel said in Verse 11 helps us understand what was in the book. *(Note: This verse is given from the King James Version.)*

11. And he said unto me, ***"THOU MUST PROPHESY AGAIN BEFORE MANY PEOPLES, AND NATIONS, AND TONGUES AND KINGS."***

To ***"prophesy"*** means ***to speak forth under Divine inspiration***. Therefore, the angel's message to John was that he was going to speak forth God's inspired message to ***"...many people, and nations, and tongues and kings."*** At that particular time John was only ***writing down*** what he was seeing and hearing in the vision, *and that was very different from* ***prophesying.*** There's no record that he ever did what Verse 11 said he was going to do. We simply don't know what happened to John after he completed the Revelation; however, he certainly didn't have a ministry of prophesying *(speaking forth)* to the very extensive audience spoken of in Verse 11. Therefore, we can only conclude that when he ate the little book, he received the information that ***he was going to be taken up to heaven without dying,*** *and that news was as sweet as honey to him.* But the rest of the little book's message was that ***he will also have to come back to the earth again, and prophesy*** *(speak forth)* ***to an extremely extensive audience, and when that part of his ministry is finished, he will finally be slain. Therefore the book was bitter to his stomach, which means that information was not at all pleasing to him.*** As we consider this, we need to remember that John was told not to write what the seven thunders said. That means he had some information that he didn't include in the Revelation, so we know that John has at least that much information that still needs to be provided to the people of this world. Therefore, it is plausible that the Apostle John may be one of the two witness spoken of in the very next chapter of Revelation. Keeping this in mind, look at how that next chapter of Revelation begins.

Revelation 11: 1 - 2 *(KNJV)*
1. Then I was given a reed like a measuring rod. And the angel stood, saying, ***"Rise and measure the temple of God, the altar, and those who worship there.***
2. ***"But leave out the court which is outside the temple, and do not measure it, for it has been given to the Gentiles. And they will tread the holy city underfoot for forty-two months."***

Do you see it? The angel gave the reed to JOHN HIMSELF, and told HIM to measure the temple, the altar and the people who were worshiping there.. That took place while John was receiving the vision of the Revelation, which was approximately A. D. 90, ***and was at least twenty (20) years AFTER Jerusalem and the temple had been completely destroyed.*** *At that time there simply wasn't a temple with people worshiping in it for John to measure. And there hasn't been a temple at any time during the nearly two thousand years since then.* Such a temple will not exist until Israel builds it as the end of the age approaches. ***Therefore, the only way John will be able to obey those instructions will be for him to come back to the earth at the end of the age AFTER ISRAEL HAS REBUILT THEIR TEMPLE AND RESUMED WORSHIPING THERE ACCORDING TO THE LAW.*** If John returns as one of the two witnesses, he will be able to measure the temple and its worshipers as he was instructed in Verses 1 & 2 above. In addition to that, he will be able to fulfill the prophecy of Revelation 10: 11 by prophesying to the entire world by means of live–TV.

Fire From Heaven. There's one other item of interest concerning the *possibility* of John being the second witness. Revelation 11: 5 says if anyone would harm the two witnesses, fire would proceed out of their mouths and devour their enemies. These men will have the power to consume their enemies with fire like Elijah did in Old Testament times *(Ref: II Kings 1: 9 - 14).* I don't know of any other prophets besides Elijah who destroyed his enemies with fire. But there is one other instance where there was a willingness to do it.

Luke 9: 51 - 54 *(NKJV)*
51. And it came to pass, when the time had come for Him *(Jesus)* to be received up, that He steadfastly set His face to go to Jerusalem,
52. and sent messengers before His face. And as they went, they entered a village of the Samaritans, to prepare for Him.
53. But they did not receive Him, because His face was set for the journey to Jerusalem.
54. And when his disciples James and John saw this, they said, ***"Lord, do You want us to command fire to come down from heaven, and consume them, just as Elijah did?"***

John was willing, *and maybe even a little eager,* to follow the example of Elijah and call down fire from heaven upon those who would not receive Jesus. Is it possible that God used that event to show that John had the willingness to execute the same kind of judgment as Elijah, against the enemies of God?

Concurrent Messages Of Law And Grace. Elijah's ministry was to call Israel back to obedience according to their covenant. At the end of the age when God again brings Israel under the covenant, Elijah will complete his ministry by once again calling upon Israel to keep their covenant to obey the law *(Ref: Malachi 4: 4 - 6).* But John's ministry was to provide the gospel of salvation through faith in Jesus Christ. Although it's true that at the end of the age God will be calling the nation of Israel to return to obedience of the law according to the covenant; ***nevertheless, the door of salvation through faith in Jesus will still be open because the Church won't be taken out of the world until AFTER the two witnesses are slain, resurrected, and caught up to heaven.*** Therefore, while Elijah is giving a powerful message specifically calling *the nation of Israel* to repentance and obedience of the law according to the covenant, ***at that same time, John as the second witness, will be preaching an equally powerful message of salvation for all those who will to repent and come to faith in Jesus Christ.***

As already discussed, the ministry of God's two witnesses will be brought to an abrupt end, when the Anti-Christ makes war against them and kills them. Their resurrection and ascension into heaven three and a half *(3½)* days later will be the signal for the seventh trumpet to sound. At that time, ***"the mystery of God"*** *(the church)* will be completed and caught up by Christ in the Rapture. After that time, nobody else will be added to the

Church, so John's ministry as the second witness, will be the end of the message of salvation as an invitation to become a part of the Church as the bride of Christ. Scripture doesn't say, *but that may also be when the door will be closed for Israel to return to God by repenting and coming to obedience according to the law.* But even it that isn't the end of Israel's opportunity, ***they won't have much longer, for their opportunity will surely be over when Jesus returns in the Second Coming.***

Part 2

Prophetic Examples About When He Is Coming

Introduction. Before considering ***EVENTS*** *in Scripture* as prophetic examples, we need to notice something God said in Isaiah.

Isaiah 46: 9 - 10 *(KJV)(This is God speaking through the prophet Isaiah.)*
9. ***"Remember the former THINGS of old, for I am God, and there is no other; I am God, and there is none like Me,***
10. ***"declaring the end from the beginning, and from ancient times things that are not yet done, saying, 'My counsel shall stand, and I will do all my pleasure.'"***

Scripture is filled with prophecy, for God used the prophets to ***declare*** *the end from the beginning;* however, those ***declarations*** of prophecy are not the only way God revealed the end from the beginning. Because of that, He exhorts us ***to "remember the former THINGS of old."*** We need to remember *those former* **THINGS**, because they ***DIDN'T JUST HAPPEN TO HAPPEN.*** The Scripture record of those former ***THINGS*** may seem to be no more than *historical accounts;* however, *in His sovereignty, God used many of those former* **THINGS** *as prophetic* **examples** *that foreshadow* what's going to happen at the end of the age.

One of those ***"things of old"*** that we're familiar with is when God told Abraham to take Isaac and offer him as a burnt offering. That was obviously an example looking forward to when God was going to offer His Son as the perfect sacrifice for our sins. There are many more of those prophetic examples that are not quite as obvious as that of Abraham and Isaac. This part of the book discusses some of those other examples you may not be as familiar with as that of Abraham and Isaac. Since God ***specifically*** told us in Isaiah that He declares ***"...the END from the BEGINNING,"*** we'll begin by looking at some of the things ***that happened in the beginning.***

Chapter 9

The Week of Creation

The Week of Creation As An Example. God worked six days to restore the earth and rested on the seventh day *(Ref: Genesis 1: 3 thru Genesis 2: 3).* As you study the week of creation in conjunction with God's plan for man's redemption, it becomes apparent that He arranged that first week to be an example of the total span of time during which He will bring forth those special people He has ordained to share with Him in His Kingdom. Accordingly, in that example each day represented a *thousand years* in His plan for man's redemption. That gives a total of seven thousand years, at the end of which God will have completed His plan of redemption. The correlation of a day to a thousand years is based on the following passage in II Peter.

II Peter 3: 3 - 8 *(KJV)(Verse 3 shows that this* ***passage relates particularly*** *to the end of the age.)*
3. Knowing this first, *that there shall come* ***in the LAST DAYS*** *scoffers,* walking after their own lusts,
4. and saying, ***"Where is the promise of His coming? For since the fathers fell asleep, all things continue as they were from the beginning of the creation."***
5. For this they willingly are ignorant of, that by the word of God the heavens were of old, and the earth standing out of the water and in the water:
6. Whereby the world that then was, being overflowed with water perished:
7. But the heavens and the earth, which are now, by the same word are kept in store, reserved unto the fire against the day of judgment and perdition of ungodly men.

8. ***But, beloved, be not ignorant of this one thing, THAT ONE DAY IS WITH THE LORD AS A THOUSAND YEARS, AND A THOUSAND YEARS AS ONE DAY.***

According to this rationale, the first six days of the week of creation represented ***the first six thousand years*** during which God is ***"bringing many sons to glory"*** *(Ref: Hebrews 2: 10)* to live with Him forever in His kingdom. The likelihood that God intended *the week of creation to* serve as an example of His plan for man is increased by the fact that He imposed that same definition of a week in the law of the Sabbath. God's *seven–day–week* is a standard recognized all over the world such that whether they realize it or not, people throughout the ages have been giving a ***weekly testimony*** *to God's time–table* for His plan of redemption for man.

The seventh day of that first week represented the seventh thousand–year period during which Christ will reign here on earth *(Ref: Revelation 20: 4- 6).* During that ***seventh*** *thousand–year–period,* Christ will complete His task of bringing every enemy under subjection, and will then deliver the restored kingdom back to God the Father *(Ref: I Corinthians 15: 24 - 28).* The Second Coming of Christ will mark the beginning of that seventh thousand–year–period during which the earth will have rest under the reign of Jesus Christ as King of kings and Lord of lords *(Revelation 20: 4).* Accordingly, the Second Coming of Christ will also mark the end of six thousand years since the week of creation. Because of that there were those who were concerned that the end of the world might come at the end of 1999. That *of course* didn't happen ***because the year 2000 did not mark the end of six thousand years since the week of creation as they supposed it would.*** The following reasons show there was no ***scriptural*** *basis* for that belief.

First: Our Gregorian calendar was based *on the* ***assumption*** that Jesus was born in the year A. D. 1; however, it's now known that Jesus was actually born three to four years before than A. D. I. Therefore, A. D. 2000 was simply the date when two thousand years had passed ***since the time Pope Gregory THOUGHT Jesus was born.***

Second: The idea that A. D. 2000 would mark the end of the first six thousand years following the week of creation was based on the work of various theologians whose research of the Old Testament indicated the first week recorded in Genesis took place four thousand years before Jesus was born. Although that was a *good* ***approximation,*** the record of time given in the Old Testament is not complete enough to determine ***precisely*** how many years passed between that first week of Genesis, and the birth of Jesus.

Third: IF the ***BIRTH of Jesus*** was really when God determined the Christian era began, *it's only reasonable that He would have given the date of Jesus's birth in Scripture.* However, Scripture doesn't even reveal the ***YEAR*** when Jesus was born, *much less the actual month and day.* Also, it wasn't Jesus's birth, ***but rather His death and resurrection*** *by which God made redemption available to man, and* **Scripture clearly reveals that Jesus *was crucified*** *in A. D. 30,* ***on the preparation day for Passover,*** *which was* ***the 14th of Abib/Nisan.*** Then, after being dead for three days and nights, He arose and on that Sunday night, He appeared to the disciples and they finally believed unto salvation, thereby becoming the first Christians. We know that is true, because they were the first ones to receive the Holy Spirit as the earnest/assurance of their salvation *(Ref: John 20: 20 - 22).* ***Therefore, that first Sunday night after Jesus's resurrection in A. D. 30 was actually the BEGINNING of the Christian era instead of the year when it was mistakenly believed He was born. Following this reasoning, the year A. D. 2030 will much more likely mark the end of six thousand years following the week of creation, instead of the year A. D. 2000.*** According to that reasoning, Jesus's coming would have taken place at the end of the first four thousand years following the first week recorded in Genesis. The following discussion of *the sun as an example of Jesus* adds to the credibility that He came at the end of those first four thousand years.

The Sun As An Example Of Jesus. The sun is an example of Jesus as ***"the light of the world."*** As a part of that example, God created the sun with light that is much more than simply ***light to see by.*** *He created the sun to give light that is* ***ABSOLUTELY ESSENTIAL FOR LIFE HERE ON EARTH.*** The cells in green plants contain chlorophyl which absorbs light from the sun *and uses that light to manufacture simple carbohydrates from water and carbon dioxide.* That process is known as photosynthesis, ***and the carbohydrates produced are the basic food source FOR ALL LIFE ON EARTH.*** *Keeping this in mind, look at the special way God introduced Jesus Christ in John's Gospel.*

John 1: 1 - 4 *(KJV)*
1. In the beginning was the Word, and the Word was with God, and the Word was God.

2. The same was in the beginning with God.
3. All things were made by Him; and without Him was not any thing made.
4. In Him was ***LIFE;*** and the ***LIFE*** was the ***LIGHT*** of men.

Long before man even knew photosynthesis existed, God created that process as the means to provide the basic food required to support natural life here on earth. ***By doing that, He made the sun a UNIQUE example of the life-giving nature of His Son, Jesus Christ.*** It makes no sense to call Jesus ***"the LIGHT of men," UNTIL*** *you see that God was relating the* ***Spirit of LIFE*** *in Jesus* ***to the example of SUNLIGHT being necessary for natural life here on earth.*** You can demonstrate the power of this example by laying a sheet of plywood on your lawn and seeing how quickly the grass under it dies. That's a good picture of how the sun is an example of Jesus, *for just as natural life cannot exist without light from the sun,* ***man cannot have God's life in his spirit without the light of the knowledge of Jesus Christ.***

John 8: 12
12. Then Jesus spoke to them again, saying, ***"I am the light of the world: he who follows Me shall not walk in darkness, BUT HAVE THE LIGHT OF LIFE."***

John 5: 24 - 26
24. ***"Verily, verily, I say unto you, 'He that hears my word, and believes on Him that sent Me, hath everlasting life, and shall not come into condemnation, BUT IS PASSED FROM DEATH UNTO LIFE.'"***
25. ***"Verily, verily, I say unto you, 'The hour is coming, and now is, when the dead shall hear the voice of the Son of God: and they that hear shall live.***
26. ***"FOR as the Father has life in Himself; SO HAS HE GIVEN TO THE SON TO HAVE LIFE IN HIMSELF.***

When The Sun Appeared, As An Example Of Jesus Christ.

When God caused the sun to become the earth's source of light is an important part of the sun's example of Jesus Christ.

Genesis 1: 1 - 4 & 14 - 18 *(UNASB)*
1. In the beginning God created the heavens and the earth.
2. And the earth was formless, and void; and darkness was over the

surface of the deep. And the Spirit of God was hovering over the surface of the waters.
3. Then God said, ***"Let there be light;"*** and there was light.
4. ***And God saw the light, that it was good; and God divided the light from the darkness.***

The light God spoke into being on that first day ***DID NOT COME FROM THE SUN.*** It simply came into being *as the result of God's* ***spoken word.*** In all likelihood, it came *from* God's own glory. The following verses show that light from the sun didn't come to the earth until the work of the fourth day.

14. Then God said, ***"Let there be lights in the expanse of the heavens to separate the day from the night; and let them be for signs and for seasons and for days and years;***
15. ***"and let them be for lights in the expanse of the heavens TO GIVE LIGHT ON THE EARTH;"*** and it was so.
16. God made two great lights, the greater light to govern the day, and the lesser light to govern the night, He made the stars also.
17. God placed them in the expanse of the heavens ***TO GIVE LIGHT ON THE EARTH,***
18. and to govern the day and the night, and to separate the light from the darkness; and God saw that it was good.
19. ***There was evening and there was morning, THE FORTH DAY.***

When Verse 16 speaks of God making the sun, moon and stars, it's not talking about what He did on the fourth day; for Verse 1 says ***"In the BEGINNING, God made the heavens and the earth."*** The sun, moon and stars comprise the heavens that God made *in the* ***beginning*** *long before that first week recorded in Genesis.* Some time before that week, light from the heavens had been completely obscured from the earth, leaving it in total darkness according to Verse 2. Most likely, the earth's darkness was caused by a shroud of clouds so thick that light from the heavens couldn't penetrate it to shine on the earth. However, during the fourth day God removed the clouds and let light from the sun, moon and stars shine through to the earth *as it had done in the beginning eons of time before.*

But this raises an interesting question. ***Since God deemed it necessary to give light to the earth on the first day, WHY did He wait til the FOURTH day TO LET THAT LIGHT COME FROM THE SUN?*** The only answer that makes sense, is that ***He was using the sun as an example of Jesus Christ.*** Because of that, God waited til the end of the fourth day to use sunlight to illuminate the earth, and He did that *as an example of the fact that Jesus Christ wasn't going to come as* ***"the light of the world," until FOUR THOUSAND YEARS AFTER THAT FIRST WEEK RECORDED IN GENESIS.*** Since the light God gave to the earth on the first day came as the result of ***His Word*** rather than from the sun, that light was also part of His example, for there was *a measure of spiritual* ***light*** *in the world* during those first four thousand years before Jesus came as the light of the world. However, the spiritual light that was in the world during those Old Testament times *came from God's* ***spoken Word of the law,*** rather than from Jesus Christ. The first glimmer of spiritual light came to Adam when God spoke, *commanding him not to eat of the tree of the knowledge of good and evil.* The rest of the spiritual light for Old Testament times came when He spoke through Moses and gave the law to Israel. However, there is a big difference between the light that came from God's Word of the law, as compared to that which came from Jesus Christ at the end of those four thousand years. We see this difference in Galatians.

Galatians 2: 16 *(KJV)*
16. Knowing that a man is not justified by the works of the law but by faith in Jesus Christ, even we have believed in Christ Jesus, that we might be justified by faith in Christ and not by the works of the law; ***for by the works of the law no flesh shall be justified.***

Galatians 3: 21 *(KJV)*
21. Is the law then against the promises of God? Certainly not! ***For if there had been a law given which could have given LIFE, truly righteousness would have been by the law.***

As blessed as the ***LIGHT*** was that came from God's Word of the law, ***it cannot IMPART the spirit–life of God to man. God revealed how that was accomplished in the first few verses of John.***

John 1: 1 - 3, 14, & 4 *(KJV)*
1. In the beginning was the Word, and the Word was with God, and the Word was God.
2. The same was in the beginning with God.
3. All things were made by Him; and without Him was not any thing made.
4. In Him was ***LIFE***; and the ***LIFE*** was the ***LIGHT*** of men.

This is talking about the spirit–life of God that was in Christ from the very beginning *because He was a part of the Trinity of God. The problem* was how to make that ***spirit–life of God*** available to man to dispel the darkness of death that was in him due to sin that had entered mankind through Adam. Verse 14 reveals how God overcame that obstacle.

14. And the Word became flesh and dwelt among us, and we beheld His glory, the glory as of the only begotten of the Father, full of grace and truth.

When the Second person of the Trinity of God become incarnate as the man Jesus, that changed everything, ***for that made the spirit–life of God Himself available to all men.*** That was true, *because Jesus Christ was a* ***MAN who was without sin or the curse of death that resulted from sin.*** Therefore the life that was in Jesus was the Divine life of God Himself, *and that life was in Jesus as a* ***seed.*** Accordingly, in John 12: 24, Jesus likened Himself to a grain *(seed)* of wheat, which abides alone until it falls into the ground and dies, but when that seed dies, the life within it is released to reproduce itself and bring forth much fruit. Therefore, when Jesus died, *just like a seed of wheat,* the Divine life within Him was released to be reproduced in every person who places his/her faith in the death of Jesus as God's sacrifice that provided life for them.

The miraculous transition ***that made the life in Jesus available to us as THE LIGHT OF THE WORLD,*** took place in A. D. 30 ***when Jesus DIED. Then, just as the life in a seed is released to give new life when the seed dies, when Jesus died, His life was released to give new life to all who receive the Gospel as the spiritual light of the world, and place their trust in Him.*** Therefore, ***that was when the first four thousand years actually came to their end.*** That *(the death and resurrection of Jesus)* was also the ***BEGINNING*** *of the Christian Era.*

Since Jesus became the light of the world in A. D. 30, *and that marked* ***the END*** *of the first* ***four*** *thousand years following the first week recorded in Genesis,* that means the church age should end two thousand years later in A. D. 2030 as discussed in Chapter 4 of this book. Accordingly, the first ***SIX thousand years*** following the week of creation should also end ***in A. D. 2030, INSTEAD of A. D. 2000*** as many believed when the year A. D. 2000 was drawing near. This brings us to *the creation of Adam* as an example of Jesus.

<u>Adam As An Example Of Jesus Christ.</u> When God made Adam on the sixth day, His creation was complete. Genesis 1 gives an over-view of the creation of Adam.

Genesis 1: 26 - 28, & 31 *(KJV)*
26. And God said, Let Us make man in Our image, after Our likeness; and let *them* have dominion over the fish of the sea, and over the fowl of the air, and over the cattle, and over all the earth, and over every creeping thing that creeps upon the earth.
27. So God created man in His own image, in the image of God created He him; *male and female created He them.*
28. And God blessed *them*, and God said unto *them*, Be fruitful, and multiply, and replenish the earth, and subdue it: and have dominion over the fish of the sea, and over the fowl of the air, and over every living thing that moves upon the earth.
31. And God saw every thing that He had made, and, behold, it was very good. And the evening and the morning were the sixth day.

We've already seen how God used the week of creation *as an* ***example*** of what He was going to do to provide redemption for man; *therefore, it's reasonable to expect that the creation of Adam was part of that* ***example***. But what did the creation of Adam exemplify? Since God made Adam in His own image, Adam had to be an example of something extremely important. In I Corinthians, God revealed what He exemplified by Adam.

I Corinthians 15: 45 - 47 *(NKJV)*
45. And so it is written, ***"The first man, Adam,*** *became a living soul."* ***The last Adam*** *became a life-giving Spirit.*
46. However, the spiritual is not first, but the natural; then the spiritual.
47. The first man *[Adam]* was of the earth, made of dust; the second Man *[Jesus]* is the Lord from heaven.

Adam was a very specific example of Jesus Christ, *and since God didn't create Adam until the sixth day,* ***that means the <u>EXAMPLE</u> of Christ presented by Adam, <u>won't be complete until the end of the sixth thousand year period.</u>*** We can understand this better when we see the part Eve played in God's example. Genesis 2 makes it obvious that *God didn't make Eve at the same time He made Adam; for* ***AFTER*** *making Adam, God planted the garden of Eden and said,* ***"It is not good that man should be alone; I will make him a helper comparable to him."****(Genesis 2: 18).* ***Then,*** God brought all the animals and birds to Adam and had him name them. But Genesis 2:

20 shows there wasn't a helper suitable for Adam among the other animals. It was only at that point in time that God proceeded to create Eve. What God ***did*** to create Eve was an important part of His example foreshadowing Jesus Christ.

God caused Adam to fall into a deep sleep, took out one of his ribs, and closed up the flesh in his side. He then made Eve out of the rib taken from Adam's side. When God opened Adam's side and took out the rib to make Eve, that was an example of Jesus's side being pierced, and the blood flowing out. In fulfillment of the example of making Eve from Adam's rib, God is now using *the* **blood** that came from Jesus's side to redeem us and make the church as the bride of Christ. Accordingly, I Peter 1: 18 & 19 says we are ***redeemed "...WITH THE PRECIOUS BLOOD OF CHRIST, as of a lamb without blemish and without spot."*** There's something else about the crucifixion that makes it even more evident that the blood that came from Jesus's side was fulfillment of the example of God taking the rib from Adam's side. When they scourged and crucified Jesus, that was an extremely bloody ordeal; however, ***the only BLOOD mentioned in any of the Gospel accounts, is the BLOOD that flowed from Jesus's side when it was pierced AFTER He had died.*** Therefore, when we're saved *(redeemed "**with the precious blood of Christ**") according to Scripture, we're redeemed by **that BLOOD** that flowed from Jesus's side, **because that's the only blood Scripture speaks of Jesus shedding.** So the rib God took from Adam's side to make Eve was an example of the blood that flowed from Jesus's side to redeem the church to become Jesus's bride.*

However, *when the soldier pierced Jesus's side,* ***WATER flowed out of His side along with the blood.*** *What part does that water play in God's creation of the church as the bride for Christ?* To answer this question we need to understand that ***our problem is not limited ONLY to sin.*** If sin was our only problem, blood is all that would have needed to flow from Jesus's side; for as we saw above, we are redeemed ***"with the precious BLOOD of Christ."***

The word ***"redeem"*** means ***"to buy back."*** In relation to our situation as sinners, *to be **redeemed** means we are bought back **from the bondage of sin**.* Therefore, when Jesus shed His blood in death; that was all that was ***necessary to REDEEM*** *(or buy back)* ***from the bondage of sin*** all who repent and place their faith in Jesus. However, *when we read God's warning to Adam, we see that his sin did more than just put him in **bondage** to sin, for God told him, **"Of every tree of the garden you may freely eat;** **but of the tree of the knowledge of good and evil you shall not eat, for in the day***

that you eat of it <u>YOU SHALL SURELY DIE.</u>" *(Which literally means,* ***"dying you shall die.")****. When Adam sinned, the life in his spirit became infected with the process of dying.* As the result, he immediately began to age and when he was nine hundred and thirty years old, his body could no longer support life and he died and was buried. But I Corinthians 15: 22 tells us that, ***"...in Adam <u>ALL DIE.</u>"*** All people whose lineage goes back to Adam, receive their spirit of life from Adam, and all Adam had to pass on to us was a spirit that was infected with sin and death. That means every one of Adam's descendants would be born, ***both in bondage to sin, <u>AND WITH DEATH ALREADY WORKING ITS DESTRUCTION IN THEIR BEING</u>.*** Accordingly, we all receive our spirit *by birth* from Adam, ***a <u>MAN</u>***; therefore, *the only solution to our problem is* ***to receive <u>ANOTHER</u> spirit by <u>ANOTHER</u> birth from <u>ANOTHER</u> man — one whose spirit has not been defiled by sin and death.*** In Romans, we see that Jesus Christ is that other man who still has a spirit that is totally alive.

Romans 8: 8 - 11 *(NKJV)*
8. So then, those who are in the flesh cannot please God.
9. But you are not in the flesh but in the Spirit, if indeed the Spirit of God dwells in you. Now if anyone does not have the Spirit of Christ, he is not His.
10. And if Christ is in you, the body is dead because of sin, but the Spirit is life because of righteousness.
11. But if the Spirit of Him who raised Jesus from the dead dwells in you, He who raised Christ from the dead will also give life to your mortal bodies through His Spirit who dwells in you.

Jesus Himself revealed that we must be born again, for He said, ***"...Verily, verily, I say unto you, 'Except a man be <u>BORN AGAIN,</u> he cannot see the kingdom of God.'"*** *(John 3: 3).* In Verse 5 He went on to add, ***"That which is born of the flesh is flesh; and that which is born of the Spirit is spirit."*** Romans 8: 8 above confirms how important this new birth is, for it says, ***"...those who are in the flesh <u>CANNOT PLEASE GOD.</u>"*** So we must be born again, but Jesus also explained in John 3 that our ***second*** *birth* is not a normal natural birth; therefore, there had to be another way for Jesus's Spirit to be released from His body and be received by us. The night before He was crucified Jesus revealed to His disciples that the only way His Spirit, *the Holy Spirit of God,* could become available to us was for Him to release it by dying.

John 16: 5 - 7 *(KJV) (Jesus had been telling His disciples it was time for Him to die, and in the following verses He revealed how essential His death was for them, and for us.)*
5. ***"But now I go My way to Him that sent Me; and none of you asketh Me; 'Whither goest thou?'"***
6. ***"But because I have said these things unto you, sorrow hath filled your heart."***
7. ***"Nevertheless I tell you the truth; it is EXPEDIENT for you that I go away: for if I go not away, the comforter will not come unto you; but if I depart, I will send him unto you."***

The only way Jesus's Spirit, *the Holy Spirit of God,* could be released from His body and thereby become available to be received by us in that mysterious new birth, ***was for Him to die.*** Accordingly, when Jesus was crucified, God gave a visual manifestation of ***His Spirit*** *being released from Jesus's body.*

John 19: 32 - 35 *(KJV)(This was when the soldiers came to break the legs of those who were crucified so they could no longer push themselves up to breathe. That hastened their death so they could be taken down and buried before the beginning of the actual day of the Passover, which was a special high Sabbath.)*
32. Then came the soldiers, and brake the legs of the first, and of the other which was crucified with Him.
33. But when they came to Jesus, and saw that He was dead already, they brake not His legs:
34. but one of the soldiers with a spear pierced His side, and forthwith came there out blood and water.

We've already discussed how we are redeemed by *the* ***blood*** that flowed from Jesus's side *when it was pierced* ***AFTER he died.*** However, we've also seen that although we needed to be redeemed from the bondage of sin that we inherited from Adam, we also received a spirit infected with death from Adam, *and being redeemed from the* ***bondage*** *of sin* ***doesn't solve our problem of death.*** That is why John also saw ***water*** flowing from Jesus's side along with the blood. The fact that *both* ***blood AND WATER*** flowed from the same wound and *remained* ***unmixed*** *so they could be distinguished one from the other* was unusual to the point of being a miracle. John was well aware of that, and went on to emphasize that it did indeed happen in just that way.

35. And he who has seen has testified, and his testimony is true; and he knows that he is telling the truth, so that you may believe.

God Himself made sure the blood and water didn't intermingle, so John could clearly distinguish that both came out together. He did that to give a visual manifestation of Jesus's Spirit coming out of His body ***AFTER*** He died. God gave that visual manifestation because Jesus had already revealed that water is one of the natural things of this world that God uses as an example of the Holy Spirit.

John 7: 37 - 39 *(NKJV)*
37. On the last day, that great day of the feast, Jesus stood and cried out, saying, ***"If anyone thirsts, let him come to Me and drink.***
38. ***"He who believes in Me, as the Scripture has said, out of his heart will flow rivers of living water."***
39. But this He spoke concerning the Spirit, ***whom those believing in Him would receive; for the Holy Spirit was not yet given, because Jesus was not yet glorified.***

There's no record in Scripture of God breathing life into Eve's body after He had formed it from Adam's rib. That was because Adam's rib was all God needed to make Eve. Eve received her life–giving spirit along with the rib God took from Adam's body. Since Adam had not yet sinned, his spirit wasn't yet infected by sin and death; therefore, when God created Eve, she was fully alive just as Adam was when God created him. Therefore, when God finished forming Eve from Adam's rib, He presented her to Adam.

Genesis 2: 22 - 24 *(KJV)*
22. And the rib, which the Lord God had taken from man, made He into a woman, and brought her unto the man.
23. And Adam said, ***"This is now bone of my bones and flesh of my flesh: she shall be called Woman, because she was taken out of Man."***
24. Therefore a man shall leave his father and mother and be joined to his wife, and they shall be one flesh.

Notice when God created the woman and presented her to Adam as his wife, He considered them to be ***"one flesh."*** *This is in agreement with what God said when He first spoke of His intention to make man, for Genesis 2: 27 says,* ***"So God created man in His own image, in the image of God created He him; MALE AND FEMALE created He them." It took BOTH the male and the female to make God's creation of MAN complete.*** Stated another way, ***God's creation of man was <u>not complete UNTIL</u> He created the woman, and joined her to Adam as his wife.*** *Therefore, according to the example of Adam and Eve,* ***<u>CHRIST will not be complete</u>*** *until God has completed the church as the* ***bride*** *of Christ, and unites Her with Christ at the end of the age in the Rapture.* Therefore, just as God completed the creation of Adam at the end of the sixth day, *in fulfillment of that example,* He will complete the Christ by uniting Jesus with His bride the Church at the end of six thousand years following that first week recorded in Genesis.

This brings us to Chapter 10, in which we consider the days of Noah as an example of when Jesus will come.

Chapter 10

The Days Of Noah

Introduction. Jesus closed His prophecy in Matthew 24 by talking about when He's going to return at the end of the age. We'll begin where He said *no one but His Father knew the day or hour of His return,* but we'll also look at what He said ***AFTER*** that.

Matthew 24: 33 - 39 *(UNASB)*
33. So you too, when you see all these things, recognize that He is near, right at the door.
34. Truly I say to you, this generation will not pass away until all these things take place.
35. Heaven and earth will pass away, but My words will not pass away.
36. But of the day and hour no one knows, not even the angels of heaven, nor the Son, but the Father alone.
37. ***For the coming of the Son of Man will be JUST LIKE the days of Noah.***
38. For as in those days before the flood, they were eating and drinking, marrying and giving in marriage, ***UNTIL THE DAY that Noah entered the ark,***
39. and they did not understand until the flood came and took them all away; so will the coming of the Son of Man be.

The most *obvious* way Jesus's return will be like the days of Noah, is that people in general will think things are normal and won't realize what is about to happen. Just like in the days of Noah, people will continue to go about their normal activities right up until Jesus comes and they will suddenly be destroyed. However, in this regard, there's something else that's ***very obvious*** about the days of Noah, ***but which is generally***

overlooked. *There was one group of people who were not going about the normal activities of life.* ***Noah and his family knew a drastic change was about to take place, <u>and they had been making very real preparations for that event for at least a hundred years.</u>*** Additionally, *they knew when the flood became imminent and they spent the last week filling the ark with animals and going in themselves. We know* ***that part of the example of the days of Noah also applies to believers,*** *because it's clearly spelled out for us in I Thessalonians.*

I Thessalonians 5: 1 - 9 *(NKJV)(This immediately follows the description of the Rapture given at the end of the previous chapter.)*
1. But concerning the time and the seasons, brethren, you have no need that I should write to you.
2. For you yourselves know perfectly that the day of the Lord so comes as a thief in the night.
3. For when they say, ***"Peace and safety!"*** then sudden destruction comes upon them, as labor pains upon a pregnant woman. And they shall not escape.

Just as in the days of Noah, ungodly people won't have any idea the coming of the Lord is near ***<u>until it actually takes place.</u>*** *But the next few verses are directed toward believers* ***and reveal that the Lord didn't mean for this <u>prophecy of IGNORANCE</u> to apply to God's children.***

4. ***<u>But YOU, brethren, are not in darkness,</u> so that this Day should overtake you as a thief.***
5. ***You are all sons of light and sons of the day. <u>WE ARE NOT OF THE NIGHT NOR OF DARKNESS.</u>***
6. ***<u>THEREFORE LET US NOT SLEEP, AS OTHERS DO, BUT LET US WATCH AND BE SOBER.</u>***
7. For those who sleep, sleep at night, and those who get drunk are drunk at night.
8. ***But let us who are of the day be sober, putting on the breastplate of faith and love, and as a helmet the hope of salvation.***
9. ***For God did not appoint us to wrath, but to obtain salvation through our Lord Jesus Christ,***
10. ***who died for us, that whether we wake or sleep, we should live together with Him.***

<u>WE</u> believers are exhorted to stay awake and watch, to be sober; that is, don't be in a ***spiritual stupor*** *so we're unaware of what's about to happen.*

Therefore, *if we* ***believers*** *are ignorant and don't know when the Lord is about to come for His Church,* ***it will only be <u>BECAUSE WE CHOOSE</u> to be that way; for God's Word provides everything we need, to KNOW when His coming is near.*** Keeping this in mind we'll look at ***"the days of Noah" as an example*** *of when Jesus will come for His Church,* ***because that's what Jesus said they are.***

<u>*When The Flood Began, as an Example.*</u>

Genesis 7: 1 - 5, & 10 - 11*(NKJV)*
1. Then the Lord said to Noah, ***"Come into the ark, you and all your household, because I have seen that you are righteous before Me in this generation.***
2. ***"You shall take with you seven each of every clean animal, a male and his female; two each of animals that are unclean, a male and his female;***
3. ***"also seven each of birds of the air, male and female, to keep the species alive on the face of the earth.***
4. ***"For after seven more days I will cause it to rain on the earth forty days and forty nights, and I will destroy from the face of the earth all living things that I have made."***
5. And Noah did according to all that the Lord commanded him.
10. And it came to pass after seven days that the waters of the flood were on the earth.
11. ***In the six hundredth year of Noah's life, in the second month, the seventeenth day of the month, <u>ON THAT DAY</u>*** all the fountains of the great deep were broken up, and the windows of heaven were opened.

The primary features of ***"the days of Noah"*** were the ***flood*** which was the manifestation of God's wrath against the wickedness of that day, and the ***ark*** by which Noah, his family, and the animals were all delivered. As we saw in Chapter 7 in the paragraph entitled, ***"The Testimony of the Twenty-four Elders,"*** the sounding of the seventh *(last)* trumpet is when Jesus will gather His church out of this world to be with Him in heaven. However, that's not all that will happen when the seventh trumpet is blown. Revelation 11: 18 tells us that when the seventh trumpet is blown the twenty-four elders will say the following: ***"And the nations were angry, and <u>THY WRATH IS COME.</u>"*** Therefore, when the seventh *(last)* trumpet is blown, that will be the day when the Rapture will take place, ***<u>AND</u> when God's <u>WRATH</u> will begin.*** Jesus also gave a second witness to that truth when He said, ***"... in those days before the flood, they were eating and drinking, marrying and giving in marriage, UNTIL THE DAY that Noah entered the ark, and they did not understand until the flood came and took them all away; SO WILL THE COMING OF THE SON OF MAN BE."****(Matthew 24: 38 - 39)***.** The flood of God's wrath began on the ***SAME DAY*** *that Noah went into the safety of the ark.* Therefore, since Jesus said ***"...the coming of the Son of Man will be JUST LIKE the days of Noah."****(Matthew 24: 37(UNASB)),* that tells us that ***God's wrath at the end of the age will begin ON THE SAME DAY as the Rapture.*** That means Jesus will come and take the church into the safety of heaven just in time to deliver us from the horror of God's wrath. That is in agreement with I Thessalonians 5: 9 *(above)* which says ***"...God did not appoint us to WRATH, but to obtain salvation through our Lord Jesus Christ."***

But this becomes even more exciting when we realize that Verse 11 above tells us that Noah went into the ark and the flood began ***ON THE SEVENTEENTH DAY OF THE SECOND MONTH, which according to the calendar of Noah's day, was the month of Heshvan,*** which falls in the October–November time–frame in our calendar. Therefore, in fulfillment of the example of the days of Noah, Jesus should come for the church on that same day *(the seventeenth of Heshvan)* at the end of the age. That means the only other thing we need to know ***is THE YEAR when it will take place.*** Although the year isn't as obvious as the month and day, when we look closely at the account of *the days of Noah,* we see that *God told us* ***Noah's age*** in a way that quite possibly reveals the year when Jesus will return for His church in fulfillment of the example of *the days of Noah.*

Noah's Age, as an Example.

Genesis 7: 1, 4, & 6 -11 *(NKJV)*
1. Then the Lord said to Noah, ***"Come into the ark, you and all your household, because I have seen that you are righteous before Me in this generation.***
4. ***"For after seven more days I will cause it to rain on the earth forty days and forty nights, and I will destroy from the face of the earth all living things that I have made.***
6. ***Noah was SIX HUNDRED YEARS OLD when the flood waters were ON the earth.***
7. So Noah, with his sons, his wife, and his sons' wives, went into the ark because of the waters of the flood.

8. Of clean animals, of animals that are unclean, of birds and of everything that creeps on the earth,
9. two by two they went into the ark to Noah, male and female, as God had commanded Noah.
10. And it came to pass ***after seven days*** that the waters of the flood were on the earth.
11. ***In the <u>SIX HUNDREDTH YEAR</u> of Noah's life, in the SECOND month, the seventeenth day of the month, <u>on that day</u>*** *all the fountains of the great deep were broken up, and the windows of heaven were opened.*

It seems unusual that within the space of six verses *(Verses 6 - 11), God called our attention* **two different times** *to how old Noah was at the time of the flood.* Since that information isn't a necessary part of the ***actual*** *story,* it must be that Noah's age is significant relative to ***<u>the days of Noah being God's EXAMPLE</u> of the coming of the Son of Man.*** Accordingly, the only logical significance Noah's age might have in that respect is for his age *in* ***hundreds*** *of years,* ***to represent*** the time *in* ***thousands*** *of years* that mankind will have been on the earth when the ***<u>EXAMPLE of the days of Noah</u>*** *is fulfilled at the end of the age.* Since Noah was six hundred years old when the flood was upon the earth, ***and <u>IF</u>*** *Noah's age was truly such an example,* it means God's wrath at the end of the age will come *when mankind has been on the earth* ***six thousand years from the time God created Adam.*** This agrees with the discussion of *the week of creation as an example* in Chapter 9.

Additionally, when God gave Noah's age in Verse 6 *(above) He used different wording from what He used in Verse 11 (above).* Although the difference is slight, it's significant. Verse 6 says, ***"Noah was six hundred years old when the flood-waters <u>WERE ON</u> the earth."*** But Verse 11 says ***the flood <u>BEGAN</u> "<u>in the six hundredth year of Noah's life.</u>"*** There's a difference between being ***six hundred years old,*** and being ***in the six hundredth year*** *of ones life.* ***To be six hundred years old*** means *six hundred years have actually passed during your life-time.* However, *to be* ***<u>IN the six hundredth year of your life</u>*** means ***you haven't yet actually had your six hundredth birthday.*** Based on this difference in wording, Verse 11 indicates the flood ***<u>BEGAN</u> during the year <u>BEFORE</u> Noah's six hundredth birthday.*** This is confirmed by Verse 6, which says ***"Noah was six hundred years old..."*** *(actually had his six hundredth birthday),* ***"...when*** *[or during the time]* ***the flood-waters were <u>ON</u> the earth."*** Therefore, according to the example of Noah's age, *God's wrath at the end of the age will be on the earth* ***in (or during) A. D. 2030,*** when mankind will have been on the earth for six thousand years. However, *God's wrath at the end of the age* will actually ***BEGIN during the preceding year of A. D. 2029.*** As previously discussed, Jesus will come for His church at the same time God's wrath ***BEGINS*** at the end of the age. Therefore, if we heed what Jesus said in Matthew 24: 37, and use *the days of Noah* as an example of the coming of the Son of Man, it tells us that Jesus should come for His church in the Rapture on the ***seventeenth day*** *of the Jewish month of Heshvan in A. D. 2029,* ***which will be on MONDAY, OCTOBER 25, 2029.***

Note:
In Chapter 7, the paragraph entitled "*When Will the Seventh Trumpet Sound?*" revealed that the seventh trumpet will sound when the two witnesses are caught up to heaven after having been slain and left lying in the streets of Jerusalem for three and a half (3½) days *(Ref: Revelation 11: 3 - 15).* Before being slain, they will minister for a thousand, two-hundred and sixty *(1260)* days. Therefore, if we back up from October 25, 2029 *(the date the seventh trumpet should sound as discussed above)* by the amount of a thousand, two-hundred and sixty *(1260)* days plus the added three and a half (3½) days, that should bring us very near the time when the two witnesses will begin their ministry. *That is important, for* ***if the two witnesses make their appearance on or about the date determined in this way, that will CONFIRM that October 25, 2029 is the time for the Lord's return almost three and a half years before He actually comes.*** Accordingly, when we work out the math, it gives us May 13, 2026 as the time when the two witnesses should begin their ministry. May 13, 2026 will be the same day as Iyar 29, 2026 in the Jewish calendar and that will be six days before the day of Pentecost following the first day of the first month in A. D. 2026, which is when God should reinstate Israel under the old covenant for the last four years of the seventieth week of Daniel *(Ref: Paragraph entitled "What Will Happen When the Last Trumpet Sounds?" in Chapter 7).* That day of Pentecost *(the Feast of Wave Loaves)* or very shortly thereafter, will be when Satan and his angels are cast out of heaven as discussed in Chapter 5. Therefore, *it would be most appropriate for God's two witnesses to begin their ministry six days earlier on May 13, 2026; for when Satan and his angels are cast down to the earth, Israel will desperately need the help of those two witnesses to stand in that time of unprecedented tribulation.*

Note: Although most believers are reluctant to even consider a specific date for the return of Jesus, as we continue to look at *the days of Noah* as an example *of the coming of the Son of Man,* we'll see that the dates God included for some of the rest of the days of Noah add considerably to the credibility of using the days of Noah as an example for when Jesus will return for His church.

<u>**_The End of The Flood, as an Example._**</u> Genesis 7: 11 &12 says the flood began when ***"..all the fountains of the great deep were broken up, and the windows of heaven were opened, and that the rain was on the earth forty days and forty nights."*** However, when the rain stopped after forty days and nights, that wasn't the end of the flood, for the waters had to decrease before the flood could actually be considered to have ended. Genesis 8 records when the flood actually ended.

Genesis 8: 1 - 4 *(NKJV)*
1. Then God remembered Noah, and every living thing, and all the animals that were with him in the ark. And God made a wind to pass over the earth, and the waters subsided.
2. The fountains of the deep and the windows of heaven were also stopped, and the rain from heaven was restrained.
3. And the waters receded continually from the earth. At the end of the hundred and fifty days the waters decreased.
4. Then the ark rested in ***the seventh month, the seventeenth day of the month,*** on the mountains of Ararat.

<u>***Note:***</u>
We need to remember that this date was also based on the calendar used in Noah's day. In Exodus 12: 2, God changed that old calendar such that its ***seventh*** month *(Abib)* became the ***first*** month of the year in the new calendar He ordained for Israel.

The flood couldn't be considered to have ended, until the waters receded enough for the ark to come to rest on the mountains of Ararat, and the day that took place was the ***seventeenth day of the seventh month.*** Therefore, for those on the ark, God's wrath of the flood came to its end on the seventeenth of Abib/Nisan. Since Jesus said the coming of the Son of Man would be like *the days of Noah,* this part of the example of *the days of Noah* indicates that God's wrath at the end of the age *will come to its end on the seventeenth of Abib/Nisan in the year after Jesus returns for His church.* However, we can't limit this example from *the days of Noah* <u>**ONLY**</u> ***to God's wrath that will be poured out at the end of the age, for the fullness of God's wrath has already been poured out once before.*** *When Jesus died almost* *two thousand years ago,* ***He had to experience the fullness of God's wrath against sin*** ***<u>BEFORE HE COULD BE RAISED FROM THE DEAD.</u>***

Jesus was crucified on the fourteenth day of Israel's first month *(Abib/ Nisan),* ***which was on a Wednesday.*** He was buried before sundown, because that was when Thursday the fifteenth of Abib began which was Passover, and a *special Sabbath (Ref: John 19: 31).* In Matthew 12: 40, Jesus said He had to remain dead and in the grave for three days and three nights. That means He was in the grave Thursday night and all day Thursday, Friday night and all day Friday, and Saturday night and all day Saturday. Therefore, God had finished pouring the fullness of His *wrath against sin* upon Jesus by the end of Saturday, ***which was the seventeenth day of Abib/Nisan.*** *That means God's wrath for the sin of the world came to its end* ***for Jesus,*** *at the end of the seventeenth day of Abib/Nisan in A. D. 30,* ***which was precisely the anniversary of the day when the ark came to rest on Mt Ararat, <u>MARKING THE END OF GOD'S WRATH OF THE FLOOD IN THE DAYS OF NOAH.</u>*** That shows how remarkably accurate Jesus was when He prophesied that the coming of the Son of Man will be ***"even as"*** *(or just like)* the days of Noah. *Since that prophecy was true with regard to* ***the end of God's wrath when it was poured out upon Jesus as our sin–bearer at the end of His first Advent, it stands to reason it will be just as true and accurate when God pours out His wrath upon the world at the end of the age when Jesus comes again. That means when God's wrath begins when Jesus comes in the Rapture of the Church on October 25, 2029 as discussed above, it should also come to its end on the seventeenth day of Abib/Nisan, which will be on Thursday, April 21, 2030.*** Next we'll look at how special it will be for Israel, when God's wrath comes to its end after the Second Coming of Jesus.

<u>The End of God's Wrath Against Israel At the End of the Age.</u> God prophesied through Isaiah that He would hide His face from Israel for a little moment, but quickly tempered that bad news with His promise of mercy and kindness.

Isaiah 54: 7 - 8 *(NKJV)*

7. ***"For a mere moment I have forsaken you, but with great mercies I will gather you.***

8. ***"With a little wrath I hid My face from you for a moment; but with everlasting kindness I will have mercy on you,"*** Says the Lord, your Redeemer.

In Romans, we see the most devastating effect of God's ***"little wrath,"*** was that He hid His face from Israel.

Romans 11: 8 - 9 *& 25 - 26(NKJV)*
8. Just as it is written: ***"God has given them a spirit of stupor, eyes that they should not see and ears that they should not hear, to this very day"***
9. And David says: ***"Let their table become a snare and a trap, a stumbling block and a recompense to them.***
10. ***"Let their eyes be darkened, so that they do not see, and bow down their back always."***

Israel refused to repent and obey God's word according to their covenant, and even continued their refusal in spite of the preaching of God's Own Son Jesus. Because of that, in His ***"little wrath,"*** God blinded Israel's eyes so they wouldn't be able to see *(recognize)* Jesus and believe, ***UNTIL they finally repent.*** However, later in Verses 25 & 26, we see that *just as in Isaiah above,* God promised to eventually remove Israel's blindness.

25. For I do not desire, brethren, that you should be ignorant of this mystery, lest you should be wise in your own opinion, that blindness in part has happened to Israel until the fullness of the Gentiles has come in. *(The fullness of the Gentiles will come in at the end of the church age.)*
26. And so all Israel will be saved, as it is written: ***"The Deliverer will come out of Zion, and He will turn away ungodliness from Jacob;***
27. ***"For this is My covenant with them, when I take away their sins."***

Because God will take away Israel's blindness at the end of the church age, a lot of things will happen when *their deliverer comes out of Zion (the Second Coming of Jesus). They will recognize that their Deliverer is actually Jesus whom their forefathers crucified. They also will realize that Jesus is their long-awaited Messiah, and that He died as God's perfect sacrifice for their sin, and hence is their Savior.* At that time, Jesus will lead Israel in observing the Passover. That ***future*** observance of Passover will fulfill the example of Joshua, when he led the children of Israel in observing the Passover after they crossed over Jordan, which is discussed in Chapter 11.

When Jesus leads Israel in observing that ***future*** Passover *after His Second Coming,* they will finally realize that He *died and* ***suffered God's wrath for THEIR sins,*** and then rose from the dead. Then, they will understand that the first Passover, *when Israel was delivered from bondage in Egypt,* was actually God's example of what He was going to do through the death of His Son Jesus *to deliver* ***THEM*** *(Israel) from* ***the bondage of SIN, AND FROM GOD'S WRATH because of that sin.*** That revelation for Israel will finally be complete on the seventeenth day of Abib/Nisan after that future Passover in A. D. 2030. That will be the anniversary of when Jesus fulfilled the example of the feast *of the Wave Sheaf* by presenting Himself before the Father to ensure that God's wrath had completely purged Him of the sin of the world *(including Israel)* that God had placed upon Him *(Ref: Isaiah 53: 6).*

At the end of the age, Israel will finally understand and accept that ***JESUS IS THEIR SUBSTITUTE*** *who has suffered all of God's wrath for their sins;* therefore, there will actually be a ***two-fold application*** by which the days of Noah exemplified the end of God's wrath against Israel. The ***FIRST*** *application* was when God's wrath *against Israel* ***came to its end FOR JESUS***, when God finished pouring all His wrath upon Him as Israel's substitute on the ***seventeenth day of (Abib/Nisan) in A. D. 30.*** Even though Jesus suffered God's wrath for Israel as their substitute when He was crucified, ***Israel hasn't yet understood that and by faith accepted it.*** Because of that, Israel has continued to experience God's ***"little wrath"*** according to Isaiah 54: 8 *(above).* That ***"little wrath"*** has continued throughout the Church age as God hid His face from Israel. But at the end of the age when Israel finally comes to repentance as God requires, He will remove their blindness and at the Second Coming, they will be able to recognize Jesus as their Messiah, Savior and Lord. ***At that time Israel will be saved*** *(Ref: Romans 11: 25 & 26).* Then, as Jesus leads them in observing that first Passover following the Second Coming, they will at last fully understand and accept *that Jesus indeed suffered God's wrath in their place for their sin.* With that understanding, they will finally come to the end of God's wrath against them because of their sin. They will come to that understanding when that first Passover following the Second Coming is over; for on the seventeenth day of Abib in A. D. 2030, they will observe the feast of first-fruits of the Wave Sheaf, and realize that feast is an example of the resurrected Jesus presenting Himself before the Father to confirm that His suffering had indeed purged away all the sins *(including Israel's sin)* that God had placed on Him according to Isaiah 53: 6.

Therefore, Jesus suffered Israel's wrath for sin in A. D. 30, ***AND*** Israel will finally understand and accept that truth two thousand years later in A. D. 2030. Nevertheless, the date for both of these events is the seventeenth day of Abib, which is the anniversary of when the ark came to rest on Mt Ararat, marking the end of God's wrath of the flood against the wickedness of that day. This is just another example of how remarkably accurate Jesus's prophecy was, when He said, ***"For the coming of the Son of Man will be just like the days of Noah."*** *(Matthew 24: 37, (UNASB)).* But the example of the days of Noah continued when Noah removed the ark's covering.

Removing The Ark's Covering, As An Example. Although the ark settled on Mt Ararat on the seventeenth day of the seventh month *(Abib, according to the calendar of Noah's day), that wasn't when Noah and his family got out of the ark.* ***In fact, Noah didn't even remove the covering and look outside when the ark came to rest on the mountain.***

Genesis 8: 13 *(NKJV)*
13. And it came to pass in the six hundred and first year, in the first month, the first day of the month, that the waters were dried up from the earth; ***and Noah removed the covering of the ark and LOOKED, and indeed the surface of the ground was dry.***

Noah waited almost five months after the ark landed before he removed the cover and looked outside. That was completely out of character with normal human behavior; therefore, *the only reason he would have waited that long,* ***was that God told him to.*** But ***why*** *did God have him wait so long?* There appear to be at least two reasons for that. ***FIRST,*** when Noah removed the cover and looked out at the earth that had been cleansed from wickedness, it marked a *new* ***beginning*** for everyone on the ark. Therefore, it was simple logic to have that take place on the first day of Tishri, ***because that was the first day of the new year according to the calendar of Noah's day.*** But might there be another reason that relates to Jesus's statement that, ***"as the days of Noah were, so shall also the coming of the Son of Man be"***? Keeping this in mind, consider the following.

We've already seen that several of the events in the days of Noah occurred on dates that coincided with the dates for feasts God ordained for Israel over eight centuries later. Is it possible God also used Noah's removal of the ark's cover as an example of one of the feasts He later ordained for Israel? If He did, it should be apparent in the date that Noah removed the cover. As we saw above, Noah removed the ark's cover on the first day of Tishri which was the beginning of the year according to the calendar of Noah's day. However, when God changed the calendar for Israel *(Ref: Exodus 12: 2),* Tishri became the seventh month, ***and the first day of Tishri was the day God ordained for the feast of Trumpets.***

Leviticus 23: 23 - 32
23. Then the Lord spoke to Moses, saying,
24. ***"Speak to the children of Israel, saying: 'In the seventh month, on the first day of the month, you shall have a sabbath-rest, a memorial of BLOWING OF TRUMPETS, a holy convocation.***
25. ***'You shall do no customary work on it; and you shall offer an offering made by fire to the Lord.'"***
26. And the Lord spoke to Moses saying;
27. ***"Also the tenth day of this seventh month shall be the Day of Atonement. It shall be a holy convocation for you; you shall afflict your souls and offer an offering made by fire unto the Lord."***

Over eight hundred years *after* Noah removed the cover from the ark, God established the feast of Trumpets for Israel, ***and ordained that it should be observed ON THE ANNIVERSARY of when Noah removed the cover from the ark.*** So, how was Noah's removing the ark's cover an example of the feast of Trumpets? The feast of trumpets was a preliminary feast observed to prepare Israel for the Day of Atonement. On the feast of trumpets, they blew trumpets to get the people's attention and remind them that they needed to afflict their souls to get ready for the Day of Atonement. As we continue in Leviticus 23, you'll see how serious it was for Israel to repent on the Day of Atonement, and you can understand why they needed to begin preparing their hearts for it ahead of time.

28. ***"And you shall do no work on that same day, for it is the Day of Atonement for you before the Lord your God.***
29. ***"For any person who is not afflicted in soul on that same day shall be cut off from his people.***
30. ***"And any person who does any work on that same day, that person I will destroy from among his people.***
31. ***"You shall do no manner of work; it shall be a statute forever throughout your generations in all your dwellings.***
32. ***"It shall be to you a sabbath of solemn rest, and you shall afflict your souls; on the ninth day of the month at evening, from evening to evening, you shall celebrate your sabbath.***

To ***"afflict"*** *or humble one's soul* is a term that expresses the self-denial and self-mortification related to fasting and prayer. In recognition of how serious this is to God, religious Jews recognize the entire ten-day period between the feast of Trumpets on the first day of Tishri, and the Day of Atonement on the tenth day of Tishri, as the ***Days of Awe.*** During those

Days of Awe, they emphasize morality, self–examination, spirituality, and holiness. Therefore, the feast of Trumpets on the first day of Tishri marks the beginning of an extended ten–day period characterized by repentance in preparation for the Day of Atonement. But how did the day when Noah removed the cover of the ark serve as an example of that period of repentance that would begin for Israel on the feast of Trumpets over eight hundred years later, when God gave them the law?

Genesis 8: 13 says that when Noah removed the covering of the ark, he also, ***"...looked, and indeed the surface of the ground was dry."*** The earth Noah saw on that day had been completely cleansed from the wickedness that had caused God to pour out His terrible wrath by such a devastating flood. For Noah and his family, that was a time of awe; *a time to reflect on the wickedness that had caused God to send the flood,* ***and to repent, resolving to keep their new earth from ever again becoming corrupt with such an abomination of wickedness.*** As such it was an example that was partly fulfilled each year after God ordained the feast of trumpets; for on that day Israel would begin reflecting on their sins of the past year and repent, in hope that God would accept their sacrifices on the forthcoming Day of Atonement and permit them to begin that new year with a fresh clean start.

However, even though that part of the example of the *days of Noah* has been partly fulfilled each year by the feast of Trumpet, when Jesus said, ***"For the coming of the Son of Man will be just like the days of Noah"*** *(Matthew 24: 37 (UNASB)), He revealed that the full and final fulfillment of the days of Noah will not take place* **UNTIL HE COMES AGAIN.** Therefore, at the end of the age, there must come a Day of Atonement when Jesus, as Israel's great High Priest, will go into the Holy of Holies in the temple in heaven and make the atonement for Israel that He hasn't yet been able to make, ***because Israel hasn't yet been in a position to do their part by afflicting their souls while He (Jesus), as their great High Priest, ministers for them before God. Israel won't be able to do that UNTIL they finally recognize and accept Jesus as their sacrifice, Savior and Lord and are saved.*** That isn't going to happen until the Second Coming when Jesus comes out of Zion as Israel's Deliverer *(Ref:"Romans 11: 25 - 26).* After the Second Coming, there's going to be a very special feast of Trumpets before the Day of Atonement. At that time, trumpets will sound in Israel calling the people to repentance in preparation for that very special Day of Atonement when Jesus will minister in the Holy of Holies in the temple in heaven, and make the atonement by which Israel will finally realize the fullness of God's forgiveness through the sacrifice of Jesus. That atonement by Jesus will prepare Israel to join with Him in His kingdom–reign here on earth, and they will be able to make that final new beginning with a clean slate. God gave a preview of that future feast of Trumpets through the prophet Joel.

Joel 2: 12 - 19 (NKJV)
12. ***"Now therefore,"*** says the Lord, ***"Turn to Me with all your heart, with fasting, with weeping and with mourning,"***
13. So, rend your heart, and not your garments; return to the Lord your God, for He is gracious and merciful, slow to anger, and of great kindness; and He relents from doing harm.
14. Who knows if He will turn and relent, and leave a blessing behind Him — a grain offering and a drink offering for the Lord your God?
15. Blow the trumpet in Zion, consecrate a fast, call a sacred assembly;
16. gather the people, sanctify the congregation, assemble the elders, gather the children and nursing babes; let the bridegroom go out from his chamber, and the bride from her dressing room.
17. Let the priests, who minister to the Lord, weep between the porch and the altar; let them say, ***"Spare Your people, O Lord, and do not give Your heritage to reproach, that the nations should rule over them. Why should they say among the peoples, 'Where is their God?'"***
18. Then the Lord will be zealous for His land, and pity His people.
19. The Lord will answer and say to His people, ***"Behold, I will send you grain and new wine and oil, and you will be satisfied by them; I will no longer make you a reproach among the nations."***

In Zechariah, God gave a preview of what the Day of Atonement will be like that will follow the feast of Trumpets prophesied by Joel above.

Zechariah 12: 10 - 14 *(NKJV)*
10. And I will pour upon the house of David, and upon the inhabitants of Jerusalem, the spirit of grace and of supplications: and they shall look upon Me whom they have pierced. Yes, they shall mourn for Him, as one mourns for his only son, and grieve for Him, as one grieves for his firstborn.
11. In that day shall there be a great mourning in Jerusalem, as the mourning of Hadad Rimmon in the valley of Megiddo.
12. And the land shall mourn, every family by itself: the family of the house of David by itself, and their wives by themselves; the family of the house of Nathan by itself, and their wives by themselves;
13. The family of the house of Levi by itself, and their wives by themselves; the family of the house of Shimei by itself, and their wives by themselves;

14. All the families that remain, every family by itself, and their wives by themselves.

At that future day the example of Noah removing the covering of the ark will finally be fulfilled. But there's one other part of the days of Noah that will still need to be fulfilled.

When Everyone Got Off the Ark, as an Example. The *last specific date* given for *the days of Noah* is when he and everybody else finally got out of the ark.

Genesis 8: 14 - 17 *(NKJV)*
14. And in the second month, on the twenty-seventh day of the month, the earth was dry.
15. Then God spoke to Noah, saying,
16. ***"Go out of the ark, you and your wife, and your sons and your sons' wives with you.***
17. ***"Bring out with you every living thing of all flesh that is with you: birds and cattle and every creeping thing that creeps on the earth, so that they may abound on the earth, and be fruitful and multiply on the earth.***

Although the waters were dried up on the first day of the first month *(Tishri)* when Noah removed the cover from the ark and looked out, *it was fifty-seven days later on the twenty-seventh day of the second month (Heshvan) before God told him to get out of the ark with his family and all the animals. Notice that Noah stayed in the ark* ***until GOD TOLD HIM TO GET OUT, so it wasn't Noah, but God who established all these dates for the days of Noah.*** *But since they had been in the ark for almost a full year,* ***WHY would God have them stay in it for fifty-seven more days AFTER the waters of the flood had dried up?*** There isn't any *apparent* **practical** *reason* for waiting almost two more months in the ark; therefore, it must have been because God was also making that event a part of the example of the days of Noah that will be fulfilled during the days of the coming of the Son of man as Jesus prophesied in Matthew 24: 37.

Therefore, since we've seen how several other events in the days of Noah occurred on the same dates as the feasts God established later for Israel, it's natural to expect that same pattern would apply to the date when God had everyone leave the ark and begin their new life on the earth. Following that reasoning, we would expect the next feast, *the Feast of Tabernacles,* would be the feast that would correspond to when everyone left the ark. That would seem to make sense, because the Feast of Tabernacles was when Israel commemorated the temporary huts they had lived in during their exodus from the land of Egypt, and also was a time to rejoice in their permanent homes in the Promised Land. What could be a better example of those at the end of the age, who will survive the final outpouring of God's wrath and return to the land of Israel to join Christ in His thousand–year reign here on earth? However, it doesn't work out that way; for they came out of the ark on the twenty-seventh day of Heshvan, but the Feast of Tabernacles begins on the fifteenth day of Tishri, *which is **fifty days before the date*** when everybody came out of the ark. In fact, none of the feasts God ordained for Israel correspond to the date when everyone came out of the ark. So why would God have varied from the pattern He established with the other major events of the days of Noah? It must be because Israel's return at the end of the age will be so completely different from their return following their Egyptian bondage. That difference will be so great that *God called attention to it* ***two separate times*** through the prophet Jeremiah.

Jeremiah 16: 14 - 15 *(NKJV)(This is talking about when God, at the end of the age, is going to bring Israel back to their homeland from their centuries–old diaspora among the nations of the world.)*
14. ***"Therefore behold, the days are coming,"*** says the Lord, ***"that it shall NO MORE BE SAID, 'The Lord lives who brought up the children of Israel from the land of Egypt,'***
15. ***"but, 'The Lord lives who brought up the children of Israel from the land of the north and from all the lands where He had driven them.' "For I will bring them back into their land which I gave to their fathers."***

Jeremiah 23: 5 - 8 *(NKJV)(This passage makes it even more obvious that the time spoken of will be after Jesus comes in His Second Coming.)*
5. ***"Behold, the days are coming,"*** says the Lord, ***"that I will raise unto David a Branch of righteousness; a King shall reign and prosper, and execute judgment and righteousness in the earth.***
6. ***"In His days Judah will be saved, and Israel will dwell safely; now this is His name by which He will be called: THE LORD OUR RIGHTEOUSNESS.***
7. ***"Therefore, behold, the days are coming,"*** says the Lord, ***"that THEY SHALL NO LONGER SAY, 'As the Lord lives who brought up the children of Israel from the land of Egypt,'***

8. ***"but, 'As the Lord lives who brought up and led the descendants of the house of Israel from the north country and from the countries where I had driven them.' And they shall dwell in their own land."***

As already discussed, at the end of the age Jesus Christ will make Israel's final atonement before God in the Holy of Holies in the temple of heaven. However, before He does that, God is going to bring ***ALL ISRAEL*** *(Ref: Ezekiel 39: 26 - 27)* back to their homeland in *a return that will be so much more glorious and complete than their exodus from Egypt,* ***that they apparently will no longer even commemorate that outdated exodus from Egypt.*** Instead they'll commemorate that final return that will take place after Christ's Second Coming. From the above passages in Jeremiah, it seems like the date for the Feast of Tabernacles may even be changed from the old date *(the fifteenth of Tishri),* when they commemorated their return from Egypt. If that should be the case; the new date for the Feast of Tabernacles would likely be the twenty-seventh day of Heshvan — *forty-three days later than the old date that was established to commemorate Israel's exodus from Egypt.* Such a change would be appropriate because the Feast of Tabernacles would then be observed on the anniversary of the date when everyone got off the ark after surviving the flood of God's wrath. That also means the Feast of Tabernacles would thereafter commemorate God's bringing Israel home again after the final completion of His wrath, and that would be a fitting end for the days of Noah *as an example of the coming of the Son of Man as Jesus prophesied in Matthew 24: 37.*

Chapter 11

Joshua As An Example Of Jesus

The Lord gave us the first hint He was using Joshua as an example of Jesus when He had Moses select the men to spy out the promised land. Of the twelve men Moses selected to spy out the land, ***he changed the name of only one of them.***

Numbers 13: 8 & 16 *(KJV)*
8. Of the tribe of Ephraim, Oshea the son of Nun.
16. These are the names of the men which Moses sent to spy out the land, *And Moses called Oshea the son of Nun,* ***Jehoshua.***

The name ***"Oshea"*** means ***"salvation,"*** but Moses changed Oshea's name to ***"Jehoshua,"*** which means ***"Jehovah is salvation."*** The shorter form of ***"Jehoshua"*** is ***"Joshua,"*** which is also pronounced ***"Yeshua"*** *(Ref: Nehemiah 8: 17), but in the Greek is translated as* ***"Jesus."*** So the Lord had Moses change Oshea's name to Joshua, ***because he was an example of Jesus.*** We see that example begin to be worked out when the spies returned and made their report to Moses and the Children of Israel.

Numbers 13: 27 - 33 & 14: 1 - 9 *(NKJV)(The ten fearful spies made their report first.)*
27. Then they told him, and said: ***"We went to the land where you sent us. It truly flows with milk and honey, and this is its fruit.***
28. ***"Nevertheless the people who dwell in the land are strong; the cities are fortified and very large; moreover we saw the descendants of Anak there.*** *(A reference to giants.)*

29. ***"The Amalekites dwell in the land of the south; the Hittites, the Jebusites, and Amorites dwell in the mountains; and the Canaanites dwell by the sea and along the banks of the Jordan."***
30. Then ***Caleb*** quieted the people before Moses, and said,***"Let us go up at once, and take possession, for we are well able to overcome it."***
31. But *the men who had gone up with him said,* ***"We are not able to go up against the people, for they are stronger than we."***
32. And they gave the children of Israel a bad report of the land which they had spied out, saying, ***"The land through which we have gone as spies is a land that devours its inhabitants, and all people whom we saw in it are men of great stature.***
33. ***"There we saw the giants; and we were like grasshoppers in our own sight, and so we were in their sight."***

Numbers 14: 1 - 9 *(NKJV)(The children of Israel chose to believe the evil report.)*
1. And all the congregation lifted up their voices and cried, and the people wept that night.
2. And all the children of Israel complained against Moses and against Aaron: and the whole congregation said to them, ***"If only we had died in the land of Egypt! Or if only we had died in this wilderness!***
3. ***"Why has the Lord brought us to this land to fall by the sword, that our wives and children should become victims? Would it not be better for us to return to Egypt?***
4. So they said to one another, ***"Let us select a leader and return to Egypt."***
5. Then Moses and Aaron fell on their faces before all the assembly of the congregation of the children of Israel.

This was Israel's first opportunity to enter the promised land, and as such, *it was an example of what would happen when they had their first opportunity to enter into the kingdom of heaven.* Caleb was the one who gave the first good report, because *he was an example of* ***John the Baptist***, who came before Jesus and urged Israel to ***"Repent, for the kingdom of heaven is at hand."*** If Israel had repented in response to John's preaching they would have been able to recognize Jesus as their Messiah, and He would have been able to lead them into the kingdom of heaven at that time. But they didn't repent, so God wouldn't let them recognize Jesus; therefore, He had to spend His earthly ministry preaching the same message of repentance that John had been preaching. We see this in Matthew 4: 17 which says, ***"From***

that time Jesus began to preach and to say, 'Repent, for the kingdom of heaven is at hand.'"

Likewise, ***in the example,*** if the children of Israel had accepted Caleb's good report, *Joshua would have replaced Moses as their leader* ***and he would have led them into the promised land at that point in time.*** However, because they rejected Caleb's good report, Joshua had to simply join with Caleb in urging the people to have faith and go take the land.

Numnbers 14: 6 - 10 *(NKJV)*

6. But ***Joshua the son of Nun***, and Caleb the son of Jephunneh, who were among those who had spied out the land, tore their clothes;

Notice that ***after*** *the people rejected Caleb,* ***JOSHUA took the lead.*** This too was part of the example, *for in its fulfillment,* after Israel rejected John's message and Jesus began preaching that same message of repentance, *the people began to follow Him rather than John the Baptist.* John explained that by saying, ***"He must increase, but I must decrease."*** *(John 3: 30).*

7. And they *(Joshua and Caleb)* spoke to all the congregation of the children of Israel, saying: ***"The land we passed through to spy out is an exceedingly good land.***

8. ***"If the Lord delights in us, then He will bring us into this land and give it us, a land which flows with milk and honey.***

9. ***"Only do not rebel against the Lord, nor fear the people of the land, for they are our bread; their protection has departed from them, and the Lord is with us. Do not fear them."***

Verse 10 shows that the children of Israel not only rejected Joshua's and Caleb's message, but rejected it ***VIOLENTLY.***

10. And all the congregation said to stone them *(Joshua and Caleb)* with stones. Now the glory of the Lord appeared in the tabernacle of the congregation, before all the children of Israel.

If God had not intervened, Israel would have stoned both Joshua and Caleb and killed them. That was part of the example showing that both John the Baptist and Jesus would be put to death because they persisted in preaching that Israel needed to repent. John the Baptist was slain by King Herod, who had him arrested and eventually slain for preaching that he, Herod was living in adultery with Herodias. Jesus was slain by the Romans *at the insistence of the religious leaders of Israel. But that wasn't the end of Joshua's example of Jesus.*

Joshua During the Forty Years in the Wilderness. Because the children of Israel rebelled against God, and refused to take the promised land, God made them wander in the wilderness for forty years *until everyone in that generation who was twenty years old or older should die with the exception of Joshua and Caleb (Ref: Numbers 14: 28 - 30).* The book of Numbers records the major events that happened to the children of Israel during those forty years; however, *their rejection of Joshua was so complete that his name isn't even mentioned in the Scripture record of those forty years.* He was mentioned in Numbers 14: 37 - 38, where Moses recorded how all the spies were slain by a plague with the exception of ***Joshua and Caleb.*** However, after that, he isn't mentioned again until the forty years were over and Moses identified Joshua and Caleb as the only ones of that faithless generation who were still alive *(Ref: Numbers 26: 63 - 65).* As far as the children of Israel were concerned, it was as though Joshua didn't exist during those forty years in the wilderness. But that also happened as a part of Joshua's example of Jesus.

Israel's forty years in the wilderness were an example of *the many centuries they would have to spend in exile among the Gentile nations for refusing to repent of their disobedience to God. It was because of their refusal to repent, that God would not permit them to recognize and accept Jesus so they could enter into the kingdom of heaven.* It's interesting that during most of the centuries Israel has been in exile among the Gentile nations, *they've been so adamantly opposed to Jesus* **that they've refused even to speak His name.** We see this in the experience of Dr. Jacob Gartenhaus, a converted Jew who spent many years faithfully presenting the Gospel to the Jewish people. He wrote a book entitled ***"Christ-Killers, Past and Present."*** In that book, he related some of his experiences as a child long before he came to faith in Jesus. He related one particular memory about how the Rabbis filled Jewish children with fear of Jesus to keep them from ever wanting anything to do with Him. Relating his own experience as a child, Dr. Gartenhaus wrote the following.

"(The author remembers how on Christmas day the Jewish 'Cheder'– ***elementary school*** **– children huddled together in the synagogue in fear and trembling, lest he – 'That Man' – might pounce upon us and snatch the souls of one or more of us.) He seldom was mentioned by the name**

'Jesus' – usually He was called 'That Man' or the 'Goysher god' (the god of the Gentiles), and other scurrilous designations." [1]

God intentionally had Joshua's name omitted from the Scriptural account of Israel's forty days in the wilderness, because that exemplified how most Jews would refuse even to speak Jesus's name during their centuries of exile scattered among the Gentile nations. Since the Jews' forty years in the wilderness was an example of their exile among the Gentile nations during the centuries between the first and second advents of Jesus, *one of the things foreshadowed by those forty years was* ***<u>how long</u> Israel's exile <u>WOULD LAST</u> before it ends when Jesus returns***. That is important *because those in Israel who survive the tribulation* will recognize Jesus and accept him when He returns, as prophesied in Romans.

Romans 11: 25 - 26 *(NKJV)*
25. For I do not desire, brethren, that you should be ignorant of this mystery, let you should be wise in your own opinion, that blindness in part has happened to Israel until the fullness of the Gentiles has come in.
26. And so all Israel will be saved, as it is written: ***"The Deliverer will come out of Zion*** *[heaven]*, ***and He will turn away ungodliness from Jacob;***
27 ***for this is My covenant with them, when I take away their sins."***

<u>Note:</u>
Even though the nation of Israel has been restored, that didn't change the fact that their exile among the nations is still an on-going reality. More Jews are still scattered among the Gentile nations of the world, than there are in the nation of Israel. However, God revealed through Ezekiel that when He brings their exile to its final end, <u>that condition will completely change.</u>

Ezekiel 39: 25 - 28 *(KJV)(This is what's going to happen after God, through the person of Jesus Christ, rises up to smite the nations of this world that come against Israel in the final battle of this age.)*
25. Therefore, thus saith the Lord God; ***"Now will I bring again the captivity of Jacob, and have mercy upon the whole house of Israel, and be jealous for My holy name;***
26. ***"After that they have born their shame, and all their trespasses whereby they have trespassed against Me, when they dwelt safely in their land, and none made them afraid.***
27. ***"When I have brought them again from the people, and gathered them out of their enemies' lands, and am sanctified in them in the sight of many nations.***

28. ***"Then shall they know that I am the Lord their God, which caused them to be led into captivity among the heathen; but I have gathered them unto their own land, AND HAVE LEFT NONE OF THEM ANY MORE THERE."***

The forty years Israel had to spend in the wilderness were based on the forty days the spies spent searching the Promised Land — a *year in the wilderness for each day the spies spent searching the Promised Land. Those forty years* ***began*** when Israel rejected Joshua's and Caleb's good report and attempted to kill them, and ***ended*** forty years later when Moses died, and Israel finally accepted Joshua as their leader to take them into the Promised Land. Since those forty years in the wilderness were God's example of the much longer time Israel was to be in exile among the nations of the world, it follows *that* ***each*** *of the forty years* in the wilderness represented a longer period of time, *forty of which will be the total time they must spend in exile among the nations of the world.* That brings us to the question — ***what is the period of time represented by each of those forty years in the wilderness?***

During the long centuries the Jews have been in exile among the nations, they have missed out on the deliverance from the bondage to sin ***that they would have had, if they had only repented so they could recognize and accept Jesus as their Savior and Lord.*** When we consider their exile from that perspective, it calls attention to an unusual provision of God's law for Israel that will help us to see what each of those forty years represents. God's law of the Sabbath provided the ***Jubilee*** as the means for people to be released from servitude in Israel.

The Jubilee As Part of God's Example. The law of the Sabbath required more than just resting on the seventh day of each week. Leviticus 25: 1 - 7 also required ***every seventh YEAR*** *to be observed as* a Sabbath. During the Sabbath years, Israel had to let their land lie at rest. They could neither plant nor harvest. In fact, they couldn't even harvest what came up on its own. Additionally, *every* ***FIFTIETH year*** was also to be observed as a Sabbath. That ***fiftieth-year-Sabbath*** was called the ***"Jubilee,"*** *and it required more* ***than just letting the land rest.***

Leviticus 25: 8 - 10, 39 - 42 & 54 - 55 (NKJV)
8. And you shall count seven Sabbaths of years for yourself, seven times seven years; and the time of the seven Sabbaths of years shall be to you forty-nine years.

9. Then you shall cause the trumpet of the Jubilee to sound on the tenth day of the seventh month; on the Day of Atonement you shall make the trumpet to sound throughout all your land.
10. And you shall consecrate the ***FIFTIETH year***, and proclaim ***liberty*** throughout all the land to all its inhabitants. It shall be a ***Jubilee*** for you; and each of you shall return to his possessions, and each of you shall return to his family.

In the year of Jubilee, all debts were cancelled in Israel. As we continue in this chapter, we'll see how far this cancellation of debts went, and also see ***WHY*** God included the Jubilee as a provision in the law.

39. And if one of your brethren who dwells by you becomes poor, and sells himself to you, you shall not compel him to serve as a slave.
40. As a hired servant and as a sojourner he shall be with thee, ***and shall serve you*** *UNTIL THE YEAR OF THE JUBILEE.*
41. And then shall he depart from you – he and his children with him – and shall return unto his own family. He shall return to the possession of his fathers.

In Israel, if a person became poor to the point of bankruptcy, he could sell himself into servitude to pay his debts, *and that servitude included his whole family.* If he should get enough money to purchase his freedom before the next year of Jubilee, he could go free. However, ***if he couldn't redeem himself, when the next year of Jubilee came, all his debts were canceled and he had to be set free from his servitude.*** This law is of particular interest to our study, because of the reason God gave it to Israel.

42. ***For they*** *(the children of Israel)* ***are My servants, whom I brought out of the land of Egypt; they shall not be sold as slaves.***
54. And if he is not redeemed in these years *(the years leading up to the next Jubilee),* then he shall be released in the year of Jubilee – he and his children with him.
55. For **the children of Israel are My servants** *whom I brought out of the land of Egypt: I am the Lord your God.*

God established the Jubilee *to prevent the children of Israel from keeping their servants* ***indefinitely.*** But in Verse 55, God said He established the Jubilee for Israel, ***because they were His servants***. When they were slaves in Egypt, they were helpless to gain their own freedom, ***so God obtained their freedom for them, and that indebted them to Him as His servants***.

However, their bondage in Egypt had only been an example of their real problem, which was their bondage to sin; for in John 8: 34, Jesus was talking directly to the Jews when He said, ***"Most assuredly, I say to YOU, 'whoever commits sin IS A SLAVE TO SIN.'"*** Therefore, when Jesus died for the sins of the world, Israel was specifically included, *and* ***HIS SACRIFICE PROVIDED THEM WITH GOD'S JUBILEE*** *— the time when they could be set free from their bondage to sin.* Therefore, when Jesus died for man's sin in A. D. 30, ***that was a year of spiritual Jubilee for Israel — the time when they could have been set free from their bondage to sin, IF ONLY THEY WOULD ACCEPT THEIR FREEDOM BY FAITH IN JESUS.*** But they didn't accept their freedom, and that meant they would have to wait for ***ANOTHER Jubilee*** before they would have another chance for freedom.

Accordingly, this is where the example of their forty years in the wilderness found its fulfillment. They had to spend one year in the wilderness for each day the spies had searched out the promised lane. In the fulfillment of that example, when Israel rejected ***the JUBILEE made available by Jesus's sacrifice for sin,*** *instead of having to wait for forty years as in their example in the wilderness,* ***they as a nation had to wait forty JUBILEES before they would have another chance to be set free from the bondage of sin.*** Since the Jubilee only came every fifty years, that meant Israel would have to wait forty times the fifty years between Jubilees, ***or two thousand (2000) years***, before they would have another chance to trust in Jesus Christ and be delivered from the bondage of sin. ***Accordingly, since their first Jubilee was in A. D. 30, their next Jubilee won't come until A. D. 2030.***

END NOTES

1. Dr. Jacob Gartenhause, *CHRIST-KILLERS Past and Present*, (Hebrew Christian Press, 1975), p 109

Chapter 12

Israel's Entry Into the Promised Land.

Introduction. Crossing over Jordan has long been recognized as an example of leaving this life and entering into new life with God. *That example* was the basis for the old hymn whose first verse is, ***"On Jordan's stormy banks I stand, and cast a wishful eye to Canaan's fair and happy land, where my possessions lie."*** When Moses died at the end of Israel's forty years in the wilderness, Joshua became Israel's new leader and he led them across Jordan into the promised land. That was an example of the end of the age when Jesus returns and Israel recognizes Him as their Messiah. At that time, *just as Joshua led Israel into the promised land,* ***Jesus will take them into His kingdom to reign with Him here on the earth.*** Therefore, when Joshua led Israel into the promised land, several things happened that were examples of what's going to happen at the end of this age. These examples began to unfold when Joshua established the arrangement of Israel's march for their crossing of the Jordan.

The Prescribed Order of The March. The way God had Joshua arrange Israel to cross Jordan was an example that revealed something important about when Jesus will come again.

Joshua 3: 1 - 4 *(KJV)*
1. And Joshua rose early in the morning; and they removed from Shittim, and came to Jordan, he and all the children of Israel, and lodged there before they passed over.
2. And it came to pass after three days, that the officers went through the host;

3. And they commanded the people, saying, When you see the ark of the covenant of the Lord your God, and the priests the Levites bearing it, then you shall remove from your place, and go after it.

The priests and Levites carried the ark of the covenant and led the children of Israel across the Jordan. The ark was a box about the size of a large trunk *and measured 45 in. by 27 in. by 27in.* It served as the support for the mercy seat in the Holy of Holies in the tabernacle, and later in the temple. As the support for the mercy seat, the ark was an example of Jesus, who made it possible for God to have mercy on all who repent and trust in Jesus as their sacrifice for sin. But the ark was more than just the box that supported the mercy seat. It was also the container for the following items.

- *The tables of stone with God's law inscribed on them, written by the finger of God.* The tables were an example of Jesus, who would come as the Word of God in human form *(Ref: John 1: 1 & 14).*
- *Aaron's rod that budded and bore fruit over night (Numbers 17: 1 - 10).* The rod was an example of Jesus as the resurrection and life – ***"...the first-fruits of them that slept."*** *(I Corinthians 15: 20).*
- *A portion of the manna.* The manna, *provided miraculously by God,* was an example of Jesus as the bread of life sent down from God *(Ref: John 6: 30 - 35).*

Each of these items played an important part as God took care of Israel in the wilderness. ***AND*** *as noted above*, each of them also gave an example of Jesus. So the ark of the covenant, *together with its contents,* provided a comprehensive example of Jesus as the Messiah, Savior and Lord. Because of that, in Verse 4 God required that the ark go before the children of Israel and lead the way as they crossed over Jordan.

4. Yet there shall be a space between you and it *(the ark of the covenant)*, about two thousand cubits by measure: come not near unto it, that ye may know the way by which ye must go: ***for ye have not passed this way heretofore.***

The ark had to lead the way because *the children of Israel had not yet been across Jordan to the promised land.* Having the ark lead the way was an example looking forward to when Jesus comes back. At that time He will lead Israel — *figuratively speaking — across the Jordan* into His kingdom. The promised land was an example of that kingdom which Israel will not enter before Jesus comes again; therefore, Jesus will lead the way because

He crossed over Jordan into the heavenly kingdom when He died, was resurrected, and ascended to be with the Father. That's what was exemplified by *the ark of the covenant* ***leading Israel across Jordan into the promised land.*** When we see that, we can understand the significance of the ***distance*** between Israel and the ark as it went before them. That order of march actually provided a prophecy of the following:

First: Having the children of Israel cross over Jordan behind the ark was a prophecy that Israel *will enter into the Messiah's kingdom,* **but not until *AFTER He first had come and both died and rose again, and had Himself entered into that heavenly kingdom.***

Second: By having Israel follow the ark by the prescribed distance of 2000 cubits was a prophecy that they would not cross over Jordan to join their Messiah *(Jesus)* in His kingdom, ***UNTIL after the time*** *had passed that was represented by that distance of 2000 cubits.* In light of the other prophecies and examples already discussed, it's apparent those 2000 cubits represented 2000 years. That's the time that would have to pass between when Jesus crossed over Jordan in death and resurrection in A. D. 30, and the time of His Second Coming when He will lead Israel over Jordan to be with Him in His kingdom. Those 2000 years will be complete in A. D. 2030. But Joshua's example of Jesus didn't end when he led the children of Israel across the Jordan.

Circumcision As An Example. The first thing Joshua did after he led the children of Israel over Jordan was circumcise them, *for none of them had been circumcised during the forty years they were in the wilderness.*

Joshua 5: 2 - 5 & 7 *(KJV)*

2. At that time the Lord said to Joshua, ***"Make flint knives for yourself, and circumcise the sons of Israel again the second time."***

3. So Joshua made flint knives for himself, and circumcised the sons of Israel at the hill of the foreskins.

4. And this is the reason why Joshua circumcised them: All the people who came out of Egypt who were males, all the men of war, had died in the wilderness on the way, after they had come out of Egypt.

5. For all the people who came out had been circumcised, but all the people born in the wilderness, on the way as they came out of Egypt, had not been circumcised.

7. Then Joshua circumcised their sons whom he raised up in their place, for they were uncircumcised, because they had not been circumcised on the way.

This raises an interesting question. Israel had continued the practice of circumcision during the four hundred years they were in Egypt; therefore, ***<u>why in the world</u> did they discontinue it for the forty years they were in the wilderness?*** The fact that Moses was leading them during those forty years even increases the puzzle, because of what he had experienced as he was returning to Egypt to lead the children of Israel out of bondage.

Exodus 4: 24 - 26 *(NKJV)(This took place while Moses and his family were on their way to Egypt.)*
24. And it came to pass on the way, at the encampment, that the Lord met him *(Moses),* and sought to kill him.
25. Then Zipporah took a sharp stone, and cut off the foreskin of her son, and cast it at Moses' feet, and said, ***"Surely you are a husband of blood to me."***
26. So He *(The Lord)* let him go. Then she said, ***"You are a husband of blood !"*** — *because of the circumcision.*

Moses and Zipporah had two sons, *but Moses had circumcised* ***<u>only one of them.</u>*** It's not hard to read between the lines and see that Zipporah was the reason he had failed to circumcise his second son. Zipporah was a Midianite and obviously wasn't familiar with the practice of circumcision, but she got a rude introduction to it when her ***first*** baby boy was eight days old and Moses proceeded to cut on him with a sharp piece of flint. You can imagine how she must have reacted when she saw her helpless little baby all bloody and screaming. She most likely told Moses he would never do that again. Numbers 12: 3 says, ***"Moses was very meek, above all the men which were upon the face of the earth."*** Therefore, because he was so meek, Moses didn't give her any argument and later when their second son was born, *rather than face Zipporah's wrath again,* Moses chose simply not to circumcise him. But God wasn't afraid of Zipporah, and because she was the source of the problem He gave her a choice — ***she herself could circumcise her son, <u>or she would lose her husband!</u>*** Therefore, she circumcised him, *but not without expressing her resentment to Moses.* What we need to see, is that circumcision was so important to God that He was willing to kill Moses rather than permit his family to continue breaking the covenant of circumcision. Circumcision was important to God ***because of what it <u>REPRESENTED.</u>*** Colossians tells us what circumcision represented.

Colossians 2: 9 - 12 *(NKJV)*
9. For in Him *(Jesus Christ)* dwells all the fullness of the Godhead bodily;

10. and you are complete in Him, who is the head of all principality and power.
11. ***In Him you were also circumcised with the circumcision made without hands, by putting off the body of the sins of the flesh, by the circumcision*** *(death and resurrection)* ***of Christ,***
12. ***buried with Him in baptism, in which you also were raised with Him through faith in the working of God, who raised Him from the dead.***

Under the old covenant, circumcision was God's natural ***example*** foreshadowing salvation — ***putting off the body of the sins of the flesh by faith in the death and resurrection of Jesus.*** Because circumcision was God's example of salvation; when He made the covenant of circumcision with Abraham, He decreed that if a Jew wasn't circumcised, he was to ***"be cut off from his people."*** God would no more permit an uncircumcised Jew to be one of His ***CHOSEN people,*** *than He will permit an unbeliever to be a part of His Church — the bride of Christ.* ***So why did Moses OF ALL PEOPLE, stop the children of Israel from continuing circumcision for the entire forty years he was leading them?*** In light of what he and Zipporah experienced, there can be only one answer: ***GOD HIMSELF TOLD HIM TO DO IT.*** And there's a very good reason why God had Moses stop circumcising Israel *during those particular forty years.* John 1: 17 says, ***"For the law was given by Moses, but grace and truth came by Jesus Christ."*** Because God *gave the law through Moses,* ***in Israel's eyes, Moses became an example of the law.*** But look at what Galatians 2: 16 says about the law. ***"Knowing that a man is not justified by the works of the law, but by the faith of Jesus Christ, even we have believed in Jesus Christ, that we might be justified by the faith of Christ, and not by the works of the law; FOR BY THE WORKS OF THE LAW SHALL NO FLESH BE JUSTIFIED."*** Since Moses represented the law ***to Israel,*** *God could not let Israel be circumcised* ***while they were under Moses's leadership.*** If Moses had continued to circumcise Israel while he was their leader, *that would have indicated salvation could come by the works of the law,* ***and that would have been a false testimony.*** Additionally, since Israel's forty years in the wilderness were an example of their exile among the Gentile nations during the Church age, *by stopping circumcision and having Moses continue as their leader during those forty years,* ***God revealed that Israel would remain UNDER THE LAW until the Second Coming of Christ at the end of the church age.***

However, when Moses died at the end of those forty years, Joshua replaced him as Israel's leader, *and Joshua was an example of Jesus.* Therefore, immediately after Joshua led Israel across Jordan into the promised land, ***he circumcised them.*** That was an example *of Israel being saved* when Jesus returns as their Deliverer at the end of the age, as prophesied in Romans 11: 26 which says, ***"And so all Israel shall be saved: as it is written, 'There shall come out of Sion the Deliverer, and shall turn away ungodliness from Jacob.'"*** When Joshua completed circumcising Israel, he immediately led them in observing the feast of Passover. By doing that, Joshua foreshadowed the fulfillment of another important example from the Old Testament.

Passover As An Example. The feast of Passover, *like the other feasts God required Israel to observe,* was an ordinance involving natural things, but it was an example of a greater spiritual reality that was going to take place as a part of God's plan of redemption. Therefore, it's generally accepted that ***when Jesus was crucified at Passover in A. D. 30,*** that fulfilled the example presented by that first Passover in Egypt. However, Jesus's crucifixion was actually ***only the BEGINNING*** of the fulfillment of the example of Passover. ***That's true because that first Passover in Egypt consisted of MUCH MORE than just KILLING the Passover Lamb.*** To keep God from killing their first-born, *every family had to do the things listed below **in addition** **to killing the Passover lamb.***

1. They had to splash the lamb's blood on the lintel and two side posts of the door to their house.
2. They had to eat the lambs' roasted flesh.
3. They had to eat it with unleavened bread and bitter herbs.

Each one** of these* things was a vital part of that original Passover, *for if a family killed their Passover lamb but neglected to do these other things, their first-born would have been slain along with the first-born of the Egyptians.* Therefore, these things also have to be satisfied in that greater Passover that's a part of God's plan of redemption, *and which is based on the death of Jesus as the Passover Lamb of God.* It's obvious that we in the church haven't done these *exact things* as a part of our fulfilling the example of that greater Passover in our salvation. However, *each of these things is an example that represents something everyone must do to be saved according to the example of that Passover long ago in Egypt.* So our next question is this: ***What do these three things from the original Passover in Egypt REPRESENT in that greater Passover in God's plan of redemption for us? When we consider what we must do to be saved, it isn't hard to see what these three things relate to as we partake in God's greater Passover based on the death of Jesus. Consider the following:

A. When Israel splashed the blood of the Passover lamb on the doorposts and lintel of the door to their houses, they were making a ***very public testimony that they were depending on that blood to protect them from God's wrath when He came to kill the first-born in Egypt.*** Therefore, for us to fulfill that example in God's greater Passover, we have to publically confess our faith in the blood Jesus shed in His death at Calvary; for I Peter 1: 18 - 19 says, ***"...you were not redeemed with corruptible things, like silver or gold, from your aimless conduct received by tradition from your fathers, but with the precious blood of Christ, as of a lamb without blemish and without spot."***

B. When Israel ate the flesh of their Passover lamb, that flesh became the sustenance for their natural lives. To fulfill that example in God's greater Passover, we have to believe God's word to the point that we commit ourselves ***to faith in Jesus <u>ALONE</u>,*** *for salvation and eternal life.* And we have to believe that to the same degree that we depend on food and drink to sustain our natural life. Jesus explained this in John 6: 54 which says, ***"Whoever eats My flesh and drinks My blood has eternal life, and I will raise him up at the last day."*** But Verse 63 goes on to clarify that by saying, ***"It is the Spirit who gives life; the flesh profits nothing. The <u>WORDS</u> that I speak to you are spirit, and they are life."***

C. Israel had to eat the Passover lamb *with unleavened bread and bitter herbs.* When Israel observed that first Passover, they hadn't yet received God's law, so they didn't know what constituted sin in their lives. Therefore, when God required them to eat *bread* **without <u>leaven</u>,** that simply indicated there was something in their lives that had to be removed before they could please Him. Now, we know that sin is what we must remove from our lives, *because we have the New Testament which reveals that* **leaven represents sin***.* Therefore, *since bread is the staff of life, to eat it without leaven,* means we must do everything we can to remove sin from our lives if we desire to please God. But Israel also had to eat bitter herbs with their Passover Lamb. The bitter herbs were a reminder to them of the bitterness of being in bondage to the Egyptians and being completely helpless to do anything about it. To fulfill the example of the bitter herbs in God's greater Passover, we must be bitter in our spirits because we're convicted of sin, and realize that we're helpless to do anything about it in our own strength. This bitterness *because of conviction to sin* is what leads us to true repentance.

So these things that were vital parts of Passover, are also examples to us showing how we have to respond to Jesus's death to receive God's deliverance from the bondage to Satan by sin and death. When we do these things we personally participate in God's greater Passover, and therefore, fulfill the example of that first Passover long ago in Egypt.

However, *even though we do these things and* ***personally*** *fulfill the example of that first Passover,* ***we need to remember that God ordained that first Passover <u>FOR ISRAEL</u>, to deliver them from their bondage in Egypt.*** Therefore, when Israel experienced Passover long ago in Egypt, in addition to delivering them from bondage, that Passover was also ***an example*** of how God was going to give His Son in a greater Passover ***to deliver <u>THEM</u> from bondage to Satan, sin and death.*** Accordingly, *Israel has indeed participated in God's greater Passover by having Jesus killed as the Passover Lamb of God;* ***<u>HOWEVER</u>, they did that in ignorance, and didn't do any of the other things discussed above that God requires before they can satisfy the ultimate fulfillment of Passover and be delivered from their bondage to Satan by sin and death.*** As a corporate people, Israel not only refused to accept Jesus as their greater Passover Lamb at His first advent in A. D. 30, *but have continued to reject Him throughout the centuries of the Church Age.* Nevertheless, there are prophecies in Scripture that give us God's assurance that Israel will eventually come to faith in Jesus, ***and that means they will accept Him as the Lamb of God who has taken away the sins of the world by His death.*** We'll look again at the prophecy in Romans 11, which we've already looked at several times in this study. Romans 11: 25 - 27 says, ***"For I do not desire, brethren, that you should be ignorant of this mystery, lest you should be wise in your own opinion, that blindness in part has happened to Israel until the fullness of the Gentiles has come in. <u>AND SO ALL ISRAEL WILL BE SAVED</u>, as it is written: 'The deliverer will come out of Zion, and He will turn away ungodliness from Jacob; for this is My covenant with them, when I take away their sins.'"*** Next, we'll look at what the children of Israel did after Joshua led them across the Jordan and circumcised them.

Joshua 5: 8 - 10 *(NKJV)*

8. So it was, when they had finished circumcising all the people, that they stayed in the camp till they were healed.

9. Then the Lord said to Joshua, ***"This day I have rolled away the reproach of Egypt from you."*** Therefore the name of the place is called Gilgal to this day.

10. ***Now the children of Israel camped in Gilgal, <u>AND KEPT THE PASSOVER ON THE FOURTEENTH DAY OF THE MONTH AT TWILIGHT</u> on the plains of Jericho.***

When Joshua circumcised all Israel, that was a prophetic example showing that Israel will be saved by belief in Jesus Christ when He returns at the Second Coming. Then, immediately after being circumcised, they observed Passover, which was another prophetic example. That example showed that when Israel sees and accepts Jesus at His Second Coming, *they will **then** fulfill those other parts of Passover — the actions that represented public confession of their faith, conviction and repentance of their sins, and their total commitment to belief and faith **in Jesus <u>ALONE</u>** for their forgiveness of sins and everlasting life.* By doing that, they will finally take part in God's greater Passover that's based on the death of Jesus, and will be delivered from their bondage to Satan by sin and death. But also ***when <u>ISRAEL</u> does that, they will finally give complete fulfillment to the example provided by that first Passover in Egypt.*** As already mentioned, the fulfillment of that example began in A. D. 30, when Israel in ignorance, killed Jesus as the Passover Lamb of God, but it will be two thousand years later before they will finally fulfill the other requirements established as a part of that Passover long ago in Egypt. When Israel is saved at the Second Coming of Jesus, they will finally fulfill the example of those other requirements exemplified in that Passover in Egypt. This brings us to one of the last things Jesus said relative to Passover, which had a distinct bearing on when Israel will finally fulfill the other requirements of that greater Passover that's based on the death of Jesus Himself.

<u>Jesus's Unusual Comment About Passover.</u> Jesus reminded His disciples that the Passover was drawing near when He would be slain.

Matthew 26: 2 *(KJV)*
2. Ye know that ***after two days*** *is the feast of the Passover,* ***and the Son of Man is betrayed to be crucified.***

Passover was one of the most revered of Israel's feast days, and Jerusalem was filled with people who had come for the sole purpose of celebrating Passover there. There wasn't a single Jew in Jerusalem who didn't already know *that Passover was just two days away.* Therefore, it may seem like it was completely unnecessary for Jesus to say Passover was only two days away. The point is this, for Jesus to say something that was *so unnecessary* was totally out of character for Him, for He never said or did anything that wasn't necessary. By His own confession, Jesus didn't do anything except what the Father led Him to do. In John 5: 19 He said, ***"Most assuredly, I say to you, the Son can do nothing of Himself, but what He sees the Father do; for whatsoever He does, the Son also does in like manner."*** We're always saying trivial and meaningless things, so it's easy to overlook it *when Jesus seemed to do the same thing.* But neither Jesus nor the Father were frivolous like we are. ***They said only what needed to be said.*** Therefore, what Jesus said about Passover may seem trivial and unnecessary, ***but it had more meaning than first meets the eye.***

It's obvious Jesus was reminding His disciples there were only two days until the Passover ***when He was going to be crucified.*** However, although ***ISRAEL*** *has observed Passover for literally thousands of years as a* ***memorial*** *of their deliverance by God from bondage in Egypt,* ***they have not yet observed it recognizing that Passover was God's EXAMPLE of how He is going to deliver them from bondage to Satan through the death of His Son Jesus.*** Therefore, the *example* God provided by Israel's historical Passover won't be completely fulfilled ***UNTIL*** *they observe their Passover with full awareness and acceptance of the fact* ***that it was actually God's example showing what He was going to do to deliver both ISRAEL AND THE GENTILES from their bondage to Satan, sin, and death.***

Accordingly, when Jesus said, ***"after two days is the feast of the Passover, and the Son of man is betrayed to be crucified,"*** He revealed that in two normal 24-hour days, it would be the Passover when He would be killed ***to fulfill the example of the Passover lambs being slain.*** However, He was also revealing that in two of God's *thousand-year days (Ref: II Peter 3: 8),* He would return and Israel will finally believe in Him and be saved, ***and THEN, Israel will finally observe a Passover with the full understanding that it has always been God's example of how He was going to redeem both Israel and the Gentiles from their bondage to Satan. When Israel does that, it will finally give full completion to the example of Passover in God's plan of salvation.*** So what Jesus said was actually a prophecy that God's greater Passover will be complete when He returns 2000 years after He was crucified in A. D. 30, which is simply another piece of evidence that He will return in A. D. 2030.

Chapter 13

Moses's Age

<u>**Introduction.**</u> Deuteronomy 34: 7 says, ***"And Moses was an hundred and twenty years old when he died; his eye was not dim, nor his natural force abated."*** If that was all Scripture said about Moses's age, there wouldn't be much significance associated with it; however, in the New Testament God provided several other facts about his age that change that situation.

Acts 7: 23 - 25, & 29 - 30 *(KJV)(This was a part of the sermon Stephen preached that got him stoned to death.)*
23. And when he *(Moses)* was full ***forty years*** *old,* it came into his heart to visit his brethren the children of Israel.
24. And seeing one of them suffer wrong, he defended him, and avenged him that was oppressed, and smote the Egyptian:
25. for ***he supposed his brethren would have understood how that God by his hand would deliver them:*** but they understood not.
29. Then fled Moses at this saying, and was a stranger in the land of Midian, where he begat two sons.
30. And *when* ***forty years*** *were expired* there appeared to him in the wilderness of mount Sinai an angel of the Lord in a flame of fire in a bush.

When Moses was forty years old, he didn't *just happen* to see the Egyptian oppressing one of the children of Israel. God had already shown Moses that He was going to use him to deliver the children of Israel from Egypt, so it didn't just come into Moses's heart to visit them. *God put that in Moses's heart, and* ***He did it because that was <u>one of the milestones</u> in the plans God had for Moses with regard to his age being one of God's examples.*** *Likewise* ***forty years later when Moses was eighty years old, that was <u>another</u>***

***milestone* in God's plan for him,** *so He got his attention by confronting him with the burning bush. Therefore,* **God presented Moses's age to us in three equal increments of *forty years* each,** *and He had to have a purpose in doing that.* Since He didn't include that information in the Old Testament as a part of the account of Moses leading Israel out of Egypt, it obviously isn't an important part of that actual story. But it must be important because God arranged Moses's life to make that breakdown of his age an example of the different stages of God's plan for man's redemption. That example becomes apparent when we see what the last forty years of Moses's life corresponded to in God's long-range plan for man's redemption. Moses died at the end of Israel's forty years in the wilderness.

Deuteronomy 34: 5 - 7 *(KJV)*
5. So Moses the servant of the Lord died there in the land of Moab, according to the word of the Lord.
6. And He buried him in the valley of Moab, over against Bethpeor: but no man knoweth of his sepulcher unto this day.
7. And Moses was an hundred and twenty years old when he died: his eye was not dim, nor his natural force abated.

When Moses died, Joshua took his place as Israel's leader, and led them across the Jordan into the promised land. That was God's example of the end of the age when Israel will finally repent and accept Jesus as their Messiah, Savior and Lord. Then, Jesus will accept Israel as His people to reign with Him in the kingdom of heaven, which will be His thousand-year reign here on the earth. *Therefore,* ***those forty years Israel had to wander in the wilderness represented this present church age.***

Israel had to wander in the wilderness as punishment for rebelling against God and refusing to go in and take the promised land when God gave them their first opportunity to do so. If they had obeyed God and taken the promised land at that first opportunity, Moses would have died then and Joshua would have become their leader. That is because the promised land was God's example of the kingdom of heaven that God offered to Israel when Jesus came in His first advent. When Israel refused to repent, and crucified Jesus instead, God punished them *as a corporate people* by blinding them so they couldn't see who Jesus actually is *(Ref: Romans 11: 7 - 10).* Consequently, the vast majority of Jews have not been open to the Gospel of salvation *and* ***have continued under the law*** *throughout the church age.* That happened in fulfillment of God's example of Moses, *who represented the law,* and had to continue as Israel's leader for the entire forty years of their wilderness wandering. Moses had to continue as Israel's leader because, when they refused to go in and take the promised land, *they also rejected Joshua, who otherwise would have replaced Moses and led them into the promised land at that time (their first opportunity).*

Since, *as we've already seen in the prophecies and examples discussed up to now,* the church age began in A. D. 30 *and very likely will end in A. D. 2030.* That means the total duration of the church age will also *very likely* be two thousand years. Therefore, Israel's forty years in the wilderness *(which were also the last forty years of Moses life)* represented the church age which constitutes the last two thousand years of God's plan for Man's redemption. That's important, because God's plan for man's redemption is divided into three separate and *basically equal* periods of time. Beginning with the last of those three periods and moving back in time, they are as follows:

- ***The church age,*** which is this present period of time during which God is offering the Gospel of salvation to the Gentiles, and during which Israel has been blinded to the Gospel and has continued under the law. They have also been *enemies of the church,* for Romans 11: 28 says, ***"As concerning the gospel, they*** *(Israel)* ***are enemies for your*** *(the Gentile believers)* ***sakes: but as touching the election, they are beloved for the fathers' sakes."***

Note:

Since the last forty years of Moses's life represented the two thousand years of the church age, it follows that the other two forty–year periods of his life likewise represented two other periods of time in God's overall plan for man's redemption, ***AND*** *that* ***each*** *of those other two periods of time* ***were also two thousand years in length.***

- ***The age from the patriarchs until Christ.*** That was the period of time beginning when God chose ***"the fathers"*** *(Abraham, Isaac and Jacob),* and lasted until Israel rejected their Messiah Jesus in A. D. 30. During that time, God's covenant of blessing was with Israel *and excluded the Gentiles;* for writing to the Gentile believers at Ephesus about those Old Testament times, Paul said, ***"Therefore remember that you, once Gentiles in the flesh – who are called Uncircumcision by what is called the Circumcision made in the flesh by hands – that at that time you were without Christ*** *(the Messiah),* ***being aliens from the commonwealth of Israel and strangers from the covenants of promise, having no hope and without God in the world. But now in Christ***

Jesus you who once were far off have been brought near by the blood of Christ." *(Ephesians 2: 11 - 13)(NKJV).*

- ***The age from Adam until the patriarchs (Abraham, Isaac and Jacob).*** That was the period of time during which God made no distinction among the different groups of people who populated the earth. All had the same opportunity to know and obey God, ***and with the exception of Noah, all of them rejected God's way and chose the way of wickedness.***

When that first two-thousand-years proved that man could not live righteously based on his own conscience and choice, God chose Abram and worked diligently with his descendants to give them the opportunity to obey His laws and show the Gentile–world how to live acceptably to God, but after two thousand years Israel totally failed to obey God's law and even crucified God's Son who came and demonstrated what it meant to live in obedience to God's law. When Israel failed, God turned to the Gentiles and gave them the chance to give the world an example of righteousness. Although God will separate out that special group *(the church)* who are repenting and accepting God's righteousness by faith in God's sacrifice of His Son Jesus Christ, *the vast majority of the Gentile world will again reject God's way of righteousness and choose wickedness instead.* Through the Apostle Paul, God gave a summary of how He has used first the Jews and later, during this present church age, the Gentiles, and in that way has been completely fair to both.

Romans 11: 30 - 32 *(NKJV) (Addressed to the predominantly Gentile church.)*
30. And as you *(Gentile believers)* were once disobedient to God, yet have now obtained mercy through their *(Israel's)* disobedience *(Ref: Romans 11: 11)*,
31. even so these *(Israel)* also have now been disobedient, that through the mercy shown you they may obtain mercy.
32. For God has committed them all *(Jews and Gentiles)* to disobedience, that He might have mercy on all.

Accordingly, at the end of the church age, when both Jews and Gentiles will have had their own separate chances to live righteously before God and will have failed, then Jesus will return and purge the world of all who have willfully rejected His righteousness, and will establish His kingdom in which He will enforce the righteousness of God with a rod of iron *(Ref: Psalms 2: 7 - 12).* At the end of the thousand years of His earthly reign, Jesus Christ will utterly destroy Satan and all those who have chosen to follow him in spite of experiencing the bliss of the perfect righteousness of God during the kingdom reign of Jesus Christ. Then with every enemy of God permanently disposed of, Jesus will present the perfectly cleansed and righteous Kingdom of God to the Father who finally, *once again and for all time to come,* will be Lord of All *(Ref: I Corinthians 15: 24 - 28).*

Therefore, it's apparent that God used Moses's age as an example of the total period of time *(six thousand years)* during which He will complete His plan for man's redemption. Accordingly, He called that example to our attention by the unusual way He divided Moses's final age of a hundred and twenty *(120)* years into three equal periods of forty years each, with each of those three forty--year periods being an example of a separate two thousand year period in His plan for man's redemption.

Chapter 14

The Stone Tables of God's Word

Introduction. God inspired John to begin his Gospel by introducing Jesus in an unusual way. He said, ***"In the beginning was the Word, and the Word was with God, and the Word was God."****(John 1: 1).* Then in verse 14 he said, ***"And THE WORD became flesh and dwelt among us, and we beheld His glory, the glory as of the only begotten of the Father, full of grace and truth."*** Later, when He was giving John the Revelation, He showed him a vision of Jesus at the end of the age when He will return at the Second Coming, and revealed that Jesus will still have that ***UNIQUE name.***

Revelation 19: 11 - 13 *(NKJV)*
11. Now I saw heaven opened, and behold, a white horse. And He who sat on him was called Faithful and True, and in righteousness He judges and makes war.
12. His eyes were like a flame of fire, and on His head were many crowns. ***He had a name written that no one knew except Himself.***
13. He was clothed with a robe dipped in blood, ***and His name is called THE WORD OF GOD.***

Verse 12 says ***"He had a name written that no one knew except Himself."*** However, that obviously doesn't mean no else can ***know what that name IS,*** for Verse 13 says, ***"and His name is called THE WORD OF GOD."*** Therefore, the fact that *no one except Jesus* ***knew*** *that name* must mean no one other than Jesus ***knew it BY EXPERIENCE.*** Jesus's name is **"The Word of God,"** *because that is what* **He actually is.** *Jesus is the complete and perfect expression of God, and no one else either is, or ever will* ***BE the kind of person defined by that name — "The Word Of God."*** *Because of that,* the first set of stone tables was one of the most fitting examples of Jesus in the Old Testament.

The First Set Of Stone Tables As An Example Of Jesus. To see how the first set of stone tables was an example of Jesus, we'll begin by looking at how God prepared them before He gave them to Moses.

Exodus 24: 12 & 18 *(KJV)*
12. And the Lord said unto Moses, ***"Come up to Me on the mount, and be there: and I will give thee tables of stone, and a law, and commandments which I have written; that thou mayest teach them."***
18. And Moses went into the midst of the cloud, and gat him up into the mount: *And Moses was in the mountain* ***forty days and forty nights.***

Exodus 32: 15 - 16 *(KJV)*
15. And Moses turned, and went down from the mountain, and the ***TWO*** *tables* of the testimony were in his hand. ***The tables were written on both their sides; on the one side and on the other were they written.***
16. Now ***the tables were the work of God,*** **AND** ***the writing was the writing of God, graven on*** *(or into)* ***the tables.***

Those stone tables were the work of God. ***No MAN had anything to do with them.*** Therefore, ***they were God's example of the VIRGIN birth of Jesus,*** conceived in Mary when the Holy Ghost came upon her and the power of God overshadowed her *(Ref: Luke 1: 34 - 35 & Isaiah 7: 14).* But this still leaves us with a question, for there were ***TWO*** tables of stone, *yet Jesus was only* ***one*** *person.* Those ***TWO tables were an example of the DUAL nature of Jesus.*** He was ***the MAN*** who came into being when He was conceived in Mary by the Holy Spirit of God; yet at the same time, He was also ***the Second Person of the Trinity of God,*** who had existed in perfect unity with God from eternity past. Therefore, there had to be ***two*** tables of stone to give an accurate example of His being.

An Example of Jesus As The Word Made Flesh. Not only were the stone tables *the* ***work*** *of God,* ***they were also the WORD of God. God engraved His law and commandments in them both on the front and the back*** *(Ref: Exodus 32: 15 - 16 above).* So the two tables of stone were filled with God's word.

Exodus 31: 18 *(KJV)*
18. And He *(God)* gave unto Moses, when He had made an end of communing with him upon mount Sinai, two tables of testimony, tables of stone ***written with the finger of God.***

Since the tables of stone contained the ***word of God***, ***they were an example of Jesus, in whom God's Word became flesh.***

John 1: 1 - 2,& 14 *(NKJV)*
1. In the beginning was the Word, and the Word was with God, and the Word was God.
2. He was in the beginning with God.
14. And ***the Word became flesh*** and dwelt among us, and we beheld His glory, the glory as of the only begotten of the Father, full of grace and truth.

As the *Word-become-flesh*, Jesus was the perfect expression of God in everything He did. He lived in unwavering obedience to God – ***totally without sin***. That doesn't mean Jesus was born with God's Word ***committed to MEMORY.*** That wasn't true of Jesus any more than it was true of any other child who has ever been born. Jesus was born as a baby in every sense of the word; for Luke 2: 52 says, ***"And Jesus increased in wisdom and stature, and in favor with God and men."*** However, as *the Word of God made flesh*, Jesus was the incarnation of the Second Person of the Trinity of God. Therefore, ***by His DIVINE nature,*** Jesus was always aware of what was pleasing or displeasing to God. Also, since He was born of a virgin, Jesus ***DIDN'T have*** what we call the ***"sin nature,"*** *that afflicts all other men because of Adam's sin. Since Jesus was the Son of God,* ***He was born with the spiritual inclination to follow His Divine nature, instead of having the irresistible compulsion to satisfy His natural human nature, like all other men.*** Jesus told us what motivated Him in everything He did.

John 8: 28 - 29 *(NKJV)*
28. Then Jesus said to them, ***"When you lift up the Son of Man, then you will know that I am He, and that I do nothing of Myself; but as My Father taught Me, I speak these things.***
29. ***"And He who sent Me is with Me. The Father has not left Me alone, for I always do those things that please Him."***

Because God made the stone tables as an example of Jesus, He didn't simply ***write*** His law and commandments ***ON*** them. Instead, He ***ENGRAVED*** His law and commandments *into them, making His word an* ***INTEGRAL PART OF THOSE TWO TABLES.*** That made them an accurate example of Jesus who didn't simply ***LEARN*** *God's* law and commandments, but had them in Himself as ***A PART OF HIS VERY NATURE.*** That doesn't mean Jesus couldn't be tempted to please His natural human desires; for Hebrews 4: 15 reveals that He "***...was in all points tempted as we are, yet without sin.***" Jesus had the same human desires we have; however, because of His Divine nature as the Son of God, *He always knew what His Father would have Him do.* Therefore, anytime He had a desire different from what He knew His Father wanted Him to do, He knew that desire came from His ***human*** nature and He chose to reject it, *because He had an* **over–riding** *desire to please His Father.* Therefore, Jesus lived His entire life in perfect obedience to His Father's will. In that way, He perfectly fulfilled the example of the first set of stone tables, which had God's word *engraved into* them as an integral part of the stones themselves. But in order for those first stone tables to be a complete example of Jesus, they also had to foreshadow His death.

An Example Of Jesus' Death. When Moses came down the mountain carrying the tables of the law, he heard the sound of revelry in the camp.

Exodus 32: 17 - 19 *(KJV)*
17. And when Joshua heard the noise of the people as they shouted, he said unto Moses, ***"There is a noise of war in the camp."***
18. And he said, ***"It is not the voice of the shout of victory, nor the noise of the cry of defeat, but the sound of singing I hear."***
19. And it came to pass, as soon as he came near the camp, that he saw the calf, and the dancing. So Moses' anger became hot, *and he cast the tables out of his hands,* ***and broke them at the foot of the mountain.***

Moses didn't just drop them; ***HE THREW THEM DOWN!*** Can you imagine having stone tables filled with God's law and commandments engraved by the finger of God, *and* ***throwing them down*** *and breaking them to pieces?* ***That was what Moses did!*** When He saw the children of Israel dancing and singing around the golden calf, he became so angry he threw the tables down to the ground and broke them to pieces. Moses didn't realize it, but he did that according to God's will. *When Moses threw the stone tables down and broke them,* ***that was an example of God sending His Son to the earth and having Him die,*** *because of His wrath against man's sin.* That made the stone tables complete as God's example of Jesus Christ. With the stone tables broken, it would appear their example of Jesus was complete. But there's still one more aspect of their being an example of Jesus that we haven't considered. ***God also revealed HOW LONG IT TOOK before God gave the stone tables to Israel by Moses.***

Exodus 24: 12 & 18 *(KJV)*
12. And the Lord said unto Moses, ***"Come up to Me on the mount, and be there: and I will give thee tables of stone, and a law, and commandments which I have written; that thou mayest teach them."***
18. And Moses went into the midst of the cloud, and gat him up into the mount: *And Moses was in the mountain* ***forty days and forty nights.***

These two verses raise a question. ***Why did it take so long to give those tables of stone to Moses?*** He didn't use that time to write His word on the stones, *because verse 12 says* ***He had already written them before He told Moses to come up to get them.*** The fact that God had already written them relates to the fact that His Word existed with Him from the beginning *(Ref: John 1: 1 - 2).*
It took forty days from the time God called Moses to come up for the stone tables, until He actually gave them to Moses, *because those forty days were* ***an example*** *of how long it would take to send Jesus to earth* ***from the time God first promised to send Him until He actually did it.*** If that was actually God's purpose for those forty days, ***then what did they relate to in His plan for bringing forth His Son here on earth?***

God first mentioned the coming of Christ in Genesis 3: 15 when He spoke to Satan saying, ***"And I will put enmity between you and the woman, and between your seed and her seed; He shall bruise your head, and you shall bruise His heel."*** This was a general statement that had no bearing on *when* Christ would actually come. It only established that *He would have a very small beginning like unto a* ***SEED.*** Centuries passed before God mentioned that ***SEED*** again in Scripture. He did that when He called Abram and told him to separate himself from his family and homeland, ***and promised him a special SEED.***

Genesis 12: 1 - 3 & 7 *(KJV)*
1. Now the Lord had said unto Abram, ***"Get thee out of thy country, and from thy kindred, and from they father's house, unto a land that I will show thee:***
2. ***"And I will make of thee a great nation and I will bless thee, and make thy name great; and thou shalt be a blessing:***

3. ***"And I will bless them that bless thee, and curse him that curseth thee: and in thee shall all the families of the earth be blessed."***
7. And the Lord appeared unto Abram, and said, ***"Unto thy <u>SEED</u> will I give this land:"*** and there builded he an altar unto the Lord, who appeared unto him.

God revealed the full meaning of this in Paul's letter to the Galatian Church.

Galatians 3: 16
16. Now to *Abraham* ***and his <u>SEED</u>*** were the promises made. He saith not, And to seeds, as of many; but as of one, ***"And to thy <u>SEED,</u>" <u>WHICH IS CHRIST.</u>***

God actually began working out His plan to send Jesus Christ when He confirmed His call to Abram by the miraculous birth of Isaac as a living example of the Christ who was to come. Isaac was born about 2066 B. C. according to the notes in the ESV Study Bible published by Crossway Bibles in Wheaton, Illinois. *(Note: The exact date of Isaac's birth isn't known, because the record of time given in the Old Testament isn't precise enough to accurately establish that date. However, the Old Testament record of time is accurate enough for us to know that Isaac was born about two thousand years before Christ.)* Therefore, the forty days Moses spent on the mountain waiting for the stone tables represented the roughly two thousand years from Isaac until Jesus came and was crucified, fulfilling the example of Isaac. Accordingly, Jesus's death at Calvary in A. D. 30 fulfilled the example of Moses throwing the stone tables down and breaking them when he came down from the mountain after the forty days were over.

However, it's evident God's ***entire plan*** wasn't completed by Jesus's death and resurrection; for after Moses broke the first tables of stone, God provided a ***<u>SECOND</u> set of stone tables*** to replace those that were broken.

<u>The Second Set Of Stone Tables.</u> Since the first set of stone tables were an example of Jesus Christ, ***<u>what did the second set exemplify?</u>*** The second set *was* ***<u>ALMOST</u> the same*** *as the first set.* But there was one important difference.

Exodus 34; 1, 4 & 28 *(KJV)*
1. And the Lord said unto Moses, ***"Hew thee two tables of stone like the first: and I will write upon these tables the words that were in the first tables, which thou brakest.***
4. And he *(Moses)* hewed two tables of stone like unto the first; and Moses rose up early in the morning, and went up unto mount Sinai, as the Lord had commanded him, and took in his hand the two tables of stone.
28. And he *(Moses)* was with the Lord forty days and forty nights; he did neither eat bread, nor drink water. And He *(the Lord)* wrote upon the tables the word of the covenant, the ten commandments.

The two sets of stone tables were just alike, *except that the stones for the first set were the work of God,* ***but He had Moses hew the stones for the second set.*** That was a significant difference because of what the two sets of stone tables exemplified. As already mentioned, the first set of tables was an example of Jesus since God Himself had hewn the stones for that set making them *an example of Jesus's* ***virgin birth.*** In contrast, God had Moses hew the stones for the second set. Therefore, ***as the work of man,*** the second set of stone tables *were an example of* ***natural people conceived by earthly fathers.*** Nevertheless, the second set was like the first in that *they also had the* ***words of God <u>ENGRAVED</u> into them by God Himself.*** Therefore, even though the second set represented natural people, they must be an example of very unusual people who will have God's words in their hearts similar to Jesus Himself. So who might those unusual people be? The answer is in Jeremiah.

Jeremiah 31: 31 - 34 *(NKJV)*
31. ***" Behold, the days are coming,"*** says the Lord, ***"when I will make a new covenant with the house of Israel, and with the house of Judah —***
32. ***"not according to the covenant that I made with their fathers in the day that I took them by the hand to lead them out of the land of Egypt, My covenant which they broke, though I was a husband to them,"*** says the Lord.
33. ***"But this is the covenant that I will make with the house of Israel after those days,"*** says the Lord: ***<u>"I will put My law in their minds, and write it on their hearts;</u> and I will be their God, and they shall be My People.***
34. ***"No more shall every man teach his neighbor, and every man his brother, saying 'Know the Lord,' for they all shall know Me, from the least of them to the greatest of them,"*** says the Lord. ***"For I will forgive their iniquity, and their sin I will remember no more."***

First of all, *we need to realize* **God meant exactly what He said.** He has not made this new covenant with us in the Church. If He had, we wouldn't be teaching one another His word *like we've been doing in the Church ever since it began almost two thousand years ago.* He will make His new covenant with the Jews to replace their first covenant when the time finally comes to do away with that old covenant. Jesus has come and paid the price necessary to make the new covenant available to the Jews; however, they haven't yet satisfied God's requirements for them under the old covenant, and until they do that they won't be able to recognize and accept Jesus as their Savior and Messiah. Only when Israel recognizes, acknowledges and repents of their disobedience to the law under the old covenant, will they understand how desperately they need the forgiveness available only through faith in the sacrifice of God's Son, Jesus Christ. Only when they do that, will God make His new covenant with them. Verse 31 above is God's promise to Israel that the day will come when they will finally satisfy His requirements and be forgiven and saved. That is when He will finally make His new covenant with them. In Romans, God confirmed that promise and also told when it will be fulfilled.

Romans 11: 25 - 27 *(NKJV)*
25. For I do not desire, brethren, that you should be ignorant of this mystery, lest you should be wise in your own opinion, that blindness in part has happened to Israel ***until the fullness of the Gentiles has come in.***
26 And so all Israel will be saved, as it is written, ***"The Deliverer will come out of Zion, and He will turn away ungodliness from Jacob;***
27. ***"<u>FOR THIS IS MY COVENANT WITH THEM, WHEN I TAKE AWAY THEIR SINS.</u>"***

"The fullness of the Gentiles" is a reference to the end of the Church age when Jesus will come and take the believers out of the world in the Rapture. At that time, Israel will finally realize they haven't obeyed God's law according to their covenant and they will repent. Then, at the Second Coming, when the Deliverer comes out of Zion, God will take away Israel's blindness and they will see Jesus, recognize Him as their Savior, Messiah, and Lord, and they will believe and be saved. Their Messiah *(Jesus)* will then take away both their sins ***<u>AND</u>*** their ***<u>UNGODLINESS,</u> according to the <u>NEW COVENANT</u>*** *of Jeremiah 31 above.* At that time, God will ***miraculously <u>TRANSFORM</u> Israel*** into a people like this world has never seen, ***except in the person of Jesus Christ.*** For in His own words, God said, ***"I will put My law in their minds, and write it on their hearts; and I will be their God, and they shall be My People."*** *(Jeremiah 31: 33).* ***When***

that happens, it will fulfill the example of God engraving His word into the second set of stone tables. But is there anything about the example provided by the second set of stone tables, that helps us know *when* God will fulfill it in His people Israel.

When Will The Example Of The Second Set Of Stone Tables Be Fulfilled? As already discussed, the forty days Moses spent on Mt Sinai waiting to receive the *first set* of stone tables, were an example of the two thousand years between Isaac *as the living* ***example*** *of Jesus*, and the death and resurrection of Jesus Himself in A. D. 30. What's interesting is that Moses had to spend another forty days and nights on Mt Sinai waiting for God to give him the *second set* of stone tables, which were an example of God putting His word in Israel's minds and writing them in their hearts according to the new covenant. Since the forty days and nights Moses waited for the *first set* were an example of *the two thousand years between Isaac (as an example of Jesus), and the coming of Jesus Himself in fulfillment of that example,* it's reasonable to expect the forty days it took God to prepare the second set of stone tables were an example of *another two thousand-year period. That will be the time between when Israel had Jesus put to death in A. D. 30, and the end of the age when God will finally save Israel and put His law in their inward parts and write it in their hearts according to the new covenant (Ref: Jeremiah 31: 31 - 34 above). Since that two thousand-year period began in A. D. 30 when Jesus was crucified, it should end in* A. D. 2030 when Jesus comes again and makes the new covenant with Israel, fulfilling the example of the second set of stone tables.

Chapter 15

Jonah

The Sign Of Jonah. Jesus Himself revealed that Jonah had been an example of His death and resurrection.

Matthew 12: 39 - 40 *(KJV)*
39. But He answered and said to them, ***"An evil and adulterous generation seeks after a sign, and no sign will be given to it except the sign of the prophet Jonah.***
40. ***"For as Jonah was three days and three nights in the belly of the great fish, so will the Son of Man be three days and three nights in the heart of the earth."***

Because God chose him to be an example of Jesus, Jonah was unique *as the only man who has been swallowed by a fish and remained alive inside the fish's belly for three days and nights.* But He was also unique in another way you may not have considered. ***He was the only Old Testament prophet whose only recorded ministry was preaching to GENTILES.*** By the covenant, God had given Israel the opportunity to become *His peculiar treasure above all other people.* Of course that would happen ***only IF*** Israel obeyed God's law according to the covenant. But the Jews throughout the ages have conveniently forgotten that, and historically have considered Gentiles to be unclean — *inferior to themselves as God's chosen people, and therefore not worthy to receive God's blessings.* That's why it was so unusual for Jonah to go and preach to the Gentile city of Nineveh. But God commanded Jonah to do it, and overcame all his objections to require him to do it. God did that, because Jonah's preaching to Nineveh was an example of another major aspect of God's plan of redemption. Jonah's unlikely ministry to the Gentile city of Nineveh exemplified a part of

God's plan for man's redemption. But just like the example of Jonah, we Gentiles didn't receive the Gospel of Jesus *without a **struggle** on the part of some of God's **Jewish** ministers.* Just as Jonah was extremely reluctant to go and preach to Nineveh, the apostles were likewise reluctant to preach the Gospel to the Gentiles. That was demonstrated first in Peter, when the Roman officer Cornelius invited Him to come to his house. Because that wasn't acceptable for a Jew, God had prepared Peter in advance by giving him a vision in which He commanded Peter to eat all manner of food, which according to the law was unclean for Jews *to eat (Ref: Acts 10: 9 - 28).* God did that because He knew Peter, *as a Jew,* wouldn't want to go to a Gentile Roman Officer's house, even to talk to him about God. It was only because of that vision that Peter was willing to preach the first Gospel sermon to the Gentiles. Nevertheless, it wasn't until about 23 years later in A. D. 63, that the example of Jonah was finally fulfilled, for that was when Paul finally turned exclusively to the Gentiles with the Gospel message.

Acts 28: 23 - 28 *(ESV)(This took place when Paul finally arrived in Rome and met the rabbis who were rulers in the numerous synagogues in Rome.)*
23. So when they had appointed him a day, many came to him at his lodging, to whom he explained and solemnly testified of the kingdom of God, persuading them concerning Jesus from both the Law of Moses and the Prophets, from morning till evening.
24. And some were persuaded by the things which were spoken, and some disbelieved.
25. So when they did not agree among themselves, they departed after Paul had said one word *(or made one last statement):* ***"The Holy Spirit spoke rightly through Isaiah the prophet to our fathers,***
26. ***saying, 'Go to this people and say: "hearing you will hear, and shall not understand; and seeing you will see and not perceive:***
27. ***For the hearts of this people have grown dull. Their ears are hard of hearing, and their eyes they have closed, lest they should see with their eyes and hear with their ears, lest they should understand with their hearts and turn, so that I should heal them."'"***
28. ***"Therefore let it be known to you that the salvation of God has been sent to the Gentiles, and they will hear it!"***
29. And when he had said these words, the Jews departed and had a great dispute among themselves.

Therefore, when Jonah preached God's message to Nineveh, that was actually God's example of the critical part of His plan to extend salvation to the Gentiles throughout this present church age. But do you remember what Jonah's message was? It was short and sweet. It's given in Jonah 3: 4 which says, ***"And Jonah began to enter into the city a day's journey, and he cried, and said, 'Yet forty days, and Nineveh shall be overthrown.'"*** He didn't try to convince them of their wickedness, or even urge them to repent. He simply warned them of God's impending judgment, ***and told them WHEN It was going to come.*** That was the message God gave Nineveh as *an **example** for the Gentiles to whom He would later send the Gospel of Salvation.* In Jonah's message, the *forty days* were literal 24–hour days which were essentially the length of time between Jonah's experience with the great fish and the time of God's judgment against Nineveh if they failed to repent. However, Jonah's experience with the great fish was God's example of Jesus's death and after three days and nights being resurrected. Therefore, it follows that the forty days were God's example representing the much longer period of time that was to pass between Jesus's death and resurrection and the end of the church age when God's judgment will come upon those who have rejected His call to repentance and salvation. There's no clue in the book of Jonah as to the length of time exemplified by those forty days; however, we've already seen a number of other places where God used that same ***forty–day** period of time* as an example of two thousand years for the length of the church age. Therefore, the example of Jonah is just another instance in which God has directed our attention to the year A. D. 2030 as the time when Jesus is likely to come back in judgment at His Second Coming. God confirmed this part of the example of Jonah, by no less than Jesus Himself.

Chapter 16

Examples In Jesus's Life

<u>The Temptation Of Jesus.</u> Temptation was a constant part of Jesus's life, yet even His temptation was a ministry in our behalf. This is pointed out in Hebrews.

Hebrews 4: 14 - 15 *(NKJV)*
14. Seeing then that we have a great High Priest who has passed through the heavens, Jesus the Son of God, let us hold fast our confession.
15. For we do not have a High Priest who cannot sympathize with our weaknesses, but was in all points tempted as we are, yet without sin.

Hebrews 2: 17 - 18 *(NKJV)*
17. Therefore, in all things He had to be made like His brethren, that He might be a merciful and faithful High Priest in things pertaining to God, to make propitiation for the sins of the people.
18. ***For in that He Himself has suffered, being tempted, He is able to aid those who are tempted.***

Jesus's temptation is important to us for more than just the fact He Himself experienced it. It's also important because He experienced it as Emmanuel, which means ***"God with us."*** Jesus's name ***"Emmanuel"*** confirms that He was in perfect unity with God the Father; therefore, even though *James 1: 13* reveals that God cannot be tempted with evil, *since Jesus was in perfect unity with God, when Jesus was tempted* ***God the Father experienced in Christ what it's like for us when we are tempted.*** So ***through Jesus's temptation,*** God is able to empathize with us and understand what we have to endure when we are tempted. Although Jesus had to endure temptation throughout

His life, at the beginning of His ministry He had to endure one particularly intense period of temptation that's especially important to us.

Matthew 4: 1 - 3 *(NKJV)(This is the record of what happened to Jesus immediately after He was baptized.)*
1. Then ***Jesus was led up by the Spirit*** into the wilderness ***to be tempted by the devil.***
2. And when He had fasted forty days and forty nights, afterward He was hungry.
3. Now when the tempter came to Him, he said, ***"If You are the Son of God, command that these stones become bread."***

It was the Spirit of God who led Jesus into the wilderness, and He did it *for the express purpose that Jesus should be tempted by the devil.* Matthew recorded only the temptations Jesus had ***after*** He had fasted for forty days and nights, but Luke adds another important bit of information about Jesus's temptation.

Luke 4: 1 - 3 *(NKJV)*
1. Then Jesus, being filled with the Holy Spirit, returned from the Jordan and was led by the Spirit into the wilderness,
2. ***BEING TEMPTED FOR FORTY DAYS by the devil.*** And in those days He ate nothing, and afterward, when they had ended he was hungry.
3. And the devil said to Him, ***"If you are the Son of God, command this stone to become bread."***

Jesus was tempted the entire forty days. The temptations ***identified*** in Matthew and Luke are only those temptations He experienced ***AFTER*** He was weak from fasting for the preceding forty days. As we consider that period of Jesus's temptations, remember that *the Church didn't even have its beginning* ***until AFTER Jesus died and was resurrected.*** *That means* ***Jesus led the way for the church, in enduring and overcoming temptations.*** In Colossians, we see that this was an important part of God's plan for Jesus and the Church.

Colossians 1: 16 - 19 (*NKJV)*
16. For by Him all things were created that are in heaven and that are on earth, visible and invisible, whether thrones or dominions or principalities or powers. All things were created through Him and for Him.
17. And He is before all things, and in Him all things consist.

18. And He is the head of the body, the church, who is the beginning, the firstborn from the dead, that in all things He may have the preeminence.
19. For it pleased the Father that in Him all the fullness should dwell.

It was God's purpose that Jesus, ***as the head of the church,*** should lead the church in everything the church must endure. Therefore, Jesus *personally, both experienced and overcame* every manner of temptation that is common to man. Accordingly, since Jesus led the way for the church in temptation, ***His temptation was an example of the temptation the church was going to experience.*** Additionally, since Jesus's temptations lasted for the very precise length of time — ***forty days and forty nights*** — that time must also be part of the example. In Chapter 13, we saw that forty days was also the length of time God took to make the second set of stone tablets, and those forty days represented the two thousand years of the church age which began at the end of Jesus's earthly ministry in A. D. 30. Therefore, the church's temptation should also cover that same two thousand year period between the first and second Advent of Christ. Since that will be the length of the church age, this is just ***one more example*** *indicating Jesus will come for His church in A. D. 2030, which should be the end of the church age.* But just as the beginning of Jesus's earthly ministry was marked by a specific period of forty days; the end of His earthly ministry was likewise marked by another time period of that same length.

<u>Jesus' Time On Earth AFTER His Resurrection.</u> After Jesus was resurrected, *even though He had completed the provision for man's salvation, He still remained on the earth for ANOTHER forty days.*

Acts 1: 1 - 3 & 9 - 11 *(NKJV)*
1. The former account I made, O Theophilus, of all that Jesus began both to do and teach,
2. until the day in which He was taken up, after He through the Holy Spirit had given commandments to the apostles whom He had chosen,
3. to whom He also presented Himself alive after His suffering by many infallible proofs, ***being seen by them during <u>FORTY DAYS</u>*** and speaking of the things pertaining to the kingdom of God.

Then, after Jesus ascended into heaven, two angels appeared to the disciples and directed their attention to that future day when Jesus will come again, ***"...<u>in like manner.</u>"***

9. Now when He had spoken these things, while they watched, *He was taken up, **and a cloud received Him** out of their sight.*
10. And while they looked steadfastly toward heaven as He went up, behold, two men stood by them in white apparel,
11. who also said, ***"Men of Galilee, why do you stand gazing up into heaven? This same Jesus, who is taken up from you into heaven, WILL SO COME IN LIKE MANNER AS YOU SAW HIM GO INTO HEAVEN."***

So we have *another* ***forty–day*** *period.* This was the forty days immediately following Jesus's resurrection. Jesus's earthly ministry was neatly sandwiched between two separate forty–day periods. At the beginning of His ministry, Jesus *as the* ***head*** *of the church* spent forty days being tempted as an example of the time *Christ's body the church would be tempted during the church age.* But this second forty–day period was the time Jesus spent on earth ***AFTER*** His death and resurrection. He spent those forty days giving His followers ***"many infallible proofs"*** that He had been raised from the dead, and also teaching them many other things about the kingdom of God. It's reasonable to anticipate that this second forty–day period was another example of the two thousand years of the church age that would follow His earthly ministry. But this leaves us with another question. Since the forty days of His temptation *at the beginning of His ministry, was an example showing that His body, the church,* would experience temptation during the two thousand years of the church age; it's reasonable that this second forty day period was an example of ***something else*** the church was going to experience during that same two thousand–years of the church age. Additionally, that something else is apparently of equal importance with the fact that the church would suffer temptation. If that is true, ***then what was that something else?***

This is one of those times when the thing we're looking for is so obvious we almost stumble over it before we notice it. *All that made that second forty–day period stand out* was the fact that ***Jesus remained on earth with His followers for forty days AFTER His resurrection.*** Therefore, that second forty–day period had to be another example of the church age that began when Jesus was resurrected, ***and exemplified the fact that Christ Himself was going to remain present here on the earth with the church throughout the entire two thousand years of the church age.*** This may not sound reasonable in light of the fact that the disciples saw Him literally ascend up into the clouds and disappear. But before you discount this as foolishness, look at several other things Jesus said to comfort and encourage His disciples both before and after He was crucified.

John 14: 15 - 18 *(KJV) (Jesus said this shortly **before** He was crucified.)*
15. *"If ye love me, keep my commandments.*
16. ***"And I will pray the Father, and He shall give you another Comforter, that He may abide with you for ever;***
17. ***even the Spirit of truth; whom the world cannot receive, because it seeth him not, neither knoweth him: but ye know Him; for He dwelleth with you, AND SHALL BE IN YOU.***

There is complete agreement that the comforter Jesus promised in Verse 16 is the Holy Spirit. In Verse 17, He said that same comforter was then ***"with"*** them, which was true for the Holy Spirit was ***IN Jesus,*** and Jesus was of course ***"WITH them."*** Then, He said that same Comforter ***"shall be IN you."*** When He said that, He was referring to the Holy Spirit they would receive ***AFTER*** His death and resurrection. But then in Verse 18, He implied that He Himself would be the comforter who would come to them.

18; ***"I will not leave you comfortless: I WILL COME TO YOU."***

A few days later, Jesus was crucified, and after three days was resurrected. Then, the next night He appeared to the disciples and when they rejoiced because they finally believed He had come back from the dead, He breathed on them and said, ***"Receive you the Holy Ghost."*** *(John 20: 22).* At that moment they became ***the very first Christians.*** And after that, every time a person has come to faith in Jesus Christ unto salvation, that person has also received the Holy Spirit *just like the disciples did that night in Jerusalem.* This is explained in Ephesians 1: 13 & 14, which says when you believed in Christ, ***"..you were sealed with the Holy Spirit of promise,"*** *which is* ***"...the earnest of our inheritance until the redemption of the purchased possession, unto the praise of His glory."*** In light of these verses, *when we believe and are saved,* ***do we receive the Holy Spirit, OR do we receive Christ?*** As you consider this, look at something else Jesus said to the disciples ***AFTER*** He was resurrected and also ***AFTER*** He had breathed on them, imparting the Holy Spirit to them.

Matthew 28: 18 - 20 *(KJV)*
18. And Jesus came and spake unto them, saying, ***"All power is given unto me in heaven and in earth.***
19. ***"Go ye therefore, and teach all nations, baptizing them in the name of the Father, and of the Son, and of the Holy Ghost:***

20. ***"Teaching them to observe all things whatsoever I have commanded you: and lo, I AM WITH YOU ALWAYS, EVEN UNTO THE END OF THE WORLD."*** Amen.

They had already received the Holy Ghost when Jesus breathed on them some time before this; however, here He promised them, ***I AM WITH YOU ALWAYS, EVEN UNTO THE END OF THE WORLD." So who is it that we receive when we believe?*** There's a passage in Romans that hopefully will clear this up.

Romans 8: 8 - 11 *(NKJV)*
8. So then, those who are in the flesh cannot please God.
9. But you are not in the flesh, but in the Spirit, ***if indeed THE SPIRIT OF GOD dwells in you.*** Now if anyone does not have ***THE SPIRIT OF CHRIST***, he is not His.
10. And if ***CHRIST is in you,*** the body is dead because of sin, but the Spirit is life because of righteousness.
11. But if the ***Spirit of HIM who raised Jesus*** from the dead dwells in you, ***HE who raised Christ from the dead will also give life to your mortal bodies through HIS SPIRIT who dwells in you.***

From this we must conclude that when we receive the Spirit of God, we also have the Spirit of Christ, which is no different from having Christ Himself. Now look at Jesus's prayer in John 17.

John 17: 11, & 20 - 23 *(NKJV)(This was Jesus's prayer immediately after the last supper.)*
11. ***"Now I am no longer in the world, but these are in the world, and I come to You. Holy Father, keep through Your name those whom You have given Me, that they may be one AS WE ARE."***
20. ***"I do not pray for these alone, but also for those who will believe in Me through their word;***
21. ***"that they all may be one, as You, Father, are in Me, and I in You; that they also may be one in Us, that the world may believe that You sent Me.***
22. ***"And the glory which You gave Me I have given them, that they may be one just as We are one:***
23. ***"I in them, and You in Me; that they may be made perfect in one, and that the world may know that You sent Me, and have loved them as You have lived Me.***

Perhaps Ephesians 4 will help you understand the unity of the Trinity of God.

Ephesians 4: 4 - 6 *(KJV)*
4. There is ***one body*** and **ONE Spirit,** just as you were called in ***one hope*** of your calling;
5. ***one Lord*** *(who is Jesus),* ***one faith, one baptism;***
6. ***one God*** and Father of all, who is above all, and through all, ***AND IN YOU ALL.***

God does not consist of three separate spirits. Instead, there is ***ONE Spirit***, which is the Holy Spirit of God, and that Spirit is manifested both in the person of the Father and of the Son. This agrees with John 4: 24, where Jesus told the Samaritan woman, ***"God is Spirit."*** Therefore, the Trinity of God consists of the Father, the Son, and the Holy Spirit, and the Holy Spirit is ***THE SPIRIT*** that perfectly unites the Father and Son in the unity that is ***the Trinity of God***. So in John 17 *(above)*, when Jesus prayed for believers, ***"that they may be made perfect in ONE,"*** *just like He and the Father are* ***ONE,*** He was actually asking the Father *to include the church in the unity* ***that prior to that time had existed ONLY AS THE TRINITY.*** However, as Jesus said in John 17: 21 & 23 above, *the closer we in the church come into unity with God,* ***the more our testimony will convince the world that Jesus is indeed the One sent from God according to God's word***.

When Jesus remained on the earth ***with His followers*** for those forty days ***AFTER*** His resurrection, that was God's example to us ***that by the indwelling presence of the Holy Spirit, we actually have God and Christ living within us right now.*** We don't yet have perfect unity with God because we're still living in bodies that effectively are still dead *(Ref: Romans 8: 10 above)*. However, since we have within us the same Holy Spirit who is the unifying agent within the Trinity, the more we walk in obedience to that indwelling Holy Spirit, the closer we will come to the unity Jesus prayed for us to have. That is God's goal for us, and should be our goal as His children. When we see that our unity with God is what will ultimately overcome the world's unbelief, it will help us understand and appreciate what God inspired David to write in Psalms 68.

Psalms 68: 1 - 2 *(NKJV)*
1. Let God arise, let His enemies be scattered, and let those that hate Him flee before Him.

2. As smoke is driven away, so drive them away; as wax melts before the fire, so let the wicked perish at the presence God.

Since God is in us, and has given us the task of spreading the Gospel to His enemies throughout the world, He doesn't act to overcome those enemies ***EXCEPT THROUGH US.*** Therefore, through David, He exhorted us is to ***"LET God arise, LET His enemies be scattered."*** Apparently God has chosen ***to arise against His enemies IN PROPORTION to how much we submit to the Holy Spirit as He works to bring us into unity with God.*** Therefore, when we believers persist in going our own way and doing our own thing, ***we are hindering God in His desire to rise up against His enemies.*** So we need to begin walking according to the Holy Spirit within us and in that way, ***"Let God arise"*** in us.

God's Special Provision For The Last Generation. As we wonder how we can enter into that deeper relationship, we need to remember that God has a special provision for the last generation. As discussed in Chapter 6, God is going to pour out the ***latter rain*** of the Holy Spirit during this last generation. That is probably what will result in the loud voice in heaven saying, ***"Now is come,...the power of His Christ."*** *(Ref: Revelation 12: 10).* The latter rains in Israel are much heavier that the former rains which were an example that began to be fulfilled at Pentecost. However, as the end of this age draws near, we can expect an outpouring of the Holy Spirit that will be both greater and more far-reaching than that which came at Pentecost. It is possible and even likely, that it will be that outpouring of the Holy Spirit by which God will bring the church into the kind of unity that will be the answer to Jesus's prayer in John 17. That is most likely how the following prophecy in Ephesians will be fulfilled.

Ephesians 5: 25 - 27
25. Husbands, love your wives, just as Christ also loved the church and gave Himself for her,
26. that He might sanctify and cleanse her with the washing of water by the word,
27. that He might present her to Himself a glorious church, not having spot or wrinkle or any such thing, but that she should be holy and without blemish.

Chapter 17

Isaac's Wedding

Introduction. Isaac is one of the most prominent examples of Jesus in the Old Testament. He was the son God promised to Abraham and Sarah for many years, and that made him an example of Jesus whom God had promised to send as the Messiah for centuries before He was finally born. When Isaac was born it was a miracle of God, for both Abraham and Sarah were past the age for having children. Romans 4: 19 speaks of both Abraham and Sarah saying, ***"And being not weak in faith, he*** *(Abraham)* ***did not consider his own body, already dead (since he was about a hundred years old) and the deadness of Sarah's womb."*** So the miracle of Isaac's birth was an example of the miracle of the virgin birth of Jesus. When God told Abraham to offer Isaac as a burnt offering, that was an example of God Himself sending His Son Jesus to die as the sacrifice for our sins. The three-day trip Abraham and Isaac made getting to the appointed place was an example of the three days Jesus was dead, for Isaac was effectively dead in Abraham's heart and mind during those three days. After God stopped Abraham from actually killing Isaac and provided a ram to offer in his place, Abraham and Isaac came down the mountain together, as an example of the resurrection of Jesus. *Therefore,* ***it was inevitable that Isaac's marriage would also be an example of the marriage of Christ.*** Accordingly, Abraham sent his eldest servant Eliezer to Haran to select a wife for Isaac. That was an example of God sending the Holy Spirit to call those God has chosen to make up the church as the bride of Christ. Rebekah accepted the offer to become Isaac's wife without first seeing Isaac. She simply believed in the word of Abraham through Eliezer concerning Isaac. That was an example of how the church is made up of people who haven't seen Jesus, but accept the call of the Holy Spirit and exercise faith in God's word. *But in addition to all this, the marriage* *of Isaac also gave an example of **<u>WHEN</u> the marriage of Christ and the church will take place.***

Genesis 25: 19 - 20 *(NKJV)*
19. This is the genealogy of Isaac, Abraham's son. Abraham begot Isaac.
20. Isaac was ***<u>FORTY</u> years old*** when he took Rebekah as wife, the daughter of Bethuel the Syrian of Padan Aram, the sister of Laban.

Here's that number ***"forty"*** again. This is unusual, ***because Isaac is one of only <u>three</u> people in Scripture whose age is given at the time they got married.*** The second person is Esau, who also married when he was forty. The third person is an obscure man named Hezron who is mentioned in I Chronicles 2: 21. He may also have a significance, but at the present time I have no idea what it may be.

However, Isaac's case is interesting because he was used in so many ways as an example of Jesus. If this is also a part of that on–going example of Jesus, then his being forty years old when he married would be *an example of how old Jesus will be when He is married to the Church at the end of the age.* Also, if the end of the age comes at or about A. D. 2030, as indicated by the other prophecies and examples already discussed in this book, then Isaac's getting married when he was forty years old would be an example of the two thousand *(plus)* years between the ***birth*** of Jesus and the end of the age when He will marry the Church as His bride. Here-to-fore we've considered the time between the end of Jesus's earthly ministry and the end of the age, which we've consistently seen indicated as two thousand years. So this example represents *essentially* the same two thousand years of the church age, but with 33 more years to go back to the ***birth*** of Jesus.

Chapter 18

The Wedding At Cana

One of the first things Jesus did in His earthly ministry, was attend an obscure local wedding in Cana of Galilee.

John 2: 1 - 4 (UNASB)
1. And the third day there was a marriage in Cana of Galilee; and the mother of Jesus was there:
2. Now both Jesus, and His disciples were invited to the marriage.
3. When they wanted wine, the mother of Jesus said unto Him, ***"They have no wine."***

When Mary told Jesus ***"They have no wine,"*** she didn't expect Him to do anything about it, for He was only an invited guest, and problems with the refreshments weren't His concern. Also, Mary had no reason to think Jesus could solve that problem, for He was a carpenter, not a wine maker, *and at that point in time **Jesus hadn't yet done any miracles***. So Mary was simply explaining why they weren't being served the refreshments that were normal at a wedding. However, Jesus responded in a way that indicated something was going on that went beyond just that local wedding.

4. Jesus saith unto her, ***"Woman, what does that have to do with you? My hour has not yet come."***

First, He acknowledged what was obvious. The lack of wine simply didn't concern either Mary or Himself. But He also said, ***"My hour has not yet come."*** That shows He knew there was going to be a similar situation when He would be responsible for providing the wine. However, *He also made it clear **that time hadn't come yet.*** He knew that when His ***"hour"*** came, it would involve ***a different wedding***. To see what He meant, we need to see what His ***"hour"*** represented.

John 7: 30 *(KJV)*
30. Then they sought to take Him: ***but no man laid hands on Him, because HIS HOUR was not yet come.***

John 8: 20 *(KJV)*
20. These words spake Jesus in the treasure, as He taught in the temple: ***and no man laid hands on Him; for HIS HOUR was not yet come.***

John 12: 27 *(KJV)*
27. ***"Now is My soul troubled; and what shall I say? 'Father, save Me from THIS HOUR': but for this cause came I unto THIS HOUR."***

John 13: 1 *(KJV)*
1. Now before the feast of the Passover, ***when Jesus knew that His HOUR was come that He should depart out of this world unto the Father,*** having loved His own which were in the world, He loved them unto the end.

Jesus's ***"hour"*** was simply *the time in God's schedule* when Jesus would be put to death. Although His hour hadn't come at the wedding in Cana, God had arranged for them to give out of wine while Jesus was at that wedding. He did that because He was using the wedding at Cana as an example of that future wedding for which Jesus does have the responsibility for providing the wine. Therefore, He had Jesus miraculously provide wine at Cana as an example of the even greater miracle He would accomplish when His ***"hour"*** finally came according to God's plan for man's redemption. It's obvious that God also spoke to Mary's heart and showed her *that Jesus was indeed going to do* **SOMETHING** *about the problem of their not having wine.* She didn't know what He would do, but she had enough faith to act on what God had shown her.

John 2: 5 - 7 *(NKJV)*
5. His mother said to the servants, ***"Whatever He says to you, do it."***

What Jesus then said was probably a surprise both to Mary and the servants.

6. Now there were set there six water–pots of stone, according to the manner of purification of the Jews, containing twenty or thirty gallons apiece.
7. Jesus said to them, ***"Fill the water–pots with water."*** And they filled them up to the brim.

What Jesus said didn't make sense to anybody, for the water in those six stone pots wasn't even used for drinking; it was for the ***"...<u>purification</u> of the Jews."*** We get a better understanding of those six pots in the book of Mark.

Mark 7: 2 - 4 *(NKJV)*
2. Now when they *[the scribes and Pharisees]* saw some of His disciples eat bread with defiled, that is, with unwashed hands, they found fault.
3. For the Pharisees, and all the Jews, do not eat unless they wash their hands in a special way, holding the tradition of the elders.
4. When they come from the marketplace, they do not eat unless they wash. And there are many other things which they have received and hold, like the washing of cups, pitchers, copper vessels, and couches.

The Jews did a lot of ceremonial washing in their efforts to be righteous before God. This explains why there was so much water — a total of 120 to 180 gallons. They needed a whole lot of water for the wedding guests to do all the washing necessary to satisfy the tradition of the elders. ***However, all that washing had nothing to do with <u>HYGIENE!</u> It was strictly a <u>RITUAL</u> that represented cleansing from sin.*** Before Jesus died as God's sacrifice for sin, *obedience to the law* was the only way man had to be righteous before God. The Jews' ceremonial washing was a ritual that represented their belief that they were obeying the law. But actually, all their washing was to no avail, for Galatians 2: 16 speaks of their efforts to *obey the law,* as "***the <u>WORKS</u> of the law,***" and it goes on to say, ***"...for by the works of the law shall no flesh be justified."***

So why did Jesus have them fill all the water-pots to the brim? It isn't reasonable that they would need that much wine for a small wedding in an obscure town like Cana. Yet, He had the pots filled to the brim, because that was an important part of the example He was presenting. In Deuteronomy 5: 13, the law said, ***"Six days thou shalt labor, and do all***

thy work." *Therefore, in Jesus's example, the* ***SIX*** ***water-pots*** *represented the Jew's* ***WORKS-OF-THE-LAW*** ***for righteousness,*** and Jesus had all ***SIX*** ***pots filled to the BRIM with water*** to show that ***ALL of GOD'S WORD for righteousness*** was then complete. In Matthew 11: 13, Jesus said, ***"For all the prophets and the law prophesied until John, and if you will receive it, this*** *[John the Baptist]* ***is Elias, which was for to come."*** Therefore the coming of John the Baptist meant the law and the prophets were complete.

However, since the ***SIX FULL water-pots*** showed that the law was complete, ***they also revealed that THE LAW ALONE WASN'T ENOUGH TO MAKE MAN RIGHTEOUS;*** *for the* ***SIX days of man's work don't make a complete week***. To make the week complete, *there must also be a* ***seventh day — THE DAY OF REST.*** So just as it takes ***SEVEN days*** *to make a complete week, Jesus's example needed* ***a SEVENTH vessel to represent the completion of God's word for man's righteousness, and which also provided for man's righteousness in REST.***

John 1: 1 - 2, & 14 *(KJV)*
1. In the beginning was the Word, and the Word was with God, and the Word was God.
2. The same was in the beginning with God.
14. And the ***Word was made flesh,*** and dwelt among us, (and we beheld His glory, the glory as of the only begotten of the Father,) full of grace and truth.

Jesus Himself was ***the SEVENTH vessel of God's word.*** That was true in two different ways. ***FIRST: As the Second Person of the Trinity of God,*** He was the ***"Word of God"*** *in the sense that He was the express image of the invisible God (Hebrews 1: 3) and,* ***SECOND: As the Son of man,*** He lived ***in perfect obedience to God's Word.*** Jesus also satisfied the requirement for man's rest, represented by the seventh day, *the day of* ***rest***. For, when we come to God by faith in Jesus Christ, ***we find REST in His righteousness.*** Because of this, Romans 10: 4 says, ***"For Christ is the end of the Law*** *[the works of the law]* ***for righteousness to every one that believes."*** Therefore, Jesus used His first miracle as an example to reveal that ***righteousness and rest before God*** can be found only by trusting in Him. A short time after He demonstrated this by the example of His first miracle, *He offered that rest in an open invitation during His Sermon on the Mount.*

Matthew 11: 28 *(KJV)*
11. "***Come unto me, all ye that labor and are heavy laden, and I will give you rest.***"

All this has been background for Jesus's miracle of turning the water into wine. We need to take a little time to look at the miracle itself.

John 2: 8-10 *(NKJV)*
8. And He said to them, ***"Draw some out now, and take it to the master of the feast."*** And they took it.
9. When the master of the feast had tasted the water that was made wine, and did not know where it came from *(but the servants who had drawn the water knew,)* the master of the feast called the bridegroom.
10. And he said to him, ***"Every man at the beginning sets forth good wine, and when guests have well drunk, then the inferior. You have kept the good wine until now."***

To fully appreciate the message in this miracle, we need to look at the end of Jesus's ministry and see how this example of turning the water into wine was actually fulfilled when ***His "HOUR" finally came.***

Matthew 26: 26 - 29 *(KJV)*
26. And as they were eating, Jesus took bread, and blessed it, and brake it, and gave it to the disciples, and said, ***"Take eat; this is My body."***
27. And He took the cup, and gave thanks, and gave it to them, saying, ***"Drink ye all of it;***
28. ***"for this is My blood of the new testament, which is shed for many for the remission of sins.***

The wine He gave the disciples at the last supper, as well as the wine Jesus made at the wedding at Cana, **were both examples that were fulfilled by the blood He shed at Calvary.** Jesus gave the context for both of those examples in John 6: 54, where He said, ***"Whoever eats My flesh and drinks My blood has eternal life, and I will raise him up at the last day."*** The Living Word of God became flesh as the man Jesus Christ, and by shedding His blood at Calvary, Jesus made His life, ***which is the same as the life of God,*** *available to all who place their faith in His shed blood for eternal life,* **and do that with the same kind of faith by which they eat bread and drink wine to sustain**

their natural life. *When we understand what the wine Jesus made actually represented, there's no wonder the master of the feast was amazed at the excellence of the wine that Jesus made.* But Verse 29 reveals one additional thing we need to see about this very special wine.

29. ***"But I say unto you, 'I will not drink henceforth of this fruit of the vine, until that day when I drink it new with you in My Father's kingdom.'"***

That night in the spring of A. D. 30 was the last time Jesus would drink the wine that represented His blood, UNTIL He drinks it with the disciples in His Father's kingdom. *He said that, referring to the end of the age,* ***when He will share wine with His bride (the church) at their wedding*** *(Ref: Revelation 19: 5 - 9).* At that time, He will drink it again ***with His disciples, AND WITH EVERYBODY ELSE WHO IS A PART OF HIS BRIDE THE CHURCH.*** Since the wedding at Cana was an example of Jesus's marriage to the church, it's reasonable to expect there was something about it that indicated when it will be fulfilled by Jesus's wedding in heaven.

When Did the Wedding in Cana Indicate Jesus's Wedding Will Take Place in Heaven? Scripture doesn't tell us precisely when the marriage of Christ and the church will take place. But Revelation 19 tells when the time for that marriage will finally come. The first five verses portray the rejoicing and praise that will take place in heaven when the judgment of the great harlot will be complete. That judgment is described in Revelation 17 & 18, and will be part of God's wrath at the end of the age. Then Revelation 19: 6 begins by describing the joy and praise that will take place in heaven *because the time will have come for the marriage of the Lamb.*

Revelation 19: 6 - 9 *(NKJV)*
6. And I heard, as it were, the voice of many waters and as the sound of mighty thunderings, saying, ***"Alleluia! For the Lord God Omnipotent reigns!"***
7. ***"Let us be glad and rejoice and give Him glory, for the marriage of the Lamb has come, and His wife has made herself ready."***
8. And to her it was granted to be arrayed in fine linen, clean and bright, for the fine linen is the righteousness of the saints.
9. Then he said to me, ***"Write: 'Blessed are those who are called to the marriage supper of the Lamb!'"*** And he said to me, ***"These are the true sayings of God."***

John was so overwhelmed that in verse 10 he said he fell at the angel's feet to worship; but was told not to do that because God is the only one to be worshiped. Then from verse 11 to the end of the Chapter, he described the Second Coming and its aftermath. This shows that the wedding of Christ to the church will probably take place sometime shortly ***after*** the Second Coming. The account of the wedding in Cana actually gives us an indication when Jesus's marriage to the church will take place; however, it's easy to miss for it's included in a way that seems to be only an incidental bit of information that has no great significance.

John 2: 1 (KJV)
1. ***<u>ON THE THIRD DAY</u>*** there was a wedding in Cana of Galilee, and the mother of Jesus was there.

When you first read this, *the* ***third*** *day* doesn't seem to be *of much,* ***if any,*** *importance,* because *it's not even obvious* ***what it was the third day <u>AFTER.</u> Also,*** *what could it matter to us almost two thousand years later, when that wedding in Cana took place?* ***It matters <u>ONLY</u> when we realize the wedding in Cana was an example foreshadowing Christ's wedding to the church in heaven.*** Accordingly, when you read John Chapter 1 carefully, you see that the wedding in Cana took place ***on the third day <u>AFTER</u>*** John the Baptist identified Jesus by saying, ***"Behold the Lamb of God who takes away the sin of the world."*** *(John 1: 29).* In Chapter 4 of this book, we saw it was that announcement that convinced the first disciples that Jesus was the Christ *(Messiah), and caused them to begin following Him.* Also in Chapter 4, we saw that John made that announcement on the first day of the first month in A. D. 27 *which marked* ***the <u>BEGINNING</u>*** *of Jesus's earthly ministry.* Three years later in A. D. 30, Jesus was crucified, ending His earthly ministry.

But Jesus's crucifixion also marked the beginning of the ***two days*** prophesied in Hosea 6: 1 - 2a as the time Israel would be smitten by God *(Ref: Paragraph entitled* ***"When Is God Going to Restore Israel into His Favor?"*** *in Chapter 4 of this book).* As discussed in Chapter 4, when we *use a thousand–years for a day (Ref: II Peter 3: 8) for the two days of Hosea 6: 1 - 2a,* it means they are prophetic of ***two thousand years*** *that will end in A. D. 2030,* at which time God will revive Israel to live in His sight ***during the <u>THIRD</u> day*** *(Ref: Hosea 6: 2b), which will be another thousand–year day.* However, when we also see the ***third*** *day for the wedding in Cana* as representing a *thousand–year–day* for the marriage of Christ and the church, it means His wedding to the church in heaven should take place during *the third* *thousand years* ***AFTER*** *John the Baptist made the announcement in A. D. 27 that identified Jesus as the Messiah (Christ).*

Scripture doesn't say exactly when Christ's marriage to the church will take place; however, Revelation 19: 7 *(above)* speaks of the Lamb's wife making herself ready for her marriage to the Lamb and the next event, *prophesied immediately after that,* is the heavens opening and Jesus and the armies of heaven coming forth on white horses, in what is obviously the Second Coming *(Ref: Revelation 19: 11 - 21).* Therefore, *as an example,* the wedding at Cana is in agreement with the other prophecies and examples discussed in this book, and all of them indicate that A. D. 2030 will be the time when Jesus will come in the Second Coming, which should take place shortly *(about four months)* after He comes for His church in the Rapture, which will mark the end of the church age.

www.ingramcontent.com/pod-product-compliance
Ingram Content Group UK Ltd.
Pitfield, Milton Keynes, MK11 3LW, UK
UKHW040603210726
13854UKWH00008B/1843